MW00814070

War and Chance

BRIDGING THE GAP

Series Editors:

Goldgeier James
Jentleson Bruce
Steven Weber

The Logic of American Nuclear Strategy:
Why Strategic Superiority Matters
Matthew Kroenig

War and Chance
Assessing Uncertainty in International Politics
Jeffrey A. Friedman

War and Chance

Assessing Uncertainty in International Politics

JEFFREY A. FRIEDMAN

April 15, 2019

Dear Bob —

Thank you for your support with this project, which has come a very long way since the workshop that you chaired, and will surely benefit from your kind words on the jacket. Please let me know if I can ever repay your generosity to you or your students. With gratitude,

Jeffrey Friedman

OXFORD
UNIVERSITY PRESS

OXFORD
UNIVERSITY PRESS

Oxford University Press is a department of the University of Oxford. It furthers
the University's objective of excellence in research, scholarship, and education
by publishing worldwide. Oxford is a registered trade mark of Oxford University
Press in the UK and certain other countries.

Published in the United States of America by Oxford University Press
198 Madison Avenue, New York, NY 10016, United States of America.

© Oxford University Press 2019

Library of Congress Cataloging-in-Publication Data
Names: Friedman, Jeffrey A. (Jeffrey Allan), author.
Title: War and chance : assessing uncertainty in international politics /
Jeffrey A. Friedman.
Description: New York, NY : Oxford University Press, 2019.
Identifiers: LCCN 2018043558| ISBN 9780190938024 (hardcover) |
ISBN 9780190938048 (epub)
Subjects: LCSH: International relations—Decision making. |
National security—Decision making. | Uncertainty—Political aspects. |
United States—Foreign relations—Decision making. | United States—National
security—Decision making. | Uncertainty—Political aspects—United States.
Classification: LCC JZ1253 .F75 2019 | DDC 327.101/9—dc23
LC record available at https://lccn.loc.gov/2018043558

1 3 5 7 9 8 6 4 2

Printed by Sheridan Books, Inc., United States of America

For my parents

CONTENTS

ACKNOWLEDGMENTS

I am delighted to have so many people to thank for their input, guidance, and support.

Stephen Walt, Monica Toft, and Robert Bates were my dissertation advisers at Harvard. In addition to providing careful feedback on my research over many years, each of them has served as a role model for producing scholarship that is interesting, rigorous, and policy-relevant. I am also especially grateful for the mentorship of Richard Zeckhauser, who inspired my interest in decision analysis, and Stephen Biddle, who played a crucial role in launching my academic career.

Dartmouth has provided an ideal environment in which to study international politics. It has been wonderful to be surrounded by so many outstanding faculty who work in this area, including Dan Benjamin, Steve Brooks, Udi Greenberg, Brian Greenhill, Jenny Lind, Mike Mastanduno, Ed Miller, Jennie Miller, Nick Miller, Katy Powers, Daryl Press, Ben Valentino, and Bill Wohlforth. I was lucky to arrive at Dartmouth along with a cohort of brilliant, supportive junior scholars, especially David Cottrell, Derek Epp, Jeremy Ferwerda, Herschel Nachlis, Paul Novosad, Julie Rose, Na'ama Shenhav, Sean Westwood, and Thomas Youle. Dartmouth's undergraduates have also served as a valuable sounding board for many of the ideas presented in this book. It has been a pleasure to work with them and to learn from their insights.

While conducting this research, I held fellowships at the Weatherhead Center for International Affairs, the Belfer Center for Science and International Affairs, the Tobin Project, the Dickey Center for International Understanding, and the Institute for Advanced Study in Toulouse, France. Each institution provided a stimulating environment for research and writing, particularly given the interdisciplinary nature of my work. The U.S. Department of Homeland Security funded portions of this research via the University of Southern California's Center for Risk and Economic Analysis of Terrorism Events. That funding was especially important in ensuring the ethical compensation of survey respondents.

I presented previous versions of the book's content to seminars at Brown University, George Washington University, Hamilton College, Harvard University, Mercyhurst University, Middlebury College, MIT, the University of Pennsylvania, the University of Pittsburgh, Princeton University, the University of Virginia, and Yale University. Just as importantly, I received invaluable feedback as a result of presenting this material to practitioners at the U.S. National War College, the U.S. National Intelligence Council, the U.S. Department of Homeland Security's Science and Technology Directorate, the Military Operations Research Society, the Canadian Forces College, and the Norwegian Defense Intelligence School. I owe particular thanks to Colonel Mark Bucknam for the vital role he played in facilitating practitioners' engagement with my work.

Portions of chapters 3 and 4 present research that I coauthored with Joshua Baker, Jennifer Lerner, Barbara Mellers, Philip Tetlock, and Richard Zeckhauser. I am grateful for their permission to use that analysis in the book, but more importantly for the opportunity to benefit from their collaboration and insight. Oxford University Press and Cambridge University Press have kindly allowed me to reprint that material. David McBride, Emily Mackenzie, and James Goldgeier played the key roles in steering the book through Oxford's review and editing process. It is a particular privilege to publish this work through Oxford's Bridging the Gap book series, a collection that reflects the highest standard of policy-relevant scholarship.

Charles Glaser and Robert Jervis chaired a workshop that reviewed an early version of the manuscript and led to several important revisions to the book's framing and content. Countless other scholars provided thoughtful comments on different portions of this research over the years, including Dan Altman, Ivan Arreguin-Toft, Alan Barnes, Dick Betts, David Budescu, Welton Chang, Walt Cooper, Greg Daddis, Derek Grossman, Michael Herron, Yusaku Horiuchi, Loch Johnson, Josh Kertzer, Joowon Kim, Matt Kocher, Jack Levy, Mark Lowenthal, David Mandel, Stephen Marrin, Jason Matheny, Peter Mattis, James McAllister, Rose McDermott, Victor McFarland, Rich Nielsen, Joe Nye, Brendan Nyhan, Randy Pherson, Paul Pillar, Mike Poznansky, Dan Reiter, Steve Rieber, Steve Rosen, Josh Rovner, Brandon Stewart, Greg Treverton, Tom Wallsten, Kris Wheaton, Justin Wolfers, Keren Yarhi-Milo, Yuri Zhukov, and two anonymous reviewers at Oxford University Press. Charlotte Bacon provided tremendous help with articulating the book's core arguments. Thanks also to Jeff, Jill, and Monte Odel, Jacquelyn and Pierre Vuarchex, Nelson Kasfir, and Anne Sa'adah for their advice and encouragement over many years.

I owe the greatest debts to my family: my parents, Barbara and Ben; my brother, John; my sister-in-law, Hilary; my uncle, Art; and my partner, Kathryn. Each of you has set a magnificent example for me to follow, both personally and professionally. I love you and will always be grateful for your support.

War and Chance

Introduction

"One of the Things You Learn as President Is That You're
Always Dealing with Probabilities"

Over the past two decades, the most serious problems in U.S. foreign policy have revolved around the challenge of assessing uncertainty. Leaders underestimated the risk of terrorism before 2001, overestimated the chances that Saddam Hussein was pursuing weapons of mass destruction in 2003, and did not fully appreciate the dangers of pursuing regime change in Iraq, Afghanistan, or Libya. Many of this generation's most consequential events, such as the 2008 financial crisis, the Arab Spring, the rise of ISIS, and Brexit, were outcomes that experts either confidently predicted would not take place or failed to anticipate entirely. Those experiences provide harsh reminders that scholars and practitioners of international politics are far less clairvoyant than we would like them to be.

The central difficulty with assessing uncertainty in international politics is that the most important judgments also tend to be the most subjective. No known methodology can reliably predict the outbreak of wars, forecast economic recessions, project the results of military operations, anticipate terrorist attacks, or estimate the chances of countless other events kinds of uncertainty that shape foreign policy decisions.[1] Many scholars and practitioners therefore believe that it is better to keep foreign policy debates focused on the facts—that it is, at best, a waste of time to debate uncertain judgments that will often prove to be wrong.

---

[1] On how irreducible uncertainty surrounds most major foreign policy decisions, see Robert Jervis, *System Effects: Complexity in Political and Social Life* (Princeton, N.J.: Princeton University Press, 1997); Richard K. Betts, *Enemies of Intelligence: Knowledge and Power in American National Security* (New York: Columbia University Press, 2006). On the limitations of even the most state-of-the-art methods for predicting international politics, see Gerald Schneider, Nils Petter Gleditsch, and Sabine Carey, "Forecasting in International Relations," *Conflict Management and Peace Science*, Vol. 20, No. 1 (2011), pp. 5–14; Michael D. Ward, "Can We Predict Politics?" *Journal of Global Security Studies*, Vol. 1, No. 1 (2016), pp. 80–91.

This skepticism raises fundamental questions about the nature and limits of foreign policy analysis. How is it possible to draw coherent conclusions about something as complicated as the probability that a military operation will succeed? If these judgments are subjective, then how can they be useful? To what extent can fallible people make sense of these judgments, particularly given the psychological constraints and political pressures that surround foreign policy decision making? These questions apply to virtually every element of foreign policy discourse, and they are the subject of this book.

The book has two main goals. The first of these goals is to show how foreign policy officials often try to avoid the challenge of probabilistic reasoning. The book's second goal is to demonstrate that assessments of uncertainty in international politics are more valuable than the conventional wisdom expects. From a theoretical standpoint, we will see that foreign policy analysts can assess uncertainty in clear and structured ways; that foreign policy decision makers can use those judgments to evaluate high-stakes choices; and that , in some cases , it is nearly impossible to make sound foreign policy decisions without assessing subjective probabilities in detail. The book's empirical chapters then demonstrate that real people are remarkably capable of putting those concepts into practice. We will see that assessments of uncertainty convey meaningful information about international politics; that presenting this information explicitly encourages decision makers to be more cautious when they place lives and resources at risk; and that, even if foreign policy analysts often receive unfair criticism, that does not necessarily distort analysts' incentives to provide clear and honest judgments.

Altogether, the book thus explains how foreign policy analysts can assess uncertainty in a manner that is theoretically coherent, empirically meaningful, politically defensible, practically useful, and sometimes logically necessary for making sound choices.[2] Each of these claims contradicts widespread skepticism about the value of probabilistic reasoning in international politics, and shows that placing greater emphasis on this subject can improve nearly any foreign policy debate. The book substantiates these claims by examining critical episodes in the history of U.S. national security policy and by drawing on a diverse range of quantitative evidence, including a database that contains nearly one million geopolitical forecasts and experimental studies involving hundreds of national security professionals.

The clearest benefit of improving assessments of uncertainty in international politics is that it can help to prevent policymakers from taking risks that they do not fully understand. Prior to authorizing the Bay of Pigs invasion in April 1961, for example, President Kennedy asked his Joint Chiefs of Staff to evaluate the

---

[2] Here and throughout the book, I use the term *foreign policy analysts* to describe anyone who seeks to inform foreign policy debates, both in and out of government.

plan's feasibility. The Joint Chiefs submitted a report that detailed the operation's strengths and weaknesses, and concluded that "this plan has a fair chance of ultimate success."[3] In the weeks that followed, high-ranking officials repeatedly referenced the Joint Chiefs' judgment when debating whether or not to set the Bay of Pigs invasion in motion. The problem was that no one had a clear idea of what that judgment actually meant.

The officer who wrote the Joint Chiefs' report on the Bay of Pigs invasion later said that the "fair chance" phrase was supposed to be a warning, much like a letter grade of C indicates "fair performance" on a test.[4] That is also how Secretary of Defense Robert McNamara recalled interpreting the Joint Chiefs' views.[5] But other leaders read the report differently. When Marine Corps Commandant David Shoup was later asked to say how *he* had interpreted the "fair chance" phrase, he replied that "the plan they had should have accomplished the mission."[6] Proponents of the invasion repeatedly cited the "fair chance" assessment in briefing materials.[7] President Kennedy came to believe that the Joint Chiefs had endorsed the plan. After the invasion collapsed, he wondered why no one had warned him that the mission might fail.[8]

---

[3] "Memorandum from the Joint Chiefs of Staff to Secretary McNamara," *Foreign Relations of the United States [FRUS] 1961-1963*, Vol. X, Doc 35 (3 February 1961). Chapter 5 describes this document in greater detail.

[4] When the historian Peter Wyden interviewed the officer fifteen years later, he found that "[then-Brigadier General David] Gray was still severely troubled about his failure to have insisted that figures [i.e., numeric percentages] be used. He felt that one of the key misunderstandings in the entire project was the misinterpretation of the word 'fair.'" Gray told Wyden that the Joint Chiefs believed that the odds of the invasion succeeding were roughly three in ten. Peter Wyden, *Bay of Pigs: The Untold Story* (New York: Simon and Schuster, 1979), pp. 88–90.

[5] In an after-action review conducted shortly after the Bay of Pigs invasion collapsed, McNamara said that he knew the Joint Chiefs thought the plan was unlikely to work, but that he had still believed it was the best opportunity the United States would get to overthrow the Castro regime. "Memorandum for the Record," *FRUS 1961-1963*, Vol. X, Doc 199 (3 May 1961).

[6] "Memorandum for the Record," *FRUS 1961-1963*, Vol. X Doc 209 (8 May 1961).

[7] James Rasenberger, *The Brilliant Disaster: JFK, Castro, and America's Doomed Invasion of the Bay of Pigs* (New York: Scribner, 2011), p. 119, explains that "the entire report, on balance, came off as an endorsement of the CIA's plan." On the CIA's subsequent use of the "fair chance" statement to support the invasion, see "Paper Prepared in the Central Intelligence Agency," *FRUS 1961–1963*, Vol. X, Doc 46 (17 February 1961). For post-mortem discussions of the invasion decision, see *FRUS 1961–1963*, Vol. X, Docs 199, 209, 210, and 221.

[8] President Kennedy later complained to an aide that the Joint Chiefs "had just sat there nodding, saying it would work." In a subsequent interview, Kennedy recalled that "five minutes after it began to fall in, we all looked at each other and asked, 'How could we have been so stupid?' When we saw the wide range of the failures we asked ourselves why it had not been apparent to somebody from the start." Richard Reeves, *President Kennedy: Profile of Power* (New York: Simon and Schuster, 1993), p. 103; Hugh Sidey, "The Lesson John Kennedy Learned from the Bay of Pigs," *Time*, Vol. 157, No. 15 (2001).

Regardless of the insight that the Joint Chiefs provided about the strengths and weaknesses of the Bay of Pigs invasion, their advice thus amounted to a Rorschach test: it allowed policymakers to adopt nearly any position they wanted, and to believe that their view had been endorsed by the military's top brass. This is just one of many examples we will see throughout the book of how failing to assess uncertainty in clear and structured ways can undermine foreign policy decision making. Yet, as the next example shows, the challenge of assessing uncertainty in international politics runs deeper than semantics, and it cannot be solved through clear language alone.

In April 2011—almost exactly fifty years after the Bay of Pigs invasion—President Barack Obama convened his senior national security team to discuss reports that Osama bin Laden might be living in Abbottabad, Pakistan. Intelligence analysts had studied a suspicious compound in Abbottabad for months. They possessed clear evidence connecting this site to al Qaeda, and they knew that the compound housed a tall, reclusive man who never left the premises. Yet it was impossible to be certain about who that person was. If President Obama was going to act on this information, he would have to base his decision on probabilistic reasoning. To make that reasoning as rigorous as possible, President Obama asked his advisers to estimate the chances that bin Laden was living in the Abbottabad compound.[9]

Answers to the president's question ranged widely. The leader of the bin Laden unit at the Central Intelligence Agency (CIA) said there was a ninety-five percent chance that they had found their man. CIA Deputy Director Michael Morell thought that those chances were more like sixty percent. Red Teams assigned to make skeptical arguments offered figures as low as thirty or forty percent. Other views reportedly clustered around seventy or eighty percent. While accounts of this meeting vary, all of them stress that participants did not know how to resolve their disagreement and that they did not find the discussion to be helpful.[10] President Obama reportedly said at the time that the debate had provided "not more certainty but more confusion." In a subsequent interview, he

[9] The following account is based on Michael Morell, *The Great War of Our Time: The CIA's Fight against Terrorism from Al Qa'ida to ISIS* (New York: Twelve, 2014), ch. 7; along with David Sanger, *Confront and Conceal: Obama's Secret Wars and Surprising Use of American Power* (New York: Crown 2012); Peter Bergen, *Manhunt: The Ten-Year Search for Bin Laden from 9/11 to Abbottabad* (New York: Crown 2012); and Mark Bowden, *The Finish: The Killing of Osama bin Laden* (New York: Atlantic, 2012).

[10] Reflecting later on this debate, James Clapper, who was then the director of national intelligence, said, "We put a lot of discussion [into] percentages of confidence, which to me is not particularly meaningful. In the end it's all subjective judgment anyway." CNN, "The Axe Files," Podcast Ep. 247 (31 May 2018).

told a reporter that his advisers' probability estimates had "disguised uncertainty as opposed to actually providing you with more useful information."[11]

Of course, President Obama's decision to raid the Abbottabad compound ended more successfully than President Kennedy's decision to invade the Bay of Pigs. Yet the confusion that President Obama and his advisers encountered when pursuing bin Laden was, in many ways, more troubling. The problem with the Joint Chiefs' assessment of the Bay of Pigs invasion was a simple matter of semantics. By contrast, the Obama administration's efforts to estimate the chances that bin Laden was living in Abbottabad revealed a deeper *conceptual* confusion: even when foreign policy officials attempted to debate the uncertainty that surrounded one of their seminal decisions, they still struggled to understand what those judgments meant and how they could be useful.

War and Chance seeks to dispel that confusion. The book describes the theoretical basis for assessing uncertainty in international politics, explains how those judgments provide crucial insight for evaluating foreign policy decisions, and shows that the conventional wisdom underestimates the extent to which these insights can aid foreign policy discourse. These arguments apply to virtually any kind of foreign policy analysis, from debates in the White House Situation Room to op-eds in the *New York Times*. As the following chapters explain, it is impossible to evaluate foreign policy choices without assessing uncertainty in some way, shape, or form.

To be clear, nothing in the book implies that assessing uncertainty in international politics should be easy or uncontroversial. The book's main goal is, instead, to show that scholars and practitioners handle this challenge best when they confront it head-on, and to explain that there is no reason why these debates should seem to be intractable. Even small advances in understanding this subject matter could provide substantial benefit—for, as President Obama reflected when the bin Laden raid was over, "One of the things you learn as president is that you're always dealing with probabilities."[12]

Subjective Probability and Its Skeptics

The military theorist Carl von Clausewitz wrote in his famous book, *On War*, that "war is a matter of assessing probabilities" and that "no other human activity is so continuously or universally bound up with chance."[13] Clausewitz believed that assessing this uncertainty required considerable intellect, as "many of the

---

[11] Bowden, *The Finish*, pp. 160–161; Bergen, *Manhunt*, p. 198; Sanger, *Confront and Conceal*, p. 93.

[12] Bowden, *The Finish*, p. 161.

[13] Carl von Clausewitz, *On War*, tr. Michael Howard and Peter Paret (Princeton, N.J.: Princeton University Press, 1984), pp. 85–86. The U.S. Marine Corps' capstone doctrine reflects this sentiment,

decisions faced by the commander-in-chief resemble mathematical problems worthy of the gifts of a Newton or an Euler." Yet Clausewitz argued elsewhere in *On War* that "logical reasoning often plays no part at all" in military decision making and that "absolute, so-called mathematical, factors never find a firm basis in military calculations."[14]

Though Clausewitz is famous for offering inscrutable insights about many aspects of military strategy, his views of assessing uncertainty are not contradictory, and they help to frame the analysis presented in this book. From a logical standpoint, it is impossible to support any foreign policy decision without believing that its chances of success are large enough to make expected benefits exceed expected costs. And that logic has rules. Probability and expected value are quantifiable concepts that obey mathematical axioms. Yet these axioms also have important limits. Rational choice theory can instruct decision makers about how to behave in a manner that is consistent with their personal beliefs, but it cannot tell decision makers how to form those beliefs in the first place, particularly not when they are dealing with subject matter that involves as much complexity, secrecy, and deception as world politics.[15] The foundation for any foreign policy decision thus rests on individual, subjective judgment.

Many scholars and practitioners see little value in debating these subjective judgments, and the book describes a range of arguments to that effect. Broadly speaking, we can divide those arguments into three camps. The book will refer to these camps as the *agnostics*, the *rejectionists*, and the *cynics*.

The *agnostics* argue that assessments of uncertainty in international politics are too unreliable to be useful.[16] Taken to its logical extreme, this argument suggests that foreign policy analysts can never make rigorous judgments about a policy's likely outcomes. As stated by the former U.S. secretary of defense, James Mattis, "It is not scientifically possible to accurately predict the outcome of [a

stating on its opening page that "War is intrinsically unpredictable. At best, we can hope to determine possibilities and probabilities." U.S. Marine Corps Doctrinal Publication 1, *Warfighting*, p. 7.

[14] Clausewitz, *On War*, pp. 80, 86, 112, 184.

[15] On how rational choice logic is contingent on personal beliefs, see Ken Binmore, *Rational Decisions* (Princeton, N.J.: Princeton University Press, 2009). Chapter 2 discusses this point in more detail. There is, for example, a large literature that describes how foreign policy analysts can use Bayesian mathematics to assess uncertainty, but Bayesian reasoning depends on subjective probability estimates.

[16] This view is premised on the notion that international politics and armed conflicts involve indefinable levels of complexity. On complexity and international politics, see Richard K. Betts, "Is Strategy an Illusion?" *International Security*, Vol. 25, No. 2 (2000), pp. 5–50; Jervis, *System Effects*; Thomas J. Czerwinski, *Coping with the Bounds: Speculations on Nonlinearity in Military Affairs* (Washington, D.C.: National Defense University Press, 1998); and Ben Connable, *Embracing the Fog of War* (Santa Monica, Calif.: Rand, 2012).

military] action. To suggest otherwise runs contrary to historical experience and the nature of war."[17]

The agnostic viewpoint carries sobering implications for foreign policy discourse. If it is impossible to predict the results of foreign policy decisions, then it is also impossible to say that one choice has a higher chance of succeeding than another. This stance would render most policy debates meaningless and it would undermine a vast range of international relations scholarship. If there is no rigorous way to evaluate foreign policy decisions on their merits, then there can also be no way to define rational behavior, because all choices could plausibly be characterized as leaders pursuing what they perceive to be sufficiently large chances of achieving sufficiently important objectives. Since this would make it impossible to prove that any decision did *not* promote the national interest, there would also be no purpose in arguing that any high-stakes decisions were driven by nonrational impulses.[18]

A weaker and more plausible version of the agnostics' thesis accepts that assessments of subjective probability provide *some* value, but only at broad levels of generality. As Aristotle put it, "The educated person seeks exactness in each area to the extent that the nature of the subject allows."[19] And perhaps that threshold of "allowable exactness" is extremely low when it comes to assessing uncertainty in international politics. Avoiding these judgments or leaving them vague could thus be seen as displaying appropriate humility rather than avoiding controversial issues.[20] Chapters 2 and 3 explore the theoretical and empirical foundations of this argument in detail.

---

[17] James N. Mattis, "USJFCOM Commander's Guidance for Effects-based Operations," *Parameters*, Vol. 38, No. 3 (2008), pp. 18–25. For similar questions about whether assessments of uncertainty provide a sound basis for decision making in international politics, see Alexander Wendt, "Driving with the Rearview Mirror: On the Rational Science of Institutional Design," *International Organization*, Vol. 55, No. 4 (2001), pp. 1019–1049; Jonathan Kirshner, "Rationalist Explanations for War?" *Security Studies*, Vol. 10, No. 1 (2000), pp. 143–150; Alan Beyerchen, "Clausewitz, Nonlinearity, and the Unpredictability of War," *International Security*, Vol. 17, No. 3 (1992/93), pp. 59–90; and Barry D. Watts, *Clausewitzian Friction and Future War*, revised edition (Washington, D.C.: National Defense University, 2004).

[18] On how any international relations theory relies on a coherent standard of rational decision making, see Charles L. Glaser, *Rational Theory of International Politics* (Princeton, N.J.: Princeton University Press, 2010), pp. 2–3. On how assessments of uncertainty play a crucial role in nearly all international relations paradigms, see Brian C. Rathbun, "Uncertain about Uncertainty: Understanding the Multiple Meanings of a Crucial Concept in International Relations Theory," *International Studies Quarterly*, Vol. 51, No. 3 (2007), pp. 533–557.

[19] Aristotle, *Nicomachean Ethics*, tr. Terence Irwin (Indianapolis, Ind.: Hackett, 1985), p. 1094b.

[20] For arguments exhorting foreign policy analysts to adopt such humility, see Stanley Hoffmann, *Gulliver's Troubles: Or, the Setting of American Foreign Policy* (New York: McGraw-Hill, 1968), pp. 87–175; David Halberstam, *The Best and the Brightest* (New York: Random House, 1972).

The *rejectionist* viewpoint claims that assessing uncertainty in international politics is not just misguided, but also counterproductive. This argument is rooted in the fact that foreign policy is not made by rational automata, but rather by human beings who are susceptible to political pressures and cognitive biases.[21] Chapter 4, for example, describes how scholars and practitioners often worry that probability assessments surround arbitrary opinions with illusions of rigor.[22] Chapter 5 then examines common claims about how transparent probabilistic reasoning exposes foreign policy analysts to unjustified criticism, thereby undermining their credibility and creating incentives to warp key judgments.[23]

The rejectionists' thesis is important because it implies that there is a major gap between what rigorous decision making entails in principle and what fallible individuals can achieve in practice when they confront high-stakes issues. That claim alone is unremarkable in light of the growing volume of scholarship that documents how heuristics and biases can undermine foreign policy decisions.[24] Yet, in most cases, scholars believe that the best way to mitigate these cognitive flaws is to conduct clear, well-structured analysis.[25] By contrast, the rejectionists suggest that attempts to clarify and structure probabilistic reasoning can backfire, exchanging one set of biases for another in a manner that would only make decisions worse. This argument raises fundamental questions about the extent

---

[21] Robert Jervis, *Perception and Misperception in International Politics* (Princeton, N.J.: Princeton University Press, 1976); Rose McDermott, *Risk-Taking in International Politics* (Ann Arbor, Mich.: University of Michigan Press, 1998); Philip E. Tetlock, *Expert Political Judgment: How Good Is It? How Can We Know?* (Princeton, N.J.: Princeton University Press, 2005).

[22] Mark M. Lowenthal, *Intelligence: From Secrets to Policy*, 3rd ed. (Washington, D.C.: CQ Press, 2006), p. 129; Yaakov Y. I. Vertzberger, *Risk Taking and Decisionmaking: Foreign Military Intervention Decisions* (Stanford, Calif.: Stanford University Press, 1998), pp. 27–28.

[23] Chapter 5 explains that this impulse is not purely self-serving. If national security analysts lose the trust of their colleagues or the general public as a result of unjustified criticism, then this can undermine their effectiveness regardless of whether that loss of standing is deserved. If analysts seek to avoid probability assessment in order to escape *justified* criticism, then this would reflect the cynical viewpoint.

[24] Jack S. Levy, "Psychology and Foreign Policy Decision-Making," in Leonie Huddy, David O. Sears, and Jack S. Levy, eds., *The Oxford Handbook of Political Psychology*, 2nd ed. (New York: Oxford University Press, 2013); Emilie M. Hafner-Burton et al., "The Behavioral Revolution and the Study of International Relations," *International Organization*, Vol. 71, No. S1 (April 2017), pp. S1–S31; Joshua D. Kertzer and Dustin Tingley, "Political Psychology in International Relations," *Annual Review of Political Science*, Vol. 21 (2018), pp. 319–339.

[25] Daniel Kahneman famously captured this insight with the distinction between "thinking fast" and "thinking slow," where the latter is less prone to heuristics and biases. Daniel Kahneman, *Thinking, Fast and Slow* (New York: Farrar, Straus and Giroux, 2011). In national security specifically, see Richards Heuer, Jr., *Psychology of Intelligence Analysis* (Washington, D.C.: Center for the Study of Intelligence, 1999).

to which traditional conceptions of analytic rigor provide viable foundations for foreign policy discourse.[26]

The *cynics* claim that foreign policy analysts and decision makers have self-interested motives to avoid assessing uncertainty. Political leaders may thus deliberately conceal doubts about their policy proposals in order to make tough choices seem "clearer than truth."[27] Marginalizing assessments of uncertainty may also allow foreign policy analysts to escape reasonable accountability for mistaken judgments.[28]

Having spoken with hundreds of practitioners while conducting my research, I do not believe that this cynical behavior is widespread. My impression is that this behavior is primarily concentrated at the highest levels of government and punditry, whereas most foreign policy analysts and decision makers are committed to doing their jobs as rigorously as possible.[29] Yet the prospect of cynical behavior, whatever its prevalence, only makes it more important to scrutinize other objections to probabilistic reasoning. As chapter 7 explains, the best way to prevent leaders from marginalizing or manipulating assessments of uncertainty is to establish a norm that favors placing those judgments front and center in high-stakes policy debates. It is impossible to establish this kind of norm—or to say whether such a norm would even make sense—without dispelling other sources of skepticism about the value of assessing uncertainty in international politics.

Though I will argue that the skepticism described in this section is overblown, it is easy to understand how those views have emerged. As noted at the beginning of the chapter, the history of international politics is full of cases in

---

[26] Wendt, "Driving with the Rearview Mirror"; Stanley A. Renshon and Deborah Welch Larson, eds., *Good Judgment in Foreign Policy* (Lanham, Md.: Rowman and Littlefield, 2003); and Peter Katzenstein and Lucia Seybert, "Protean Power and Uncertainty: Exploring the Unexpected in World Politics," *International Studies Quarterly*, Vol. 62, No. 1 (2018), pp. 80–93.

[27] Dean Acheson, *Present at the Creation: My Years at the State Department* (New York: Norton, 1969), p. 375; John M. Schuessler, *Deceit on the Road to War* (Ithaca, N.Y.: Cornell University Press, 2015); Uri Bar-Joseph and Rose McDermott, *Intelligence Success and Failure: The Human Factor* (New York: Oxford University Press, 2017). In other cases, decision makers may prefer to leave assessments of uncertainty vague, so as to maintain freedom of action. Joshua Rovner, *Fixing the Facts: National Security and the Politics of Intelligence* (Ithaca, N.Y.: Cornell University Press, 2011); Robert Jervis, "Why Intelligence and Policymakers Clash," *Political Science Quarterly*, Vol. 125, No. 2 (Summer 2010), pp. 185–204.

[28] H. R. McMaster, *Dereliction of Duty* (New York: HarperCollins, 1997); Philip E. Tetlock, "Reading Tarot on K Street," *The National Interest*, No. 103 (2009), pp. 57–67; Christopher Hood, *The Blame Game: Spin, Bureaucracy, and Self-Preservation in Government* (Princeton, N.J.: Princeton University Press, 2011). As mentioned in note 23, the desire to avoid *unjustified* blame falls within the rejectionists' viewpoint.

[29] This is consistent with the (much more informed) views of Robert Jervis, "Politics and Political Science," *Annual Review of Political Science*, Vol. 21 (2018), p. 17.

which scholars and practitioners misperceived or failed to recognize important elements of uncertainty.[30] Yet there is an important difference between asking how good we are at assessing uncertainty on the whole and determining how to assess uncertainty as effectively as possible. Indeed, the worse our performance in this area becomes, the more priority we should place on preserving and exploiting whatever insight we actually possess. The book documents how a series of harmful practices interfere with that goal; it demonstrates that these practices reflect misplaced skepticism about the logic, psychology, and politics of probabilistic reasoning; and it shows how it is possible to improve the quality of these judgments in nearly any area of foreign policy discourse.

Chapter Outline

The book contains seven chapters. Chapter 1 describes how foreign policy analysts often avoid assessing uncertainty in a manner that supports sound decision making. This concern dates back to a famous 1964 essay by Sherman Kent, which remains one of the seminal works in intelligence studies.[31] But chapter 1 explains that aversion to probabilistic reasoning is not just a problem for intelligence analysts and that the issue runs much deeper than semantics. We will see how scholars, practitioners, and pundits often debate international politics without assessing the most important probabilities at all, particularly by analyzing which policies offer the best prospects of success or by debating whether actions are necessary to achieve their objectives, without carefully assessing the chances that high-stakes decisions will actually work. Chapter 1 shows how this behavior is ingrained throughout a broad range of foreign policy discourse, and it describes how these problematic practices shaped the highest levels of U.S. decision making during the Vietnam War.

Chapter 2 explores the theoretical foundations of probabilistic reasoning in international politics. It explains that, even though the most important assessments of uncertainty in international politics are inherently subjective, foreign policy analysts always possess a coherent conceptual basis for debating these judgments in clear and structured ways. Chapter 3 then examines the

---

[30] See, for example, Jack Snyder, *Myths of Empire: Domestic Politics and International Ambition* (Ithaca, N.Y.: Cornell University Press, 1991); John Lewis Gaddis, *We Now Know: Rethinking Cold War History* (New York: Oxford University Press, 1997); Dominic D. P. Johnson, *Overconfidence and War* (Cambridge, Mass.: Harvard University Press, 2004); and John Mueller, *Overblown: How Politicians and the Terrorism Industry Inflate National Security Threats, and Why We Believe Them* (New York, Free Press 2006).

[31] Sherman Kent, "Words of Estimative Probability," *Studies in Intelligence*, Vol. 8, No. 4 (1964), pp. 49–65.

empirical value of assessing uncertainty in international politics. By analyzing a database containing nearly one million geopolitical forecasts, it shows that foreign policy analysts can reliably estimate subjective probabilities with numeric precision. Together, chapters 2 and 3 refute the idea that there is some threshold of "allowable exactness" that constrains assessments of uncertainty in international politics. Avoiding these judgments or leaving them vague should not be seen as displaying appropriate analytic humility, but rather as a practice that sells analysts' capabilities short and diminishes the quality of foreign policy discourse.

Chapter 4 examines the psychology of assessing uncertainty in international politics, focusing on the concern that clear probabilistic reasoning could confuse decision makers or create harmful "illusions of rigor." By presenting a series of survey experiments that involved more than six hundred national security professionals, the chapter shows that foreign policy decision makers' choices are sensitive to subtle variations in probability assessments, and that making these assessments more explicit encourages decision makers to be more cautious when they are placing lives and resources at risk.[32] Chapter 5 then explores the argument that assessing uncertainty in clear and structured ways would expose foreign policy analysts to excessive criticism. By combining experimental evidence with a historical review of perceived intelligence failures, chapter 5 suggests that the conventional wisdom about the "politics of uncertainty and blame" may actually have the matter exactly backward: by leaving their assessments of uncertainty vague, foreign policy analysts end up providing their critics with an opportunity to make key judgments seem worse than they really were.

Chapter 6 takes a closer look at how foreign policy decision makers can use assessments of uncertainty to evaluate high-stakes choices. It explains why transparent probabilistic reasoning is especially important when leaders are struggling to assess strategic progress. In some cases, it can actually be impossible to make rigorous judgments about the extent to which foreign policies are making acceptable progress without assessing subjective probabilities in detail. Chapter 7 concludes by exploring the book's practical implications for improving foreign policy debates. It focuses on the importance of creating norms that place assessments of uncertainty front and center in foreign policy analysis, and explains how the practice of multiple advocacy can help to generate those norms.

---

[32] One irony of these findings is that the national security officials who participated in the experiments often insisted that fine-grained probabilistic distinctions would *not* shape their decisions, even as the experimental data unambiguously demonstrated that this information influenced their views. The notion that decision makers may not always be aware of how they arrive at their own beliefs is one of the central motivations for conducting experimental research in political psychology. Yet, unlike areas of political psychology that show how decision makers' views are susceptible to unconscious biases, the book's empirical analysis suggests that national security officials are more sophisticated than they give themselves credit for in handling subjective probabilities.

This argument further highlights that the goal of improving assessments of uncertainty in international politics is not just an issue for government officials,
but that it is also a matter of how scholars, journalists, and pundits can raise the
standards of foreign policy discourse.

Methods and Approach

If presidents are always dealing with probabilities, then how can there be so
much confusion about handling that subject? And if this topic is so important,
then why have other scholars not written a book like this one already?

One answer to these questions is that the study of probabilistic reasoning
requires combining disciplinary approaches that scholars tend to pursue separately. Understanding what subjective probability assessments mean and how
they shape foreign policy decisions (chapters 2 and 6) requires adapting general principles from decision theory to specific problems of international politics. Understanding the extent to which real people can employ these concepts
(chapters 3 and 4) requires studying the psychological dimensions of foreign
policy analysis and decision making. Understanding how the prospect of criticism shapes foreign policy analysts' incentives (chapter 5) requires merging
insights from intelligence studies and organizational management.

In this sense, no one academic discipline is well-suited to addressing the
full range of claims that skeptics direct toward assessing uncertainty in foreign
policy discourse. And though the book's interdisciplinary approach involves an
inevitable trade-off of depth for breadth, it is crucial to examine these topics
together and not in isolation. As the rejectionists point out, well-intentioned
efforts to mitigate one set of flaws with probabilistic reasoning could plausibly
backfire by amplifying others. Addressing these concerns requires taking a
comprehensive view of the logic, psychology, and politics of assessing uncertainty in international affairs. To my knowledge, *War and Chance* is the first
book to do so.

A second reason why scholars and practitioners lack consensus about the
value of probabilistic reasoning in international politics is that this subject is notoriously difficult to study empirically. Uncertainty is an abstract concept that no
one can directly observe. Since analysts and decision makers tend to be vague
when they assess uncertainty, it is usually hard to say what their judgments actually mean. And even when analysts make their judgments explicit, it can still
be difficult to evaluate them. For instance, if you say that an event has a thirty
percent chance of taking place and then it happens, how can we tell whether
you were wrong or just unlucky? Chapters 3 through 5 will show that navigating
these issues requires gathering large volumes of well-structured data. Most areas

of foreign policy do not lend themselves to this kind of data collection. Scholars have therefore tended to treat the assessment of uncertainty as a topic better-suited to philosophical debate than to empirical analysis.[33]

In recent years, however, social scientists have developed new methods to study probabilistic reasoning, and governmental organizations have become increasingly receptive to supporting empirical research on the subject. Chapter 3's analysis of the value of precision in probability assessment would not have been possible without the U.S. Intelligence Community's decision to sponsor the collection of nearly one million geopolitical forecasts.[34] Similarly, chapter 4's analysis of how decision makers respond to assessments of uncertainty depended on the support of the National War College and the willingness of more than six hundred national security professionals to participate in experimental research. Thus, even if none of the following chapters represents the final word on its subject, one of the book's main contributions is simply to demonstrate that it is possible to conduct rigorous empirical analysis of issues that many scholars and practitioners have previously considered intractable.

This book also differs from previous scholarship in how it treats the relationship between explanation and prescription. Academic studies of international politics typically prioritize the explanatory function of social science, in which scholars focus on building a descriptive model of the world that helps readers to understand why states and leaders act in puzzling ways. Most scholars therefore orient their analyses around theoretical and empirical questions that are important for explaining observed behavior. Although such studies can generate policy-relevant insights, those insights are often secondary to scholars' descriptive aims. Indeed, some of the most salient insights that these studies produce is that there is relatively little we can do to improve problematic behavior, either because foreign policy officials have strong incentives to act in a harmful fashion or because their choices are shaped by structural forces outside of their control.[35]

This book, by contrast, prioritizes the prescriptive value of social science. It aims to understand what sound decision making entails in principle and how close we can get to that standard in practice. To serve these objectives, the following chapters focus on theoretical and empirical questions that are important for understanding how to *improve* foreign policy analysis and decision making,

---

[33] Mandeep K. Dhami, "Towards an Evidence-Based Approach to Communicating Uncertainty in Intelligence Analysis," *Intelligence and National Security*, Vol. 33, No. 2 (2018), pp. 257–272.

[34] Philip E. Tetlock and Daniel Gardner, *Superforecasting: The Art and Science of Prediction* (New York: Crown, 2015).

[35] For a critique of how international relations scholars often privilege descriptive aims over prescriptive insights, see Alexander George, *Bridging the Gap: Theory and Practice in Foreign Policy* (Washington, D.C.: U.S. Institute of Peace, 1993); and Bruce W. Jentleson, "The Need for Praxis: Bringing Policy Relevance Back In," *International Security*, Vol. 26, No. 4 (2002), pp. 169–183.

not just to explain the current state of affairs in this field. As with most social science, however, the book's prescriptive and descriptive aims overlap. By showing how scholars and practitioners often exaggerate the obstacles to assessing uncertainty in international politics, the following chapters reveal how many key aspects of this subject remain understudied and misunderstood.

Key Concepts and Scope Conditions

Since probabilistic reasoning is an abstract endeavor, it is important to define some key terms up front.

The book applies the term *probability assessment* to any description of the chances that a statement is true. This does not simply refer to the kinds of numeric estimates that President Obama's advisers made when discussing the probability that Osama bin Laden was living in Abbottabad. Any description of uncertainty, no matter how vague, falls within the scope of the book's analysis.

Assessments of probability are distinct from assessments of confidence. *Analytic confidence* describes the extent to which analysts believe that they have a sound basis for making probabilistic judgments.[36] For example, a coin flip has a fifty percent probability of coming up heads, and most people would have high confidence when making that estimate. But when you discuss the outcome of an election that you have not been following closely, you might say that a candidate's chances of success are fifty-fifty simply because you have no idea what those chances are. In that case, you would still offer a probability estimate of fifty percent, but you would assign low confidence to your judgment. The importance of disentangling probability and confidence appears in several places throughout the book, and we will see how scholars and practitioners regularly conflate these concepts.[37]

There is also an important distinction to draw between making probability assessments and evaluating high-stakes decisions themselves. Any decision made under uncertainty requires assessing probabilities—without some key

[36] Elsewhere, I have argued that analytic confidence comprises three distinct attributes: the availability of reliable evidence supporting a judgment, the range of reasonable opinion surrounding that judgment, and the extent to which analysts expect their judgment to change in response to new information. See Jeffrey A. Friedman and Richard Zeckhauser, "Analytic Confidence and Political Decision Making: Theoretical Principles and Experimental Evidence from National Security Professionals," *Political Psychology*, Vol. 39, No. 5 (2018), pp. 1069–1087.

[37] See, for example, James Clapper's description of "percentages of confidence" in note 10, above. For further discussion of how scholars and practitioners conflate probability and confidence, see Jeffrey A. Friedman and Richard Zeckhauser, "Assessing Uncertainty in Intelligence," *Intelligence and National Security*, Vol. 27, No. 6 (2012), pp. 834–841.

element of a decision being probabilistic, there would be no uncertainty to deal with. But rigorous decision making under uncertainty requires tackling many challenges besides assessing probabilities, such as identifying the range of different outcomes than an action could influence, assigning costs and benefits to those outcomes, and judging the potential value of delaying action or gathering additional information.[38]

Assessing uncertainty is thus not sufficient to ensure sound foreign policy decisions. But assessing uncertainty is a *necessary* component of making sound foreign policy decisions, and it is a topic that generates unusual controversy. For example, I am unaware of any serious scholar or practitioner who argues that foreign policy officials should deliberately avoid defining their interests, or that it would be counterproductive to analyze the details of how much a policy might cost. The fact that many foreign policy experts *do* level those arguments against assessing uncertainty reveals how the subject raises special skepticism.

Finally, while the book focuses on assessing uncertainty in international politics—and while most of its examples are drawn from U.S. national security policy, in particular—the book's basic themes are relevant to any area of high-stakes decision making. Debates about the value of probability assessment appear in most domains of public policy, and indeed throughout daily life. Medical decisions, for example, require assessing uncertainty surrounding contentious diagnoses or treatment options. Yet physicians, like foreign policy analysts, can be reluctant to describe uncertainty when speaking with their patients.[39] By law, some government agencies are required to quantify the degree to which they expect proposed regulations to reduce the probability of unfavorable outcomes. Some critics find this practice to be absurd and potentially counterproductive.[40]

---

[38] Robert Winkler, *An Introduction to Bayesian Inference and Decision*, 2nd ed. (Sugar Land, Tex.: Probabilistic Publishing, 2003). Decision scientists further distinguish between situations of "risk," where all probabilities relevant to decision making are known; situations of "uncertainty," where decision makers know all the relevant outcomes, but those outcomes have ambiguous probabilities of occurrence; and situations of "ignorance," where decision makers do not know all the relevant outcomes that their choices would affect. See Richard Zeckhauser, "Investing in the Unknown and Unknowable," in Francis Diebold, Neil Doherty, and Richard Herring, eds., *The Known, the Unknown, and the Unknowable in Financial Risk Management* (Princeton, N.J.: Princeton University Press, 2010).

[39] One study of more than three thousand doctor-patient interactions found that physicians described uncertainty about treatment outcomes in just seventeen percent of complex procedures (and in four percent of procedures overall). See Clarence H. Braddock et al., "Informed Decision Making in Outpatient Practice," *Journal of the American Medical Association*, Vol. 282, No. 24 (December 1999), pp. 2313–2320.

[40] For competing views on this subject, see Cass R. Sunstein, *Valuing Life: Humanizing the Regulatory State* (Chicago, Ill.: University of Chicago Press, 2014); and Frank Ackerman and Lisa Heinzerling, *Priceless: On Knowing the Price of Everything and the Value of Nothing* (New York: W. W. Norton, 2004).

For more than a decade, climate scientists have engaged in a vigorous debate over the proper methods for communicating uncertainty to the public regarding projections of global warming, sea level rise, and other environmental issues.[41]

In one of the most salient examples of how vague probabilistic reasoning shapes civil society, the U.S. criminal justice system reaches verdicts by asking jurors to determine whether the probability of a defendant's guilt lies "beyond a reasonable doubt." Judges, juries, and attorneys hold strikingly divergent views of what the reasonable doubt standard entails. Some of the ways that lawyers and judges have described this standard in court include "60 percent," "kind of like 75 percent," "somewhere between the 75- and 90-yard line on a 100-yard-long football field," and "a 1,000-piece puzzle with sixty pieces missing."[42] One survey that asked federal judges to quantify the "beyond a reasonable doubt" standard produced answers with a minimum of fifty percent, a maximum of one hundred percent, an average of ninety percent, and a standard deviation of eight percentage points.[43] A related survey found several real juries in which a majority of jurors believed that a seventy percent probability of guilt lay beyond a reasonable doubt.[44] These seemingly arbitrary interpretations raise troubling questions about the application of criminal justice. Yet, as in international politics, many scholars and practitioners of the law oppose assessing uncertainty in clearer and more structured ways.

Empirical findings from one field do not always apply to others. Yet the book's conceptual framework and empirical methodology can be extended to nearly any domain of high-stakes decision making. And to the extent that international politics are typically understood to be particularly complex and subjective, this domain should pose a high degree of difficulty for improving the quality and rigor of probabilistic reasoning. Thus, to the extent that the book pushes back against entrenched skepticism about the nature and limits of assessing uncertainty in international politics, it suggests that other disciplines might also benefit from revisiting their own views of this subject.

[41] David V. Budescu, Stephen Broomell, and Han-Hui Por, "Improving Communication of Uncertainty in the Report of the Intergovernmental Panel on Climate Change," *Psychological Science*, Vol. 20, No. 3 (2009), pp. 299–308.

[42] Peter Tillers and Jonathan Gottfried, "Case Comment—*United States* v. *Copeland*, 369 F. Supp. 2d 275 (E.D.N.Y. 2005): A Collateral Attack on the Legal Maxim That Proof beyond a Reasonable Doubt Is Unquantifiable?" *Law, Probability, and Risk*, Vol. 5, No. 2 (June 2006), pp. 135–157.

[43] C. M. A. McAuliff, "Burdens of Proof: Degrees of Belief, Quanta of Evidence, or Constitutional Guarantees?" *Vanderbilt Law Review* 35 (November 1982), p. 1325.

[44] James Franklin, "Case Comment—*United States* v. *Copeland*, 369 F. Supp. 2d 275 (E.D.N.Y. 2005): Quantification of the 'Proof Beyond Reasonable Doubt' Standard," *Law, Probability, and Risk*, Vol. 5, No. 2 (June 2006), p. 165.

1

Pathologies of Probability Assessment

This chapter describes how foreign policy officials often avoid assessing uncertainty in a manner that supports sound decision making. This problem extends beyond the fact that foreign policy analysts are generally unwilling to articulate their judgments precisely. Instead, we will see how foreign policy officials often appear reluctant to assess basic elements of uncertainty at all. For example, the chapter shows that foreign policy officials frequently orient debates around determining what policies offer the best prospects for success or what actions are necessary to achieve strategic objectives, without analyzing the chances that these measures will actually work. This behavior is ingrained throughout foreign policy discourse, from day-to-day intelligence reports to the highest levels of national security decision making.

The chapter describes this problem in two ways. First, it reviews official guidelines for assessing uncertainty in the U.S. military, Intelligence Community, and other national security agencies. These guidelines demonstrate a widespread aversion to probabilistic reasoning. The chapter then presents a case study that describes how U.S. officials debated their strategic prospects during the Vietnam War between 1961 and 1965. Through qualitative and quantitative analysis of key documents from this period, we will see that senior leaders consistently avoided assessing the uncertainty that surrounded their decisions to escalate the war.

The Vietnam case holds special significance considering that Secretary of Defense Robert McNamara and his staff were some of the most analytically inclined decision makers in the history of U.S. foreign policy. Conventional narratives of Vietnam War decision making portray these so-called Whiz Kids as being overly committed to methodological rigor, especially when it came to conducting the kinds of quantitative, cost-benefit analyses that Secretary McNamara had pioneered as an executive at Ford Motors. This narrative may accurately characterize the immense analytic firepower that the Pentagon devoted to measuring tactical progress during the war. Yet we will also see that

100% Certainty		
The General Area of Possibility		
93%	give or take about 6%	Almost certain
75%	give or take about 12%	Probable
50%	give or take about 10%	Chances about even
30%	give or take about 10%	Probably not
7%	give or take about 5%	Almost certainly not
0% Impossibility		

Figure 1.1 Sherman Kent's odds table. Source: Kent, "Words of Estimative Probability."

U.S. officials put virtually no systematic effort into assessing the chances that their overall strategy would succeed.

Seen from this vantage point, the McNamara Pentagon did not suffer from an excess of methodological rigor when guiding the Vietnam War, but rather from an almost complete absence of attention to the logical foundations of their most important choices. The fact that even the Whiz Kids could not bring themselves to address these matters in clear and structured ways highlights a basic divergence between the theory and the practice of foreign policy decision making. Although virtually every theory of decision making in international politics depends on assessing uncertainty in one form or another, this chapter shows that foreign policy officials can place lives and resources at risk without carefully evaluating what those risks entail.

"Words of Estimative Probability"

In 1950, an intelligence official named Sherman Kent supervised the production of a report that warned of a "serious possibility" that the Soviet Union would invade Yugoslavia within a year. Kent later asked his analysts to explain how they interpreted the phrase "a serious possibility." Their answers ranged from twenty percent to eighty percent. Surely, Kent reasoned, intelligence reports meant little if their own authors disagreed so strongly about what their judgments meant. Kent described this experience in a 1964 essay, titled "Words of Estimative Probability," in which he recommended that intelligence analysts articulate assessments of uncertainty using the odds table shown in Figure 1.1.[1]

---

[1] Sherman Kent, "Words of Estimative Probability," *Studies in Intelligence*, Vol. 8, No. 4 (1964), pp. 49–65. Kent defined the numeric ranges in the odds table by surveying how foreign policy officials intuitively quantified probabilistic phrases. This method of eliciting "inferred probabilities" is now

Sherman Kent was one of the most influential figures in the early years of the United States Intelligence Community. A former history professor at Yale, Kent became the director of the Board of National Estimates, an organization similar to today's National Intelligence Council. Kent is known as the "founding father of intelligence estimation" in the United States, and the Central Intelligence Agency training center is named in his honor. But despite his position of authority, Kent could not convince his colleagues to use the odds table or to clarify their assessments of uncertainty in any other systematic way.

In his essay, Kent described receiving pushback from a group of analysts he called the "poets" (in contrast to the "mathematicians," who supported making assessments of uncertainty more precise). Kent wrote that the poets "appear to believe the most a writer can achieve when working in a speculative area of human affairs is communication in only the broadest general sense. If he gets the wrong message across or no message at all—well, that is life." To the extent that the poets saw the odds table as reflecting "bogus precision," Kent argued, it represented a "fundamentally defeatist" attitude. The poets nevertheless retained the upper hand in this debate for four decades, defeating subsequent attempts by other high-ranking officials, including National Intelligence Council chairman Joseph Nye, to clarify assessments of uncertainty in intelligence.[2]

The poets were ultimately forced to cede ground following mistaken assessments of Saddam Hussein's weapons of mass destruction (WMD) programs, which President George W. Bush used to justify the 2003 invasion of Iraq. A National Intelligence Estimate (NIE) on this subject opened by stating, "We judge that Iraq has continued its weapons of mass destruction programs in defiance of UN resolutions and restrictions."[3] Phrases like "we judge" are what

a standard tool in the decision sciences. See Ruth Beyth-Marom, "How Probable Is Probable?" *Journal of Forecasting*, Vol. 1 (1982), pp. 257–269; Frederick Mosteller and Cleo Youtz, "Quantifying Probabilistic Expressions," *Statistical Science*, Vol. 5, No. 1 (1990), pp. 2–12; and David R. Mandel, "Accuracy of Intelligence Forecasts from the Intelligence Consumer's Perspective," *Policy Insights from the Behavioral and Brain Sciences*, Vol. 2, No. 1 (2015), pp. 111–120.

[2] Joseph S. Nye, Jr., "Peering into the Future," *Foreign Affairs*, Vol. 73, No. 4 (1994), pp. 82–93. Reviewing a corpus of 379 NIEs written between 1964 and 1994, Richard Zeckhauser and I found that only 4 percent of key judgments assessed uncertainty using quantitative indicators, whereas 18 percent of key judgments did not convey even a qualitative sense of the chances that a statement was true. Jeffrey A. Friedman and Richard Zeckhauser, "Assessing Uncertainty in Intelligence," *Intelligence and National Security*, Vol. 27, No. 6 (2012), p. 837. For similar descriptions of the aversion to transparent probabilistic reasoning in Israeli and Canadian intelligence, respectively, see Zvi Lanir and Daniel Kahneman, "An Experiment in Decision Analysis in Israel in 1975," *Studies in Intelligence*, Vol. 50, No. 4 (2006), pp. 11–19; and Alan Barnes, "Making Intelligence Analysis More Intelligent: Using Numeric Probabilities," *Intelligence and National Security*, Vol. 31, No. 1 (2016), pp. 327–344.

[3] NIE 2002-16HC, *Iraq's Continuing Programs for Weapons of Mass Destruction* (Oct. 2002).

intelligence analysts call "estimative verbs." In principle, estimative verbs are meant to emphasize the presence of uncertainty. A statement that analysts *judge* to be true is thus distinct from a statement that analysts *know* to be true. Yet most people read the NIE's key judgments as though they conveyed facts, not inferences. It was widely believed that intelligence analysts had presented the evidence on Iraq's weapons programs as a "slam dunk," and almost every post-mortem analysis of the episode emphasized that the Iraq NIE was unclear on this point.[4]

This lack of clarity ran much deeper than confusing semantics. Several prominent postmortem analyses of the Iraq NIE argued that the document's lack of linguistic clarity reflected a more fundamental failure to grapple with the uncertainty surrounding key judgments. For instance, Robert Jervis describes how intelligence analysts' perceptions in this case were heavily conditioned by assumptions drawn from Saddam Hussein's intentions and past behavior. Because these assumptions seemed reasonable and were widely shared, it was easy to overlook how heavily they relied on circumstantial evidence. Jervis thus concludes that "the central analytic error [with the Iraq NIE] was not that inferences were driven by their plausibility [instead of direct evidence] . . . but that the analysts did not make this clear and probably did not even understand it."[5] Former deputy director of intelligence Michael Morell has similarly argued that "By far the biggest mistake made by the analysts . . . was not that they came to the wrong conclusion about Iraq's WMD program, but rather that they did not rigorously ask themselves how confident they were in their judgments."[6] Morell specifically singled out a line in the NIE that assigned "high confidence" to the judgment that Saddam Hussein was developing chemical, biological, and nuclear weapons, explaining that

> the analysts did not really think about that statement before making it. It was a reflection of their gut view. It did not reflect a thorough

[4] See, for example, Michael Schrage, "What Percent Is Slam Dunk?" *Washington Post*, February 20, 2005, p. B01. Chapter 5 will return to this episode, describing how the "slam dunk" term was mistakenly (but foreseeably) used to characterize the Iraq NIE. Richard Betts similarly argues that the principal error in intelligence on Iraqi weapons programs was a "failure to make clear how weak the direct evidence was for reaching any conclusion." Richard K. Betts, *Enemies of Intelligence: Knowledge and Power in American National Security* (New York: Columbia University Press, 2006), p. 116.

[5] Robert Jervis, "Reports, Politics, and Intelligence Failures: The Case of Iraq," *Journal of Strategic Studies*, Vol. 29, No. 1 (2006), p. 44.

[6] Michael Morell, *The Great War of Our Time: The CIA's Fight against Terrorism from Al Qa'ida to ISIS* (New York: Twelve, 2014), p. 102.

assessment of the question of confidence levels. Such a rigorous assessment was missing. It was simply not part of an analyst's toolkit in those days.[7]

The Iraq WMD controversy provoked widespread pressure to improve analytic standards in intelligence reporting. Congress even translated this pressure into law, requiring intelligence analysts to "properly caveat and express uncertainties" in their published work.[8] Yet because Congress did not explain what "properly" assessing uncertainty meant, intelligence agencies responded by creating idiosyncratic standards as opposed to common doctrine. Figure 1.2 presents four examples.[9] Nodding to Sherman Kent, scholars call these expressions "words of estimative probability," though it is worth noting that this phrase is usually a misnomer, as most such spectrums do not include the kinds of explicit definitions that Kent had originally recommended.

While these guidelines all possess important advantages over unstructured communication, they also reveal how intelligence agencies remain reluctant to provide policymakers with clear assessments of uncertainty. Indeed, these guidelines show that intelligence agencies are willing to take special steps to avoid transparent probabilistic reasoning. The Defense Intelligence Agency's doctrine is especially outspoken on this matter, stating—emphasis in the original—that *"DIA does not condone the use of probability percentages in its products to portray likelihood."*[10] But each of the guidelines shown in Figure 1.2 conveys a similar sentiment. To apply these guidelines properly, analysts must determine where their probability estimates fall along the number line, after which analysts are instructed to coarsen their beliefs into broader categories, most of which lack clear definitions.

The application of these analytic standards also remains inconsistent. For example, the guidelines shown at the bottom of Figure 1.2 appear in an Intelligence

[7] Ibid. Note that in this and the previous quotation, Morell uses the term "confidence" as a synonym for probability. The Iraq NIE conflates these concepts in similar ways—or, at least, never draws a clear distinction between the chances that a statement is true and the basis on which analysts have drawn those conclusions. Chapter 2 returns to the distinction between probability and confidence.

   [8] 2004 Intelligence Reform and Terrorism Prevention Act, Section 1019(b)(2)(A).

   [9] The Defense Intelligence Agency guidelines in Figure 1.1 have been redrawn for clarity; each of the other guidelines in Figure 1.2 is a facsimile based on original documents.

   [10] Defense Intelligence Agency Tradecraft Note 01-15, *Expressing Analytic Certainty* (January 2015), p. 1. The Defense Intelligence Agency (DIA) guidelines contain other peculiarities. For example, they do not give analysts any clear option for communicating probability estimates that are near fifty percent. Terms in the middle of the DIA's spectrum, such as "undetermined" and "perhaps," suggest lack of knowledge as opposed to considered judgments, and the guidelines state that these phrases should only be used to reflect "purely exploratory analysis."

From the 2007 National Intelligence Estimate, "Prospects for Iraq's Stability":

Intelligence judgments pertaining to likelihood are intended to reflect the community's sense of the probability of a development or event. Assigning precise numerical ratings to such judgments would imply more rigor than we intend. The chart below provides a rough idea of the relationship of terms to each other.

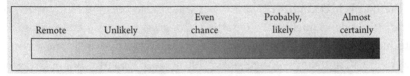

| Remote | Unlikely | Even chance | Probably, likely | Almost certainly |

From the Defense Intelligence Agency's 2015 Tradecraft Standards:

Likelihood expresses the probability that an event or development will **or will not** happen.

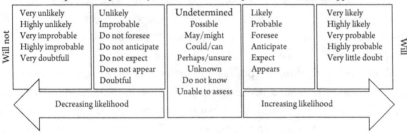

Will not				Will
Very unlikely Highly unlikely Very improbable Highly improbable Very doubtfull	Unlikely Improbable Do not foresee Do not anticipate Do not expect Does not appear Doubtful	Undetermined Possible May/might Could/can Perhaps/unsure Unknown Do not know Unable to assess	Likely Probable Foresee Anticipate Expect Appears	Very likely Highly likely Very probable Highly probable Very little doubt
Decreasing likelihood			Increasing likelihood	

From the 2015 Intelligence Community Directive on "Analytic Standards":

(a) **For expressions of likelihood or probability, an analytic product must use one** of the following sets of terms:

almost no chance	very unlikely	unlikely	roughly even chance	likely	very likely	almost certain(ly)
remote	highly improbable	improbable (improbably)	roughly even odds	probable (probably)	highly probable	nearly certain
01–05%	05–20%	20–45%	45–55%	55–80%	80–95%	95–99%

From the 2017 National Intelligence Community Assessment on Russian Hacking:

Percent

| Almost no chance | Very unlikely | Unlikely | Roughly even chance | Likely | Very likely | Almost certainly |

| 0 | 20 | 40 | 60 | 80 | 100 |

| | Highly improbable | Improbable | Roughly even odds | Probable | Highly probable | Nearly certain |
| Remote | | | | | | |

Figure 1.2 Words of estimative probability in intelligence analysis.

Community Assessment describing Russia's attempts to influence the 2016 U.S. presidential election. These guidelines indicate that intelligence analysts should communicate probabilistic judgments using fourteen "words of estimative probability" grouped into seven segments along the number line. One could argue about whether or not this is the best way to communicate important assessments of uncertainty. But that argument would be largely irrelevant in this case, given that the report's key judgments did not actually use those terms to convey key judgments. Instead, the report described uncertainty about Russian interference in the 2016 election using estimative verbs and confidence levels, as in the following statements:

> *We assess* Russian President Vladimir Putin ordered an influence cam-
> paign in 2016 aimed at the US presidential election. Russia's goals were to
> undermine public faith in the US democratic process, denigrate Secretary
> Clinton, and harm her electability and potential presidency. *We further
> assess* Putin and the Russian Government developed a clear preference
> for President-elect Trump. *We have high confidence in these judgments.*
>
> *We also assess* Putin and the Russian Government aspired to help
> President-elect Trump's election chances when possible by discrediting
> Secretary Clinton and publicly contrasting her unfavorably to him. All
> three agencies agree with this judgment. *CIA and FBI have high confi-
> dence in this judgment; NSA has moderate confidence.*[11]

It is hard to say exactly what these judgments mean. One plausible interpretation is that analysts conflated assessments of probability (which reflect the chances that a statement is true) with assessments of confidence (which reflect the extent to which analysts believe they have a sound basis for drawing conclusions).[12] This would raise further questions about what probabilities a "high confidence" or "moderate confidence" judgment might reflect. If analysts *did* intend to distinguish between probability and confidence, then their conclusions would be even harder to interpret, because the only other probabilistic term these judgments use is the estimative verb, "we assess." Either way, these judgments are not consistent with the analytic standards for assessing

[11] ICA 2017-01D, *Assessing Russian Activities and Intentions in Recent U.S. Elections* (January 2017). Emphasis added. See https://www.dni.gov/files/documents/ICA_2017_01.pdf.

[12] Chapter 2 expands on this conceptual distinction. Friedman and Zeckhauser, "Assessing Uncertainty in Intelligence," pp. 834–841, show that intelligence analysts appear to regularly conflate the language of probability and the language of confidence, particularly when they are dealing with uncertainty about questions to which the answers are knowable. Intelligence analysts are thus more likely to use the language of confidence to describe uncertainty about events that have occurred in the past; they are more likely to use the language of probability to describe uncertainty about events that will occur in the future; and they rarely employ both concepts when offering a single judgment.

RISK ASSESSMENT MATRIX						
		Probability				
Severity		**Frequent** **A**	**Likely** **B**	**Occasional** **C**	**Seldom** **D**	**Unlikely** **E**
Catastrophic	**I**	E	E	H	H	M
Critical	**II**	E	H	H	M	L
Marginal	**III**	H	M	M	L	L
Negligible	**IV**	M	L	L	L	L
E - Extremely High		**H-High**		**M - Moderate**		**L- Low**

Assess Each Hazard on the Probability of the Event or Occurrence

1-23.   Probability is the likelihood of an event. This is your estimate, given what information you know and what others have experienced. The probability levels estimated for each hazard are based on the mission, COA, or frequency of a similar event. For the purpose of CRM, there are five levels of probability—frequent, likely, occasional, seldom, and unlikely:

•   Frequent – Occurs very often, known to happen regularly. In illustration, given 500 or so exposures to the hazard, expect that it will definitely happen to someone. Examples of frequent occurrences are vehicle rollovers, rear-end collisions, and heat injury during a battalion physical training run with hot weather or nonacclimated Soldiers.

•   Likely – Occurs several times, a common occurrence. In illustration, given 1000 or so exposures without proper controls, it will occur at some point. Examples might include improvised explosive devices (IEDs), wire strikes for aircraft, controlled flights into terrain, and unintentional weapons discharges.

•   Occasional – Occurs sporadically, but is not uncommon. You may or may not get through your deployment without it happening. Some examples might include unexploded ordnance (UXO) and fratricide.

•   Seldom - Remotely possible, could occur at some time. Usually several things must go wrong for it to happen. Examples might include things like heat-related death or electrocution.

•   Unlikely – Can assume will not occur, but not impossible. Examples might include detonation of containerized ammunition during transport.

Figure 1.3 U.S. Army guidelines for risk assessment. *Source:* U.S. Army Field Manual 5-19, *Composite Risk Management.*

uncertainty that the document itself put forth. This discrepancy highlights how intelligence analysts remain ambivalent about the importance of assessing uncertainty in clear and structured ways, despite decades of effort spent promoting that goal.

Words of Estimative Probability Outside Intelligence Studies

Official guidelines for assessing uncertainty are most commonly debated in intelligence studies, but similar controversies appear in other areas of foreign policy analysis. For example, Figure 1.3 presents current U.S. Army doctrine on risk assessment. This doctrine instructs planners to describe probability using five terms. These terms superficially resemble the words of estimative probability spectrums shown in Figure 1.2, but they convey very different meanings. For example, the term *frequent* describes a hazard that "occurs very often, [and is] known to happen regularly. In illustration, given 500 exposures to the hazard, expect that it will definitely happen to someone." The word "likely" means that a hazard "will occur at some point" given "1000 or so exposures without proper controls."[13]

Even though the guidelines shown in Figure 1.3 define key terms using numbers, the resulting definitions remain extremely vague. What does it mean to "expect that something will definitely happen"? Does an "exposure" refer to a single action, so that we would need to take that action 1,000 times before a "likely" risk would occur? Or is every person exposed to the risk separately, so that the risk would occur if a unit with 1,000 people took that action once? And why is a "likely" risk only defined with respect to actions undertaken "without proper controls"? How would planners express a risk that would occur one time in 1,000 trials *with* proper controls?

Figure 1.4 presents a different set of guidelines, used by the Joint Chiefs of Staff to assess the risks surrounding military strategies.[14] This scale involves four categories of risk: low, moderate, significant, and high. Each designation reflects a complex array of vaguely defined factors. Moreover, none of the terms allows the Joint Chiefs to indicate that a military strategy is unlikely to succeed—the category of "high risk" indicates only that achieving desired objectives "requires extraordinary measures." Later in the chapter, we will see how U.S. officials sent combat forces to Vietnam thinking that, even if this strategy was unlikely to work, its chances of success were still large enough to justify a high-stakes gamble. As of this writing, the U.S. military is committed to "destroying" the Islamic State, an outcome that most senior leaders presumably see as unlikely, at least in the short run. The Joint Chiefs of Staff's risk assessment system makes it impossible to describe that logic, let alone to grapple in a meaningful way with the uncertainty it entails.

Figure 1.5 presents the analytic standards that U.S. military interrogators use when describing the reliability of human sources.[15] Whenever foreign policy analysts consider information from a human source, it is crucial to assess the probability that the source could be lying. One of the principal critiques of

[13] U.S. Army Field Manual 5-19, *Composite Risk Management* (2006), paras. 1–23. U.S. Army doctrine can be found online at https://usacac.army.mil/cac2/Doctrine.asp.

[14] "CJCS Joint Risk Assessment System" (2004), accessed October 5, 2016, http://dde.carlisle.army.mil/LLL/DSC/ppt/L14_CRA.pdf.

[15] U.S. Army Field Manual 2-22.3, *Human Intelligence Collector Operations* (2006), p. B-1.

	Low	Moderate	Significant	High
Strategic Objectives	Strategic objective: Assured	Strategic objective: Very likely	Strategic objective: Likely	Strategic objective: Requires extraordinary measures
Authorities	Full authorities provided to achieve all strategic objectives	Authorities provided to achieve most strategic objectives	Authorities are insufficient to achieve key strategic objectives	Critical authorities are not provided; ability to achieve strategic objectives is compromised
Plans	SCG/CPG/JSCP direct advanced planning: OPLANS (Level IV) or CONPLANS (Level III)	SCG/CPG/JSCP direct preliminary planning: Base Plans (Level II) or CDR's Estimate (Level I)	SCG/CPG/JSCP do not direct planning but local plans exist or are being developed	SCG/CPG/JSCP do not direct plans and planning is not in progress
Resources	As planned	Additional resources from other plans and operations	Additional resources from other plans & operations; some significant capability shortfalls	Significant resources from other operations; some resources severely deficient or absent altogether
Resources: Timelines	As planned	Extended	Significant adjustments	Significant adjustments; may not achieve desired end-states
Resources: Unanticipated Requirements	Easily managed, minimal impact	May necessitate adjustments to plans	Will necessitate significant adjustments to plans	Unable to manage
Resources: Force Provider	Full capacity to source COCOM rqmts	Can source all rqmts. Worldwide force allocation solutions may result in limited duration capability gaps	Can source priority COCOM rqmts. Worldwide force allocation solutions may result in extended duration capability gaps	Require full mobilization to sustain sourcing solutions to achieve strategic objectives
Resources: Services Functions, Force Management, Institutional Capacity	Full capacity to source COCOM rqmts	Requires intra-Service adjustments to source COCOM rqmts	Requires joint source solutions and force substitutions to source COCOM rqmts	COCOM rqmts exceed Joint Force capacity to substitute capabilities

Figure 1.4 Joint Chiefs of Staff risk assessment system.

A	Reliable	**No doubt** of authenticity, trustworthiness, or competency; has a history of complete reliability
B	Usually Reliable	**Minor doubt** about authenticity, trustworthiness, or competency; has a history of valid information most of the time
C	Fairly Reliable	**Doubt** of authenticity, trustworthiness, or competency but has provided valid information in the past
D .	Not Usually Reliable	**Significant doubt** about authenticity, trustworthiness, or competency but has provided valid information in the past
E	Unreliable	**Lacking** in authenticity, trustworthiness, and competency; history of invalid information
F	Cannot Be Judged	**No basis** exists for evaluating the reliability of the source

Figure 1.5 U. S. Army guidelines for source reliability assessment. *Source:* U.S. Army Field Manual 2-22.3, Human Intelligence Collector Operations.

prewar intelligence on Iraq, for instance, was that analysts should have been more skeptical of the source known as "Curveball," who had fabricated information about biological weapons. Even though several intelligence officials doubted Curveball's reliability, that skepticism was not clearly conveyed in reports that drew on Curveball's interviews.[16]

To help avoid such problems, collectors of human intelligence generally attach source reliability assessments to their reports. The source assessment doctrine shown in Figure 1.5 encourages analysts to communicate these evaluations using six qualitative terms. These assessments of reliability are defined in relation to another set of qualitative terms describing doubt. The doctrine then provides no indication of how either reliability or doubt relates to the probability that a source is telling the truth.

The guidelines described in this section reflect just a handful of relevant examples of how intelligence agencies and military organizations encourage analysts to leave probability assessments vague.[17] Nevertheless, the guidelines

[16] Senate Select Committee on Intelligence, *Report on the U.S. Intelligence Community's Prewar Intelligence Assessments on Iraq* (2004), ch. IV.

[17] This behavior is not limited to the United States. The current "NATO Common Standard" for assessing probability in intelligence analysis involves five terms: *highly unlikely* (less than 10 percent), *unlikely* (10 to 40 percent), *even chance* (40 to 60 percent), *likely* (60 to 90 percent), and *highly likely* (more than 90 percent). NATO Standard AJP 2.1, *Allied Joint Doctrine for Intelligence Procedures*, pp. 3–15. For NATO standards on source reliability assessment that are similar to the doctrine shown in Figure 1.5, see Dan Irwin and David Mandel, "Standards for Evaluating Source Reliability

described in this section cover a vast range of consequential analyses. In principle, they shape every key judgment in every intelligence report, every risk assessment in every Army strategy and plan, and every source assessment provided by military interrogators.

Chapters 3 and 4 will show that this imprecision discards information that can improve the accuracy of foreign policy analysis and the effectiveness of foreign policy decision making. For the moment, however, the purpose of describing these standards is simply to demonstrate the lengths to which foreign policy agencies are willing to go to in order to avoid transparent probabilistic reasoning: accepting the risk of miscommunication, creating divergent definitions of key words, and requiring analysts and decision makers to memorize a bewildering array of phrases—the analytic standards described in this section alone contain more than eighty distinct terms. Yet the chapter's next section explains why imprecision is actually the least concerning form of vagueness that surrounds assessments of uncertainty in foreign policy discourse. Two other problems, which I call *relative probability* and *conditioning*, pose even greater obstacles to making sound decisions.

Relative Probability and Conditioning

As the Taliban gained ground throughout Afghanistan in 2009, President Obama appointed General Stanley McChrystal to command allied forces in the country. Two months later, General McChrystal submitted an assessment in which he recommended a new counterinsurgency strategy to be bolstered by forty thousand additional troops. McChrystal argued that his proposal would "improve effectiveness" and that that it offered "the best prospect for success in this important mission."[18] When the document leaked to the press, it helped to build political momentum behind the policy known as the Afghan Surge.[19]

and Information Credibility in Intelligence Production," in David Mandel, ed., *Assessment and Communication of Uncertainty in Intelligence to Support Decision-Making* (Brussels, Belgium: NATO Science and Technology Organization, in press). For additional examples drawn from Britain, Canada, and Israel, see Mandeep K. Dhami, *Understanding and Communicating Uncertainty in Intelligence Analysis* (London, U.K.: Report Prepared for H.M. Government, 2013); Barnes, "Making Intelligence Analysis More Intelligent"; and Lanir and Kahneman, "Experiment in Decision Analysis in Israel."

[18] Commander, International Security Assistance Force-Afghanistan, *COMISAF Initial Assessment*, August 2009, pp. 1–3, 1–4, and 2–22. See http://www.washingtonpost.com/wp-dyn/content/article/2009/09/21/AR2009092100110.html.

[19] Kevin Marsh, "Obama's Surge: A Bureaucratic Politics Analysis of the Decision to Order a Troop Surge in the Afghanistan War," *Foreign Policy Analysis*, Vol. 10, No. 3 (2014), pp. 265–288.

General McChrystal's report presented a candid, detailed argument for strategic change. Yet it was essentially trivial to argue that deploying forty thousand additional troops would improve effectiveness. The key question was *how much* those forces would improve effectiveness, and whether their expected benefit justified their expected cost. Similarly, saying that the Afghan Surge represented the best prospect for success did not imply that the strategy was worth pursuing, especially given growing concerns about whether the United States had the resources and political will to defeat the Taliban. Logically speaking, there was no way to evaluate General McChrystal's proposal without estimating the extent to which his recommendations would raise the chances of strategic success. Yet the proposal itself left that judgment to the reader.

McChrystal's report exemplifies the use of *relative probability*: a probability assessment that conveys an analyst's beliefs with respect to an unspecified baseline. Relative probability provides limited information, and it can bias assessments of expected value. Pharmaceutical companies, for example, often encourage customers to purchase drugs that reduce risks even if those risks are already vanishingly small.[20] Regardless of the extent to which foreign policy officials consciously seek to fool their colleagues in this manner, it is reasonable to expect their use of relative probability to produce a similar result. Decision makers may thus find it easier to accept a strategy billed as their best chance of success over a strategy whose odds of succeeding are roughly one in five, even if those strategies are the same.

Of course, there is no reason why decision makers should not seek to minimize risks or to maximize their chances of success, so long as they are cognizant of what those risks and chances entail. Yet the analytic standards that guide military planning often revolve exclusively around relational judgments. U.S. Army operations doctrine thus states that when commanders evaluate potential courses of action, they should define the problem, gather information, develop possible solutions, and "select the best solution."[21] To do this,

> the staff compares feasible COAs [courses of action] to identify the one with the *highest probability* of success.... The selected COA should also pose the *minimum risk* to the force and mission accomplishment; place the force in the *best posture* for future operations; provide *maximum*

[20] Jonathan Baron, "Confusion of Relative and Absolute Risk in Valuation," *Journal of Risk and Uncertainty*, Vol. 14 (1997), pp. 301–309; and Gerd Gigerenzer, *Calculated Risks: How to Know When Numbers Deceive You* (New York: Simon and Schuster, 2002). On how governments likewise spend inordinate resources reducing risks that are already very small, see Cass R. Sunstein, *Worst-Case Scenarios* (Cambridge, Mass.: Harvard University Press, 2007); and John Mueller and Mark G. Stewart, *Terror, Security, and Money: Balancing the Risks, Benefits, and Costs of Homeland Security* (New York: Oxford University Press, 2011).

[21] Emphasis added. U.S. Army Field Manual 5-0, *The Operations Process* (2009), para. 2–19.

latitude for initiative by subordinates; provide the *most flexibility* to
meet unexpected threats and opportunities; provide the *most secure* and
stable environment for civilians in the AO; [and] *best facilitate* initial
information themes and messages.[22]

Army doctrine on staff organization similarly states that planners should
"compare feasible courses of action to identify the one that has the highest probability of success."[23] Army doctrine on tactical intelligence recommends a series of exercises that help to "identify the [course of action] that has the highest
probability of success."[24] Official guidelines for strategic assessment instruct
commanders to "determine which COA (or combination) hold the greatest
promise of success."[25] These analyses demonstrate that General McChrystal's
report on the Afghan Surge was not unusual in presenting a recommendation based on minimizing risk and maximizing strategic prospects rather than
evaluating what those risks and prospects were. This was, in fact, consistent with
the instructions that military commanders are asked to follow when making
high-stakes decisions.

Part of what makes this doctrine problematic is that choosing the course of
action with the highest probability of success is almost never the correct decision
to make. It is usually possible to increase the probability of success by devoting
more resources to a task. Yet short of all-out existential warfare, decision makers
must at some point determine where additional resource commitments are no
longer worth the expense.[26]

One could attempt to skirt this issue by redefining "success" as an outcome
for which an action's benefits exceed its costs. Perhaps Army planning doctrine
aims to channel that idea by instructing commanders to select the strategy with
the highest chances of success among all "feasible" courses of action. But that
would not present a valid basis for decision making either. If a policy has a very
small chance of becoming a very large disaster, then it might be wise to pursue
an alternative course of action that trades a smaller chance of success for less
downside risk.[27] The fact of the matter is that it is impossible to judge a policy's

[22] Ibid., para. B-173.

[23] U.S. Army Field Manual 101-5, *Staff Organization and Operations* (1997), para. 5–24.

[24] U.S. Army Field Manual 34-130, *Intelligence Preparation of the Battlefield* (1994), p. A-7.

[25] U.S. Joint Forces Command, *Commander's Handbook for an Effects-Based Approach to Joint Operations* (2006), pp. 3–14.

[26] Alain C. Enthoven and K. Wayne Smith, *How Much Is Enough? Shaping the Defense Program, 1961–1969* (Santa Monica, Calif.: Rand, 2005).

[27] George W. Downs and David M. Rocke, "Conflict, Agency, and Gambling for Resurrection: The Principal-Agent Problem Goes to War," *American Journal of Political Science*, Vol. 38, No. 2 (1994), pp. 362–380.

expected value without estimating its chances of success in absolute terms. Any heuristic that avoids doing this will generate systematic biases.

The terrorism advisory system of the Department of Homeland Security (DHS) offers another example of how relative probability provides limited and potentially misleading information. Starting in 2003, the system involved five color-coded threat levels: red (severe risk), orange (high risk), yellow (elevated/significant risk), blue (guarded/general risk), and green (low risk). Since none of these terms received a clear definition, the primary way in which DHS used the system to communicate information was by shifting the color-coded threat levels over time. These shifts essentially instructed citizens to adjust their prior assumptions about the risk of terrorism up or down. But since most people already hold dramatically inflated perceptions about what the risk of terrorism entails, raising official threat levels may have only created unnecessary alarm.[28] Faced with mounting critiques, the DHS scrapped this framework in 2011. The department's new National Terrorism Advisory System provides information about specific threats, whose risk levels are classified into three tiers ("elevated," "intermediate," and "imminent"), none of which receives a definition that maps to a discernible segment of the number line.[29]

Relative probability plays a prominent role in intelligence analysis, too. For example, the most widely taught "structured analytic technique" for assessing uncertainty in intelligence is called analysis of competing hypotheses (ACH).[30] ACH instructs analysts to create a matrix in which the columns represent plausible conclusions and the rows represent pieces of available evidence. Analysts populate this matrix by indicating the extent to which each piece of evidence is inconsistent with each hypothesis. When the analysis is complete, the hypothesis with the lowest inconsistency score is considered to be the most likely conclusion.

ACH combats confirmation bias by ensuring that analysts consider alternative judgments and at the same time fosters a falsificationist mindset that prevents jumping to conclusions. These goals are undeniably important. Yet identifying

<hr/>

[28] Rose McDermott and Philip G. Zimbardo, "The Psychological Consequences of Terrorist Alerts," in Bruce Bongar et al., eds., *Psychology of Terrorism* (New York: Oxford University Press, 2007), pp. 357–370; and Jacob N. Shapiro and Dara Kay Cohen, "Color Blind: Lessons from the Failed Homeland Security Advisory System," *International Security*, Vol. 32, No. 2 (Fall 2007), pp. 121–154.

[29] For example, an "elevated" alert "warns of a credible terrorism threat," and an "imminent" alert "warns of a credible, specific, and impending terrorism threat." See Department of Homeland Security, "National Terrorism Advisory System (NTAS)," https://www.dhs.gov/national-terrorism-advisory-system, accessed August 6, 2018.

[30] Richards Heuer and Randolph Pherson, *Structured Analytic Techniques for Intelligence Analysis* (Washington, D.C.: CQ Press, 2010), pp. 160–169.

the most probable conclusion says little about what that probability entails. Just as a strategy that offers the best chances of success might not be worth pursuing, the most likely conclusion is not necessarily worth betting on.[31]

This was indeed the heart of the critiques we encountered earlier regarding intelligence on Iraq's weapons of mass destruction programs. Though the National Intelligence Estimate may have reflected the most plausible interpretation of the available evidence, it was still important to assess the probability that this interpretation was true. Highlighting the presence of this uncertainty could then have provoked important questions about why existing evidence about Iraq's weapons programs could just sustain more conclusive judgments. As Morell describes it,

> The way analysts talked and wrote about their judgments would have led anyone to think that it was a slam dunk—that is, that Saddam definitively had active WMD programs. No one ever said to me, [CIA Deputy Director for Intelligence Jami] Miscik, [Deputy Director of Central Intelligence John] McLaughlin, [CIA Director George] Tenet, [Secretary of State Condoleezza] Rice, or the president, "You know, there is a chance he might not have them." Such a statement would have gotten everyone's attention.[32]

Conditioning

A third way that assessments of uncertainty can be too vague to support sound foreign policy decision involves a practice that I call *conditioning*. This occurs when analysts describe the conditions that must hold in order for a statement to be true. Conditioning is the least informative approach to assessing uncertainty described in this chapter. The logic of conditioning states that *if* a statement is true, *then* an assumption must hold. Note, however, that this logic does not flow in the opposite direction. If the assumption holds, this implies nothing about the probability that the statement is true.

[31] Indeed, there is remarkably little systematic evidence that proves that ACH improves judgmental accuracy. See David R. Mandel, Christopher W. Karvetski, and Mandeep K. Dhami, "Boosting Intelligence Analysts' Judgmental Accuracy: What Works, What Fails?" *Judgment and Decision Making*, forthcoming; Welton Chang and Philip Tetlock, "Rethinking the Training of Intelligence Analysts," *Intelligence and National Security*, Vol. 31, No. 6 (2016), pp. 903–920.

[32] Morell, *Great War of Our Time*, p. 103. Note how this statement implies that the proper way to assess the impact of the Iraq NIE is not to speculate about what would have happened if the NIE had never been published, but rather to explore what might have happened if the NIE had been researched and written in a manner that gave higher priority to the importance of assessing and communicating uncertainty.

One vivid example of conditioning involves recent debates over force sizing for counterinsurgency. In 2006, the U.S. military released a new counterinsurgency doctrine known as Field Manual 3-24 (FM 3-24).[33] Here is the guidance that FM 3-24 offered for sizing forces in counterinsurgency wars:

> Most [troop] density recommendations fall within a range of 20 to 25 counterinsurgents for every 1,000 residents in an AO [area of operations]. Twenty counterinsurgents per 1,000 residents is often considered the minimum troop density required for effective COIN [counterinsurgency] operations; however, as with any fixed ratio, such calculations remain very dependent upon the situation.[34]

At a glance, this paragraph appears to offer clear guidance, saying that if counterinsurgents wish to succeed, then they should deploy at least twenty troops per thousand residents in an area of operations. But even if that claim had been correct,[35] FM 3-24 still said nothing about the chances that a counterinsurgent who met this threshold would achieve its goals. FM 3-24 only claimed that if counterinsurgents deployed twenty troops per thousand inhabitants in an area of operations, then their probability of success might be greater than zero. Even *that* judgment was hedged by the caveat that troop-density thresholds vary across cases.

Taken literally, FM 3-24 thus stated that if counterinsurgents deploy a particular number of forces, then it is possible that success would then be possible. And though that insight clearly fell short of a rigorous basis for sending large numbers of soldiers into harm's way, FM 3-24's guidance on force sizing played a major role in building support for the eventual troop surges in both Iraq and Afghanistan.[36] Part of the problem with these arguments was that their flaws were subtle: on a first read, FM 3-24 appeared to offer clear instructions for conducting successful counterinsurgency operations, even though the doctrine's actual empirical claim was far weaker than that. It is also easy to see how these kinds of judgments can bias policy evaluations. Warning decision makers that they will fail without taking some action surely provides more encouragement for committing resources than saying that this action has a negligible chance of succeeding, even though both statements can be true simultaneously.

---

[33] The manual's formal title was U.S. Army Field Manual 3-24/Marine Corps Warfighting Publication 3-33.5, *Counterinsurgency*.

[34] Field Manual 3-24, *Counterinsurgency*, para. 1–67.

[35] This is highly dubious: see Jeffrey A. Friedman, "Manpower and Counterinsurgency: Empirical Foundations for Theory and Doctrine," *Security Studies*, Vol. 20, No. 4 (2011), pp. 556–591.

[36] Peter Mansoor, *Surge* (New Haven, Conn.: Yale University Press, 2013), ch. 2.

In principle, one could offer a clear probability assessment *and* identify the conditions that must hold for a statement to be true. In practice, however, many scholars and practitioners argue that foreign policy analysts should limit their focus to the latter of those tasks. Intelligence scholars call this the "linchpins and drivers" approach to foreign policy analysis.[37] The basic idea behind this approach is that analysts should lay out the key assumptions that are required to sustain a conclusion under uncertainty, but then leave it to readers to assess those assumptions' collective plausibility. Some intelligence estimates explicitly define their scope along these lines. For example, the National Intelligence Council's *Global Trends 2025* report opened by explaining, "The study as a whole is more a description of the factors likely to shape events than a prediction of what will actually happen. By examining a small number of variables that we judge probably will have a disproportionate influence on future events and possibilities, the study seeks to help readers to recognize signposts indicating where events are headed." *Global Trends 2030* similarly describes its aim as being to identify "megatrends" and "game-changers" that could potentially lead to "alternative worlds," but not to make predictions about the chances that those worlds will actually materialize.

Yet analysts cannot speak about the future without engaging in some form of probabilistic reasoning. There is little practical value in analyzing events that truly have no chance of taking place. And since analysts cannot devote equal text to describing every global trend or possible future that they can imagine, those judgments depend—however implicitly—on the premise that these statements are sufficiently likely to deserve the reader's attention. Leaving these judgments vague only defers the challenge of assessing uncertainty from analysts to decision makers, who generally have much less time, expertise, and incentive to make accurate judgments.[38]

Relative probability and conditioning are important because they demonstrate how foreign policy officials' aversion to probabilistic reasoning runs much deeper than semantics. The problem is not just that analysts and decision makers are reluctant to assess uncertainty in clear and structured ways. Indeed,

---

[37] Douglas J. MacEachin, "The Tradecraft of Analysis," in Roy Godson, Ernest R. May, and Gary Schmitt eds., *U.S. Intelligence at the Crossroads: Agendas for Reform* (Washington, D.C.: Brassey's, 1995); Jack Davis, *A Compendium of Analytic Tradecraft Notes* (Washington, D.C.: Central Intelligence Agency, 1997); and Thomas Fingar, *Reducing Uncertainty: Intelligence Analysis and National Security* (Stanford, Calif.: Stanford Security Studies, 2011), pp. 53–74.

[38] As Richard Betts puts it, "The greater the ambiguity, the greater the impact of preconceptions." Richard K. Betts, *Surprise Attack: Lessons for Defense Planning* (Washington, D.C.: Brookings, 1982), p. 103. Joshua Rovner, *Fixing the Facts: National Security and the Politics of Intelligence* (Ithaca, N.Y.: Cornell University Press, 2011), further explains how decision makers can exploit judgmental ambiguity for political ends.

this section has shown how intelligence agencies and military organizations deliberately develop heuristics that allow analysts and decision makers to avoid grappling with crucial probabilities entirely.

It is also important to note that while all of the examples described in this chapter come from official government sources, similar problems recur throughout broader foreign policy discourse. Recent works by Daniel Gardner, Chaim Kaufmann, John Mueller, Nate Silver, Mark Stewart, and Philip Tetlock, among others, document a range of strategies that foreign policy commentators use to appear insightful without actually making falsifiable claims.[39] These strategies include focusing excessive attention on hypothetical scenarios or worst-case outcomes, defending policies based on desirability rather than feasibility, and lacing statements with vague caveats and contingencies. In many cases, it is virtually impossible to define the outcomes that analysts are assessing, let alone to understand how probable analysts think these outcomes might be. Here, too, the problem is not just that foreign policy analysts use imprecise language to express their beliefs, but that they avoid addressing the uncertainty that surrounds high-stakes choices.

The remainder of the chapter shows how these problems surround the highest levels of foreign policy decision making. To do this, I present a mixed-method case study that examines Vietnam War decision making, focusing on how senior leaders assessed the risks of escalating U.S. involvement in Vietnam between 1961 and 1965. I devote special attention to this case for four reasons.

The first of these reasons is that, if any group of leaders should have been expected to evaluate the logical foundations of high-stakes choices in clear and structured ways, it would have been the group that shaped Vietnam War policy from 1961 to 1965. President Kennedy appointed Robert McNamara as secretary of defense based on his reputation for conducting rigorous cost-benefit analyses as an executive at Ford Motor Company. McNamara staffed his office with the so-called Whiz Kids, who possessed an unusual zeal for quantitative analysis.[40] The Whiz Kids found a receptive audience among the Kennedy administration's roster of public intellectuals, including National Security Advisor McGeorge Bundy, a political scientist who had previously served as

[39] Daniel Gardner, *Future Babble* (New York: Plume, 2011); Chaim Kaufmann, "Threat Inflation and the Failure of the Marketplace of Ideas," *International Security*, Vol. 29, No. 1 (Summer 2004), pp. 5–48; Nate Silver, *The Signal and the Noise* (New York: Penguin, 2012); Philip Tetlock and Daniel Gardner, *Superforecasting* (New York: Crown, 2015); John Mueller, *Overblown: How Politicians and the Terrorism Industry Inflate National Security Threats, and Why We Believe Them* (New York: Free Press 2006); John Mueller and Mark G. Stewart, *Chasing Ghosts: The Policing of Terrorism* (New York: Oxford University Press, 2016).

[40] David Halberstam, *The Best and the Brightest* (New York: Penguin, 1983); John A. Byrne, *The Whiz Kids* (New York: Doubleday, 1993).

dean of Harvard's Faculty of Arts and Sciences. If even these leaders assessed uncertainty in the problematic ways that this chapter describes, that would lend credibility to the notion that these are consistent flaws in foreign policy decision making.[41]

Debates about escalating the Vietnam War also provide exactly the kind of context in which we would expect rational decision makers to assess uncertainty as carefully as possible. U.S. officials knew that all available strategies in Vietnam presented serious risks. They had genuine doubts about whether those risks were worth accepting, and several years to develop opinions on this issue. In this sense, the escalation of U.S. involvement in Vietnam presents a case where leaders should have had both the motivation and the opportunity to study their strategic options in detail.[42]

The documentary record of Vietnam War decision making is, furthermore, unusually thorough. Collections such as the *Foreign Relations of the United States*, the *Pentagon Papers*, and the National Intelligence Council's *Estimative Products on Vietnam* provide scholars with a broad base of well-known, widely available, trusted primary sources. We will see how these documents contain candid discussions of U.S. strategy, as public officials did not yet anticipate that sensitive opinions voiced in private would consistently leak to the press.[43] Debates over Vietnam War strategy thus present a case where assessments of uncertainty were especially important, where decision makers were especially capable of confronting this challenge directly, and where transparent discussions of those issues should be especially accessible to scholars.

Finally, Vietnam War decision making is important because it relates so closely to the theoretical frameworks that international relations scholars use to study coercion. During this period, international relations theorists developed the contemporary view that the primary purpose of coercion is to influence how opponents perceive their strategic prospects.[44] Secretary McNamara himself wrote in 1965 that the basic goal of military operations in Vietnam was "to create

---

[41] For a similar logic of selecting cases as a window into the (ir)rationality of foreign policy decision making, see Brian Rathbun, "The Rarity of Realpolitik: What Bismarck's Rationality Reveals about International Politics," *International Security*, Vol. 43, No. 1 (2018), pp. 7–55.

[42] Leslie Gelb and Richard K. Betts, *The Irony of Vietnam: The System Worked* (Washington, D.C.: Brookings, 1979); Fredrik Logevall, *Choosing War: The Lost Chance for Peace and the Escalation of War in Vietnam* (Berkeley, Calif.: University of California Press, 1999).

[43] Yuen Foong Khong, *Analogies at War: Korea, Munich, Dien Bien Phu, and the Vietnam Decisions of 1965* (Princeton, N.J.: Princeton University Press, 1992).

[44] Prominent articulations of this view include Thomas Schelling, *Arms and Influence* (New Haven, Conn.: Yale University Press, 1966); Robert A. Pape, *Bombing to Win: Air Power, Coercion, and War* (Ithaca, N.Y.: Cornell University Press, 1996); and Branislav Slantchev, "The Principle of Convergence in Wartime Negotiations," *American Political Science Review*, Vol. 97, No. 4 (2003), pp. 621–632.

conditions for a favorable settlement by demonstrating [to the Communists] that the odds are against their winning."[45] Yet we will see how McNamara and his senior colleagues consistently avoided analyzing their own odds of winning in a meaningful way. This presents a clear divergence between the theory and practice of strategic decision making, even according to U.S. officials' own standard of rational leadership.

The case study presented here involves a combination of qualitative and quantitative evidence. The analysis begins by describing how U.S. officials assessed their chances of success in documents that historians have identified as shaping President Kennedy's decision to expand the United States' advisory role in Vietnam in 1961, as well as President Johnson's decisions to escalate the air and ground campaigns in 1964–1965. Then it looks at the broader patterns in how U.S. officials assessed uncertainty when debating Vietnam War strategy, using a database of 1,757 probabilistic statements gathered from primary sources.

This mixed-method approach demonstrates how the pathologies of probability assessment described in this chapter appeared at key junctures of Vietnam War decision making, while confirming that these examples reflect systematic trends in how U.S. officials assessed uncertainty across a fifty-four-month period. The empirical record shows that officials were overwhelmingly vague in assessing key elements of uncertainty surrounding the war, and that their judgments were least informative on the issue that mattered most—namely, the chances that U.S. strategy would succeed. This account departs sharply from the conventional idea that the Whiz Kids were excessively devoted to methodological rigor. Instead, we will see how the Kennedy and Johnson administrations progressively committed the United States to war without carefully considering the risks their decisions involved.

The Probability of Success in Vietnam, 1961–1965

When John F. Kennedy became president in 1961, Vietnam was not a top priority for U.S. foreign policy. There were fewer than seven hundred U.S. soldiers in the country at the time, employed in noncombat roles as "advisers." Yet the situation in Vietnam was deteriorating. The Communist insurgency known as the Viet Cong was gaining strength, and the regime in Saigon led by South

---

[45] McNamara to Johnson, *Foreign Relations of the United States, 1964–1968*, Vol. III, Doc 38 (1 July 1965). Hereafter cited as *FRUS*. On U.S. officials' conception of coercion in Vietnam, see Wallace J. Thies, *When Governments Collide: Coercion and Diplomacy in the Vietnam Conflict, 1964–1968* (Berkeley, Calif.: University of California Press, 1980).

Vietnamese President Ngo Dinh Diem was rapidly losing public support. President Kennedy thus asked Secretary McNamara to write a report analyzing how the United States could respond to this growing crisis.

Secretary McNamara presented his views to the president in November 1961. He wrote, "The chances are against, probably sharply against, preventing [the fall of South Vietnam] by any measures short of the introduction of U.S. forces on a substantial scale." McNamara rejected proposals for limited escalation, saying that if the Kennedy administration introduced just eight to ten thousand additional soldiers, then they would be "almost certain to get increasingly mired down in an inconclusive struggle." McNamara recommended sending up to 220,000 troops to Vietnam. But he never assessed the chances that the United States would succeed in this effort, writing only that large-scale commitments were necessary to keep Saigon from falling to the Communists.[46]

Kennedy had solicited a second report on the growing crisis in Vietnam, which was coauthored by General Maxwell Taylor and the deputy national security adviser, Walt Rostow. They argued that "morale in Viet-Nam will rapidly crumble" without "a hard U.S. commitment to the ground." But when Taylor and Rostow recommended that the United States commit combat forces to stop the insurgency's momentum, they indicated only that this initiative was more likely to succeed than the alternatives, explaining that "intervention under SEATO [Southeast Asian Treaty Organization] or U.S. plans is the best means of saving SVN [South Vietnam] and indeed, all of Southeast Asia."[47] Employing a similar emphasis on relative probability, the Joint Chiefs of Staff argued that defeating the Viet Cong insurgency required expanding U.S. involvement and that "the over-all objective could best be served" by attacking North Vietnam directly.[48]

These documents established a pattern that recurred throughout debates about Vietnam War strategy from 1961 to 1965. When U.S. officials evaluated existing strategies, they candidly acknowledged that the war's current trajectory offered little chance of success. But when they turned their focus to recommending new strategies, their probabilistic reasoning shifted as well. Instead of directly assessing the odds that their recommendations would work, U.S. officials typically justified new measures through relative probability or

[46] *FRUS, 1961–1963*, Vol. I, Doc 214 (5 November 1961). Also see ibid., Doc 222, indicating concurrence from the secretary of state, Dean Rusk, and the Joint Chiefs of Staff.

[47] *FRUS, 1961–1963*, Vol. I, Doc 210 (3 November 1961); and *Pentagon Papers*, Vol. V.B.4, pp. 331–342. Taylor and Rostow called for 6,000–8,000 combat troops to be sent to Vietnam, while acknowledging that there would be "no limit to our possible commitment" once U.S. forces were committed in this way.

[48] JCS to McNamara, *Pentagon Papers*, Vol. V.B.4, p. 288 (9 October 1961).

conditioning, saying that new policies offered the best chance of success or that they were necessary to prevent Saigon's collapse. These forms of probabilistic reasoning were not just semantically imprecise—they reflected a deeper lack of engagement with the uncertainty surrounding strategic choices that would come to dominate U.S. foreign policy for the next decade.

This method of analysis was not limited to proponents of military escalation.[49] In several letters to President Kennedy, for instance, foreign policy adviser John Kenneth Galbraith denounced military measures for their "high risk and limited promise," arguing that "there is scarcely the slightest practical chance" that President Diem would implement the needed reforms. There was "no chance of success," Galbraith concluded, if the United States continued to back Diem and his family. Galbraith thus recommended that Washington shift its support to other Vietnamese leaders without expanding its military commitments. But beyond arguing that this course was "not hopeless," Galbraith did not evaluate the odds that his proposal would work—he simply wrote that it was "the only solution" worth considering.[50] The chairman of the Joint Chiefs of Staff, Lyman Lemnitzer, rebutted Galbraith using the same style of argumentation, writing that "the President's policy of supporting the Diem regime . . . appears to be the only practicable alternative at this time," without explaining how practicable the policy actually was.[51]

Again, the problem with this debate was not just that U.S. officials articulated their proposals in an imprecise manner that made it difficult to determine which argument was more likely to be correct. It is indeed plausible that *both* sides of this debate offered valid arguments: the United States may have had little chance of creating a stable noncommunist South Vietnam through political measures or through military measures, with or without the Diem regime. Focusing on which measure was the most likely to succeed concealed deeper uncertainty about whether the United States was pursuing feasible objectives.[52] Secretary McNamara himself later wrote that failing to address this uncertainty was one of the key factors that led the United States into the Vietnam quagmire. In his memoirs, McNamara acknowledged that "we never carefully debated what

[49] See Logevall, *Choosing War*, on how Ball and other opponents of Americanization rarely went into depth in articulating alternative proposals.

[50] *FRUS, 1961–1963*, Vol. I, Doc 209 (3 November 1961); Galbraith to Kennedy, *Pentagon Papers*, Vol. V.B.4, pp. 406–407 (20 November 1961); Galbraith to Kennedy, ibid., pp. 414–416 (21 November 1961).

[51] Lemnitzer to McNamara, *Pentagon Papers*, Vol. V.B.4, p. 465 (13 April 1962).

[52] Aaron Rapport, *Waging War, Planning Peace: U.S. Noncombat Operations in Major Wars* (Ithaca, N.Y.: Cornell University Press, 2015), argues that this reflects a broader tendency for foreign policy decision makers to base high-stakes decisions on the desirability of their objectives rather than the feasibility of their methods.

U.S. force would ultimately be required, what our chances of success would be, or what the political, military, financial, and human costs would be if we provided it. Indeed, these basic questions went unexamined. We were at the beginning of a slide down a tragic and slippery slope."[53]

Expanding the War, 1964–1965

President Kennedy responded to the crisis in Vietnam by sending fifteen thousand additional soldiers to the country, but he also refused to expand their mission beyond an advisory role. This limited investment was unable to halt the growth of the Viet Cong insurgency or to stop Saigon's political decay. In November 1964, a group of Vietnamese military officers assassinated President Diem. The coup plotters then failed to consolidate a stable regime. When Lyndon Johnson became president in December 1964, he thus faced renewed questions about the basic tenets of U.S. strategy in Vietnam. As Johnson's advisers debated those questions, they fell back on their previous style of argumentation, offering clear judgments that the current strategy was failing without assessing the chances that alternative proposals would succeed.

National Security Advisor McGeorge Bundy led the push to expand air strikes against Hanoi. "The situation in Vietnam is deteriorating," he wrote, "and without new U.S. action defeat appears inevitable." Bundy then identified strategic bombing as "the most promising course available . . . the best available way of increasing our chance of success in Vietnam." But Bundy also wrote that "we cannot estimate the odds of success with any accuracy— they may be somewhere between 25% and 75%."[54] (This statement was even less informative in context, because Bundy had defined success in terms of whether strategic bombing would "change the course of the contest in Vietnam," not whether the United States would ultimately achieve its strategic objectives.) Maxwell Taylor, now the U.S. ambassador to Saigon, concurred that an escalated bombing program "offers the best available means of exerting increasing pressure on the DRV [Democratic Republic of Vietnam] leaders to induce them to cease their intervention in SVN," without indicating how that policy was likely to fare.[55]

[53] Robert S. McNamara with Brian VanDeMark, *In Retrospect: The Tragedy and Lessons of Vietnam* (New York: Times Books, 1995), p. 107.
[54] McG. Bundy to Johnson, *FRUS, 1964–1968*, Vol. II, Doc 84 (7 February 1965).
[55] Taylor to State Department, *FRUS, 1964–1968*, Vol. II, Doc 93 (9 February 1964).

The Joint Chiefs of Staff played an ambivalent role in this debate.[56] They agreed that the United States could not succeed in Vietnam without committing additional forces. In an October 1964 memorandum, the chairman of the Joint Chiefs of Staff Earle Wheeler stated, "Unless we move now to alter the present evolution of events, there is great likelihood of VC [Viet Cong] victory."[57] However, the Joint Chiefs believed that civilian leaders underestimated the importance of directly attacking Hanoi. Wheeler thus explained: "The military course of action which would contribute most to defeating insurgencies in Southeast Asia remains the destruction of the DRV will and capabilities as necessary to compel the DRV to cease providing support to those insurgencies." Wheeler repeatedly backed this position with relational judgments, arguing that bombing North Vietnam offered "the best probability of success," the "greatest assurance of success," and the "best probability of achieving our objectives."[58] Yet despite warning that existing U.S. policy would almost surely fail, Wheeler and the Chiefs did not describe the chances that their preferred strategy might succeed.

As in 1961, opponents of escalating the war also presented recommendations without assessing their chances of success. The most prominent internal critic of escalation during this period was the undersecretary of state, George Ball. In a sixty-seven-page memorandum, Ball argued that his colleagues offered implausible justifications for expanding the war.[59] Ball instead recommended that the White House attempt to negotiate a neutral political status for South Vietnam. But though Ball wrote that this strategy's prospects were "at least as good as the chance of success through military action alone," he did not describe what those chances were.[60] In his memoirs, Ball admitted that he never tried to "do more than outline the possibilities of such a settlement."[61] Thus, though Ball advocated a different strategy than most of the other high-ranking members of the Johnson administration, he mirrored his colleagues' style of argumentation, identifying the risks and logical flaws in other proposals without evaluating the chances that his own recommendations would succeed.

---

[56] Herbert R. McMaster, *Dereliction of Duty: Lyndon Johnson, Robert McNamara, the Joint Chiefs of Staff, and the Lies That Led to Vietnam* (New York: HarperCollins, 1997).

[57] Wheeler to McNamara, *FRUS, 1964–1968*, Vol. I, Doc 388 (27 October 1964). The JCS also wrote to McNamara saying that "if present trends are not reversed, the counterinsurgency campaign in South Vietnam will be lost" and that U.S. combat troops were required "to turn the tide of the war." JCS to McNamara, *FRUS, 1964–1968*, Vol. II, Doc 208 (18 March 1965).

[58] Wheeler to McNamara, *FRUS, 1964–1968*, Vol. I, Doc 420 (7 February 1964).

[59] George Ball, "How Valid Are the Assumptions Underlying Our Viet-Nam Policies?" 5 October 1964. Lyndon B. Johnson Presidential Library, National Security File, Vietnam Country File, Box 222.

[60] *FRUS, 1964–1968*, Vol. II, Doc 300 (13 May 1965).

[61] George Ball, *The Past Has Another Pattern* (New York: Norton, 1982), p. 383.

Measuring Tactical Progress without
Assessing Strategic Prospects

The manner in which high-ranking U.S. officials avoided assessing their chances of strategic success throughout this period struck a sharp contrast with the unprecedented analytic firepower they devoted to measuring tactical progress.[62] This elaborate effort created the impression that Secretary McNamara and his colleagues were unusually committed to methodological rigor. The McNamara Pentagon's failures in Vietnam have thus generated lasting mistrust among scholars and practitioners regarding the extent to which sophisticated analytic tools can provide value for assessing military strategy.[63]

Both impressions are misplaced. Regardless of how extensively the McNamara Pentagon analyzed tactical progress in Vietnam, this was a separate matter from analyzing the chances that U.S. strategy would ultimately succeed. Even though U.S. Army tactical reporting requirements alone used up to fourteen thousand pounds of paper per day,[64] the Pentagon undertook just one formal study of whether the United States had the capacity to ultimately achieve its central objectives.[65] And even that report, written by Andrew Goodpaster, ducked the central question by debating whether the United States *could* win the war instead of assessing the chances that the United States *would* win the war: "There appears to be no reason we cannot win if such is our will," Goodpaster explained. Goodpaster even wrote in this document that he did not believe it was necessary to offer any "assessment of the assurance the U.S. can have of winning."[66]

U.S. decision makers regularly discussed the probability of making progress in Vietnam as though progress itself were the strategic objective. A Defense Department memorandum of discussion from fall 1964 stated that the "guiding principle" for bombing Hanoi was that "the situation in Southeast Asia can be improved over what it would otherwise be if pressure is brought to bear on North Vietnam."[67] The memorandum then discusses which measures had the

---

[62] Thomas C. Thayer, *War without Fronts: The American Experience in Vietnam* (Boulder, Colo.: Westview Press, 1985); Gregory Daddis, *No Sure Victory: Measuring U.S. Army Effectiveness in the Vietnam War* (New York: Oxford University Press, 2011).

[63] On the Vietnam War's legacy for debates about methodological rigor and military strategy, see Halberstam, *The Best and the Brightest*; Ben Connable, *Embracing the Fog of War* (Santa Monica, Calif.: Rand, 2012).

[64] Daddis, *No Sure Victory*, p. 121.

[65] Gelb and Betts, *Irony of Vietnam*, p. 125.

[66] *FRUS, 1964–1968*, Vol. III, Doc 69 (21 July 1965).

[67] *FRUS, 1964–1968*, Vol. I, Doc 361 (25 September 1964).

potential to make these improvements, without presenting any conclusions about the extent to which those measures would influence the overall chances of winning the war. In an August 1964 memorandum to President Johnson that recommended deploying major combat forces to Vietnam, McGeorge Bundy similarly wrote that "the larger question is whether there is any course of action that can improve the chances in this weakening situation."[68] Of course, that question remained substantially narrower than asking whether the United States could actually achieve the goals for which it was preparing to sacrifice so much blood and treasure.

Estimating the chances of making progress is an inherently indirect way to evaluate policy. For example, many historians use a January 1961 report from Brigadier General Edward Lansdale to mark the start of serious debate about escalating U.S. commitment to Vietnam. Lansdale explained to President Kennedy that although the Viet Cong were making headway, "We still have a chance of beating them if we can give the people some fighting chance of gaining security and some political basis of action."[69] Assistant Secretary of State William Bundy used similarly convoluted language that fall in writing: "An early and hard-hitting operation has a good chance (70% would be my guess) of arresting things and giving Diem a chance to do better and clean up."[70] In other words, Bundy argued that expanding the war had a chance of giving Diem a chance to do something that would, in turn, improve the chances of success in Vietnam. Part of what makes this statement remarkable is that even though Bundy attempted to clarify part of his reasoning with a numeric estimate, the broader sentence conveys virtually no useful information about the strategic value of placing U.S. forces in harm's way.

None of this is to say that U.S. officials were unaware of the uncertainty surrounding the decision to escalate the Vietnam War. Most historians agree that senior officials in the Kennedy and Johnson administrations realized that the odds were against them as they deepened their commitment to Saigon. If the stakes are high enough, it can be rational for decision makers to accept low-probability gambles. And when debating Vietnam War strategy, senior leaders like Secretary McNamara, National Security Advisor Bundy, and President Johnson appear to have genuinely believed that losing Vietnam would represent a major blow to U.S. interests. It furthermore seemed implausible that a relatively small and economically undeveloped country would not eventually reach

[68] Ibid., Doc 335 (31 August 1964).

[69] Lansdale to McNamara, *Pentagon Papers*, Vol. V.B.4, p. 11 (17 January 1961).

[70] W. Bundy to Rusk, ibid., p. 312 (10 October 1961).

its breaking point when confronting the might of United States military.[71] Leslie
Gelb and Richard Betts thus titled their famous book on decision making during
this period *The Irony of Vietnam: The System Worked*. Even though U.S. strategy in
Vietnam ultimately failed, Gelb and Betts argued, it might have still represented
a reasonable, calculated risk.[72]

Yet to conclude that escalating the Vietnam War reflected reasonable
logic, one must show that decision makers actually attempted to analyze
their choices in a logical, reasonable manner. If McNamara, Bundy, and their
colleagues had carefully considered whether the chances of success were high
enough to justify escalating the war, then critics might have to accept that this
was a subjective matter over which reasonable people could disagree. Instead,
we have seen how senior U.S. officials repeatedly avoided assessing the uncertainty that surrounded their most important strategic choices and focused
instead on identifying which measures were necessary or which strategies
had the highest probability of success. As Gelb and Betts describe it themselves, debates about U.S. strategy in Vietnam "revolved around how to do
things better, and whether they could be done, not whether they were worth
doing."[73]

Seen from this perspective, the McNamara Pentagon's approach to decision
making during the Vietnam War was not characterized by an excess of methodological rigor, but rather by a nearly complete absence of debate about the logical foundations of U.S. strategy. In his memoirs, Robert McNamara reflected on
how he of all people should have understood this. "I had spent twenty years as a
manager," McNamara wrote, "identifying problems and forcing organizations—
often against their will—to think deeply and realistically about alternative
courses of action and their consequences. I doubt I will ever fully understand
why I did not do so here."[74]

---

[71] John Mueller, "The Search for the 'Breaking Point' in Vietnam: The Statistics of a Deadly
Quarrel," *International Studies Quarterly*, Vol. 24, No. 4 (1980), pp. 497–519; Stanley Hoffmann et al.,
"Vietnam Reappraised," *International Security*, Vol. 6, No. 1 (1981), p. 9.

[72] Gelb and Betts, *Irony of Vietnam*.

[73] Leslie Gelb and Richard K. Betts, "Vietnam: The System Worked," *Foreign Policy*, No. 3 (1971),
p. 146. Furthermore, saying that these officials shared a sense of pessimism does not mean that further analysis was unwarranted. There are situations in which decision makers might accept a thirty
percent chance of success, but not a five percent chance of success, and certainly not a zero percent
chance of success, even though all of these assessments could be described as pessimistic. When
decision makers are pessimistic about their prospects, this is in fact exactly when it should be most
important to parse probability estimates carefully, because a strategy's chances of success may be too
low to justify moving forward.

[74] McNamara, *In Retrospect*, pp. 202–203.

Patterns of Probability Assessment across *Foreign Relations* Documents

The previous section used qualitative analysis of key documents to show how senior foreign policy officials were consistently vague when analyzing their strategic prospects in Vietnam, and how their judgments were especially uninformative when it came to evaluating proposals for escalating the war. One might nevertheless question the extent to which the individual documents described in the last section reflected general patterns. To substantiate an argument that senior leaders systematically avoided debating their chances of success in Vietnam, I need to analyze the documentary record systematically myself.

To do that, I constructed a database of probabilistic statements drawn from documents in the Foreign Relations of the United States (FRUS) series. FRUS is an anthology of primary sources compiled by the U.S. State Department's Office of the Historian; it constitutes "the official documentary historical record of major U.S. foreign policy decisions."[75] The six FRUS volumes that cover Vietnam War decision making from January 1961 through June 1965 contain 2,199 documents, drawn from sources that include presidential libraries, the Departments of State and Defense, the National Security Council, the Central Intelligence Agency, and private papers of individuals involved with formulating U.S. policy.

The editors of the FRUS series explain that they "choose documentation that illuminates policy formulation and major aspects and repercussions of its execution."[76] These documents thus tend to focus on the views of the high-ranking officials who set policy in Washington, as opposed to the experiences of personnel who implement those decisions in the field. Moreover, written reports and memoranda of discussions are bound to offer oversimplified versions of foreign policy officials' actual beliefs. Although these are significant drawbacks for many areas of Vietnam War scholarship, the main aim of this case study is to describe how senior leaders like Robert McNamara and McGeorge Bundy assessed their strategic prospects when they were debating escalation in Vietnam. The fact that these debates often excluded critical information is exactly why one should be concerned with how this discourse shaped the highest levels of foreign policy decision making.

---

[75] "About the *Foreign Relations of the United States* Series," Historical Documents, *Office of the Historian* website, https://history.state.gov/historicaldocuments/about-frus, accessed May 18, 2017.

[76] Ibid.

To analyze these documents systematically, I composed a list of twenty-one probabilistic terms based on previous scholarship exploring the meanings of qualitative expressions of uncertainty.[77] Then I collected every statement in the FRUS documents that contained any of these terms.[78] These statements made it possible to build a database containing 1,757 assessments of uncertainty, spanning 600 separate documents.

I coded each assessment as representing one of four categories. *Precise* assessments of probability establish unambiguous meaning. I defined this category liberally to include qualitative expressions such as "even chance" and "almost certain." *Imprecise* assessments of probability use qualitative expressions or numeric ranges to give a vague sense of what an analyst's belief entails. *Relative probability* assessments indicate that some conclusion is more likely than another without specifying the relevant reference point. Statements that involve *conditioning* indicate that a conclusion would be impossible to sustain unless some logical condition were met, without assessing the probability that the conclusion is actually true.

To examine how these forms of probability assessment varied across different kinds of judgments, I divided statements in the database into nine categories. First, I identified 94 statements that involved U.S. officials describing the chances that their strategic recommendations would succeed. Next, I identified 58 statements that involved U.S. officials describing the probability of success in Vietnam *without* making a strategic recommendation, usually in the context of critiquing other people's proposals or explaining why the status quo was not viable. The remaining seven categories dealt with elements of uncertainty besides the probability of strategic success. These categories, which were neither mutually exclusive nor exhaustive, included predictions about coups or Government of Vietnam (GVN) leadership succession; assessments of the chances that other states would turn

[77] The terms were "almost certain," "cannot rule out," "chance," "conceivable," "doubt," "doubtful," "fifty-fifty," "improbable," "inconceivable," "liable," "likelihood," "likely," "odds," "percent," "probability," "probable," "probably," "prospect," "remote," "risk," and "unlikely." I chose these search terms because they appear in other scholars' empirical studies of verbal uncertainty expressions, specifically, Kent, "Words of Estimative Probability"; Beyth-Marom, "How Probable Is Probable?"; and Mosteller and Youtz, "Quantifying Probabilistic Expressions."

[78] I applied three criteria for inclusion in this database. First, I only retained statements that expressed the beliefs of the document's author or that were recorded in a memorandum of discussion. Second, I only retained statements that reflected the beliefs of U.S. government officials; though independent scholars or members of the press appear frequently in FRUS documents, the goal of this study is to analyze how U.S. officials debated uncertainty. Third, I only included documents and memoranda intended for an internal audience, on the assumption that public speeches, letters to President Diem, or other public statements would not reliably reflect officials' true beliefs.

Table 1.1. **Patterns of Probability Assessment across *Foreign Relations* Documents**

	Precise assessments	Imprecise assessments	Relative probability or conditioning
Probability of a proposed strategy succeeding (N = 94)	0%[**]	9%[***]	91%[***]
Probability of any other strategy succeeding (58)	2%	88%	10%
All statements (1,759)	8%	78%	14%
Coups/South Vietnamese succession (213)	9%	74%	17%
Other states turning Communist (30)	20%[*]	67%	13%
GVN domestic policies (432)	5%[*]	88%[***]	7%[***]
GVN economic/fiscal policies (39)	0%	95%[**]	5%
Communist strategy/perceptions (472)	12%[***]	76%	12%
Foreign policies of noncombatants (106)	10%	85%	36%[***]
Chances of tactical policy success (136)	7%	87%[**]	25%[**]

Asterisks reflect statistical significance levels when comparing each category to baseline patterns across the data as a whole, as follows: $^* = p < 0.05$, $^{**} = p < 0.01$, $^{***} = p < .0.001$.

or lean Communist; assessments of GVN domestic policies; assessments of GVN economic or fiscal policies; assessments of Communist combatants' strategies or intentions; assessments of noncombatant countries' foreign policies or intentions; and the chances that specific policies would succeed in meeting tactical objectives.

The database strongly confirms the patterns shown in the previous section's qualitative analysis. As shown by the top row of Table 1.1, U.S. officials were overwhelmingly vague when describing the chances that their recommendations would succeed. Ninety-one percent of those statements involved either relative probability or conditioning. Most of the remaining statements were not especially informative either. Some involved unspecified logic, such as Ambassador Frederick Nolting's claim that "we have better than [a] 50-50 chance of winning on this policy line provided the border with Laos is reasonably well protected," in which Nolting neither explained what it meant to "reasonably" protect the border nor assessed the probability that this could be accomplished.[79] Other statements convey extremely vague sentiments, such as the argument of Deputy National Security Advisor Rostow that escalation would produce "a fair chance of avoiding war," General Wheeler's assessment that "victory is now a hopeful prospect," or Director of Central Intelligence John McCone's reporting to President Johnson that winning the war would be "formidable and difficult, but not impossible."[80]

The database also confirms that U.S. officials consistently provided more informative probability assessments when critiquing the strategies they opposed. Fifty-eight statements in the database involve U.S. officials describing the current strategy's prospects or critiquing other officials' recommendations. Although only one of these statements could reasonably be considered precise,[81] just six (ten percent) involved relative probability or conditioning. Most of these statements offer at least some rough way to gauge U.S. officials' pessimism: for example, stating that "the chances of a turn-around in South Vietnam remain less than even," explaining that current U.S. strategy "would probably not save South Viet-Nam from eventual loss," or warning that "our present course of action . . . is very likely to fail."[82]

The database also confirms that the manner in which U.S. officials discussed their strategic prospects contrasted with how they assessed other aspects of uncertainty about the war.[83] Though these officials almost never made their probability assessments explicit, just fourteen percent of the statements across the database as a whole involved either relative probability or conditioning. No other category of statements employed these forms of probabilistic reasoning nearly as frequently as when officials described the chances

---

[79] Frederick Nolting, "Telegram from the Embassy in Vietnam to the Department of State," *FRUS, 1961–1963*, Vol. 1, Doc 147 (6 October 1961). Similarly, Major General Charles Bonesteel argued in a meeting of the Presidential Task Force on Vietnam that "if we had a reasonably workable settlement in Laos, bolstered by the barrier between Laos and Viet-Nam and along the 17th parallel, we could probably succeed." *FRUS, 1961–1963*, Vol. 1, Doc 43 (4 May 1961).

[80] Rostow to Johnson, *FRUS, 1961–1963*, Vol. 1, Doc 251 (14 November 1961); JCS Team Report on South Vietnam, *FRUS, 1961–1963*, Vol. II, Doc 26 (January 1963); McCone to Johnson, *FRUS, 1961–1963*, Vol. IV, Doc 375 (23 December 1963).

[81] This is a memorandum written by the Defense Department's Office of International Security Affairs, which argues that continuing U.S. policy toward President Diem would "almost certainly seal the fate of Vietnam." *FRUS, 1961–1963*, Vol. II, doc. 35 (26 January 1962).

[82] McG. Bundy to Johnson, *FRUS, 1964–1968*, Vol. II, Doc 183 (6 March 1965); Maxwell Taylor, "The Current Situation in South Vietnam," *FRUS, 1964–1968*, Vol. I, Doc 426 (November 1964); Chester Bowles to Kennedy, "Recommendations for a Fresh Approach to the Vietnam Impasse," *FRUS, 1961–1963*, Vol. III, Doc 52 (7 March 1963).

[83] The statistical significance tests reported in Table 1.1 reflect two-way t-tests comparing differences in means.

that their favored strategies would succeed. Altogether, these data support the chapter's qualitative description of how U.S. officials were overwhelmingly vague when assessing uncertainty in Vietnam; of how this problem ran much deeper than the use of imprecise language; and of how assessments of uncertainty were least informative when it came to proposals for escalating the war.

Beyond "Words of Estimative Probability"

This chapter began by describing the famous 1964 essay by Sherman Kent, titled "Words of Estimative Probability." In that essay, Kent criticized intelligence analysts for making imprecise assessments of uncertainty. More than a half-century later, Kent's writing on this topic remains an effective vehicle for sparking discussion about the nature and limits of foreign policy analysis. Yet the chapter described three ways in which Kent did not go far enough in describing the degree to which foreign policy analysts avoid probabilistic reasoning.

First, Kent's essay suggests that vague assessments of uncertainty are mainly a problem for intelligence analysts. The chapter has explained, by contrast, how similar issues recur across a broad range of foreign policy agencies, in public debates among scholars and pundits, and among decision makers forming policy at the highest levels.

Second, when Kent offered his critiques in 1964, he was raising an issue to which foreign policy analysts had previously devoted little attention. In recounting his experience writing a report describing a "serious possibility" that the Soviet Union would invade Yugoslavia, Kent admitted that he had not given this phrase much thought. This chapter has shown, by contrast, that aversion to probabilistic reasoning in foreign policy discourse is now entirely deliberate, guided by official doctrine that encourages intelligence analysts and military planners to avoid assessing uncertainty in clear and structured ways.

Third, and most importantly, this chapter has demonstrated how problems with assessing uncertainty in international politics run much deeper than semantics. It is even more worrisome to see that foreign policy analysts often avoid assessing crucial probabilities at all, especially by engaging in the practices that this chapter called relative probability and conditioning. These are not just inefficient methods for assessing uncertainty: these kinds of analysis are fundamentally unsuited to supporting sound decisions. Nor do these problems appear solely among the so-called poets who are uncomfortable with advanced analytics. Even Robert McNamara and the Whiz Kids systematically avoided assessing the uncertainty surrounding their most important foreign policy choices.

This experience motivates a broader concern that will run throughout the remainder of the book. In most areas of policy and scholarship, it is generally assumed that rigor, objectivity, and analytic precision go together.[84] Yet that is not the case when it comes to probabilistic reasoning in international politics. Any attempt to assess uncertainty in this domain is inherently subjective, and that is indeed one of the main reasons why foreign policy analysts are typically reluctant to describe their judgments explicitly. The Whiz Kids' experience in Vietnam highlights the dangers of failing to grapple with this challenge—of privileging objectivity over rigor in foreign policy analysis. But if the most important elements of uncertainty in international politics are inherently subjective, then what would rigorously analyzing these issues look like? How well can fallible individuals handle this challenge? And how can decision makers incorporate these judgments into real foreign policy decisions? These are the questions that occupy the rest of the book.

---

[84] For a history of debates about rigor, objectivity, and quantification in public policy analysis, see Theodore Porter, *Trust in Numbers: The Pursuit of Objectivity in Science and Public Life* (Princeton, N.J.: Princeton University Press, 1995).

2

Subjective Probability and International Politics

This chapter examines the theoretical foundations of assessing uncertainty in international politics. The chapter's first section explains that all major foreign policy decisions depend on perceptions of subjective probability. Even when foreign policy analysts base their judgments on statistical analyses or mathematical models, their assessments still reflect personal convictions rather than objective truths. The chapter's second section explains why it is logically acceptable to believe that subjective probabilities are meaningless, but shows that this premise has consequences that no foreign policy analyst can accept. The chapter's third section demonstrates how, conditional on believing that assessments of subjective probability contain any meaningful insight, it is always possible to form and communicate that insight in clear and structured ways. The subjective nature of probabilistic reasoning in international politics is, in fact, exactly what makes it possible to debate that reasoning directly, because foreign policy analysts can always describe their personal convictions however precisely they like.

This theoretical analysis has several practical implications. For instance, the chapter explains how it is always possible to resolve the kind of confusion that President Obama encountered in reconciling different views about the chances that Osama bin Laden was living at Abbottabad. We will see that there is no situation in which foreign policy analysts can communicate their beliefs using qualitative language but not numeric percentages. And I will argue that the impulse that leads foreign policy analysts to prize objectivity is better served by drawing clear distinctions between the concepts of probability and confidence. Altogether, the chapter shows how foreign policy analysts always possess a coherent theoretical basis for assessing uncertainty in international politics.

Theoretical Foundations of Probability Assessment

What did it mean to estimate a "sixty percent chance" that Osama bin Laden was living in Abbottabad? Ultimately, bin Laden was there or he wasn't—how could any other judgment be considered meaningful? And if foreign policy analysts cannot accurately model phenomena as complex as international politics and armed conflict, then how can they form coherent estimates of the uncertainty that these phenomena contain? These are nontrivial questions that raise long-standing debates about the conceptual foundations of probabilistic reasoning and the nature of foreign policy analysis.[1]

Broadly speaking, there are three ways to define what probability assessments represent. These frameworks are called the *frequency, propensity,* and *subjective* theories of probability.[2] This section explains how the subjective theory of probability is the only viable foundation for assessing uncertainty in international politics.

Much of the discussion in this section revolves around the distinction between the concepts of *aleatory* and *epistemic* uncertainty. Aleatory uncertainty applies to situations in which outcomes are unknown because they reflect processes involving genuine randomness. Epistemic uncertainty applies to situations in which outcomes are unknown because analysts possess incomplete information.[3] Uncertainty about Osama bin Laden's location or the status of Saddam Hussein's nuclear weapons programs are both examples of epistemic uncertainty. Epistemic uncertainty is always subjective, because it depends on the state of an analyst's personal knowledge. In brief, this section argues that all probabilistic reasoning in international politics involves epistemic uncertainty in one form or another.[4]

---

[1] Ian Hacking, *The Emergence of Probability: A Philosophical Study of Early Ideas about Probability, Induction, and Statistical Inference* (New York: Cambridge University Press, 1975); Donald Gillies, *Philosophical Theories of Probability* (New York: Routledge, 2000); Gerd Gigerenzer et al., *The Empire of Chance: How Probability Changed Science and Everyday Life* (New York: Cambridge University Press, 1989); and David Howie, *Interpreting Probability: Controversies and Developments in the Early Twentieth Century* (New York: Cambridge University Press, 2002).

[2] This typology omits two paradigms: the classical theory of probability of Bernoulli and Laplace, and Keynes's theory of logical probability. These theories played an important role in the history of probabilistic thought, but they are no longer considered viable. See Gillies, *Philosophical Theories of Probability,* for an overview of these concepts.

[3] This "dual nature" of probability assessment is a central theme in Hacking, *Emergence of Probability.*

[4] Note that the contrast between aleatory and epistemic uncertainty is different from the way in which intelligence scholars distinguish between *puzzles* and *mysteries.* In intelligence studies, puzzles represent questions that have knowable right answers, whereas mysteries represent questions about which it is impossible to provide conclusive judgments. Some kinds of epistemic uncertainty (like Osama bin Laden's location in 2011) are indeed puzzles, but other forms of epistemic uncertainty

The Frequency Theory of Probability

The first way of defining what probability assessments represent is called the *frequency theory* of probability. According to the frequency theory, probability assessments reflect inferences drawn from analyzing a series of previous identical events.[5] When you say that a coin flip has a fifty percent chance of turning up heads, the frequency theory's interpretation for this statement is that you have previously witnessed many such coins being flipped, and half of those coins have landed facing up. Probability assessments based on the frequency theory are considered to be "correct" to the extent that they accurately characterize the patterns observed across these previous, identical events.

The frequency theory serves as the basis for many statistical techniques. Nevertheless, the frequency theory does not provide a coherent foundation for probabilistic reasoning in international politics. It cannot, for example, resolve uncertainty over factual matters. When intelligence analysts debated the chances that Saddam Hussein was pursuing nuclear weapons, their judgments reflected incomplete information, and not inferences drawn from a stream of prior cases. And though foreign policy analysts can often use statistical patterns to inform their expectations about the likely outcomes of a policy, those patterns almost never reflect a series of previous, identical events. Richard von Mises, the German mathematician who made seminal contributions to the frequency theory, was clear on this point. " 'The probability of winning a battle,' " he explained, "has no place in our theory of probability, because we cannot think of a collective to which it belongs."[6]

This does not mean that statistical analysis is useless for informing foreign policy debates. Yet the moment statistical analysts can no longer consider data points to be identical to the specific issue they are assessing, they can no longer defend their conclusions on the basis of the frequency theory alone. This is what von Mises meant by saying that battles do not naturally belong to "collectives": constructing a statistical model of battle outcomes requires determining which data points belong in the analysis, assessing how similar the cases are, and speculating about what kinds of confounds a statistical model might

(such as judging a foreign leader's intentions) are essentially impossible to resolve, and should thus be considered mysteries. Meanwhile, some kinds of aleatory uncertainty (such as estimating the probability that a coin flip will come up heads) do yield "correct" answers, and should therefore be considered puzzles. On the distinction between mysteries and puzzles, see Wilhelm Agrell and Gregory F. Treverton, *National Intelligence and Science: Beyond the Great Divide in Analysis and Policy* (New York: Oxford University Press, 2015), pp. 32–35.

[5] Richard von Mises, *Probability, Statistics and Truth* (Mineola, N.Y.: Dover Publications, 1981 [1928]).

[6] von Mises, *Probability, Statistics, and Truth*, pp. 11–15.

be unable to measure.[7] These are all subjective judgments that reflect epistemic uncertainty about the quality of a statistical model's assumptions, rather than objective properties of randomness.[8] In this sense, even if the statistical methods used in foreign policy analysis are often described in terms of "frequentist statistics," they are properly viewed as analogies to the frequentist paradigm, rather than strict applications of that conceptual framework.[9]

The Propensity Theory of Probability

The second way to describe what probability assessments represent is called the *propensity theory* of probability. According to the propensity theory, probability assessments reflect an analyst's knowledge of the manner in which physical systems generate random output.[10] When you say that a coin flip has a fifty percent chance of turning up heads, the propensity theory's interpretation of this statement is that you have studied the coin's physical properties, and you have concluded that they will cause the coin to land face up half of the time. Probability assessments based on the propensity theory are considered to be "correct" to the extent that they accurately characterize the properties of mechanical systems.

The propensity theory plays a major role in the natural sciences, particularly when it comes to grounding quantum mechanics. But like frequency theory, propensity theory is inappropriate for describing probability assessments in international politics. Once again, the theory cannot capture what analysts are saying when they describe uncertainty surrounding factual matters. When Michael Morell said there was a sixty percent chance that bin Laden was living

[7] The subjective nature of determining what it means for cases to be "comparable" in this fashion is known as the *reference class problem*. See John Venn, *The Logic of Chance* (London, U.K.: Macmillan, 1888); Hans Reichenbach, *The Theory of Probability*, tr. Ernest H. Hutten and Maria Reichenbach (Berkeley, Calif.: University of California Press, 1949).

[8] Charles F. Manski, *Public Policy in an Uncertain World: Analysis and Decision* (Cambridge, Mass.: Harvard University Press, 2013), explains that statistical probability estimates present an incomplete (and usually narrower) picture of the overall uncertainty that surrounds empirical inference.

[9] In other words, the use of frequentist statistics in foreign policy analysis is properly understood as a tool for generating subjective probability estimates. It is, then, an empirical question as to whether those statistical methods are more reliable than other forms of subjective judgment. For more on how frequentist statistics rarely adhere to the frequency theory of probability itself, see Harold Jeffreys, "Probability and Scientific Method," *Proceedings of the Royal Society of London A*, Vol. 146, No. 856 (1933), pp. 9–16; E. T. Jaynes, *Probability Theory: The Logic of Science*, ed. G. Larry Brethorst (New York: Cambridge University Press, 2003).

[10] The propensity theory originates with Karl Popper, "The Propensity Interpretation of Probability," *British Journal for the Philosophy of Science*, Vol. 10, No. 37 (1959), pp. 25–52.

at Abbottabad, he was not implying that some mechanical process had randomly assigned bin Laden to this location six times out of ten. And though foreign policy analysts can use physical models and simulation techniques to guide some elements of policy design, no one would claim that these analyses depict the actual properties of social systems. Even the most sophisticated models of armed conflict and international politics reflect extreme simplifications of reality. Interpreting these models' results thus requires making subjective judgments about the appropriateness of simplifying assumptions.[11]

Moreover, even if foreign policy analysts could create a deterministic model of international politics, that would *still* be insufficient to make objective predictions, because many of the model's key parameters would remain uncertain. When waging wars or bargaining over contentious issues, leaders have incentives to conceal their intentions, capabilities, and resolve. Since any model of conflict or cooperation should account for these variables, those models' output will reflect epistemic uncertainty about underlying conditions.[12] This is another reason why even the most sophisticated piece of foreign policy analysis could never meet the propensity theory's standards of objectivity.[13]

Of course, there is no need to invoke probability theory just to understand the difficulties of predicting international politics. The purpose of this discussion is

[11] On the limits to objectivity in military modeling in particular, see Joshua M. Epstein, *Strategy and Force Planning* (Washington, D.C.: Brookings, 1987); Thomas J. Czerwinski, *Coping with the Bounds: Speculations on Nonlinearity in Military Affairs* (Washington, D.C.: National Defense University Press, 1998); Michael E. O'Hanlon, *The Science of War* (Princeton, N.J.: Princeton University Press, 2009).

[12] On the pervasiveness of this uncertainty, see Robert Jervis, *System Effects: Complexity in Political and Social Life* (Princeton, N.J.: Princeton University Press, 1997); John Mearsheimer, *The Tragedy of Great Power Politics* (New York: Norton, 2001), pp. 29–54; and Kristopher W. Ramsey, "Information, Uncertainty, and War," *Annual Reviews of Political Science*, Vol. 20 (2017), pp. 505–527. For practitioners' views of this subject, see James N. Mattis, "USJFCOM Commander's Guidance for Effects-Based Operations," *Parameters*, Vol. 38, No. 3 (2008), pp. 18–25; and Paul K. Van Riper, "EBO: There Was No Baby in the Bathwater," *Joint Forces Quarterly*, No. 52 (2009), pp. 82–85. On the limits of academic forecasting in international politics, see Gerald Schneider, Nils Petter Gleditsch, and Sabine Carey, "Forecasting in International Relations," *Conflict Management and Peace Science*, Vol. 20, No. 1 (2011), pp. 5–14; and Michael D. Ward, "Can We Predict Politics?" *Journal of Global Security Studies*, Vol. 1, No. 1 (2016), pp. 80–91.

[13] Furthermore, even if foreign policy analysts *could* somehow develop a purely objective probability assessment, most decision makers would be unable to know that this was the case. Decision makers do not possess the time or expertise to scrutinize every data point and assumption behind the estimates that analysts give them. Indeed, the purpose of delegating analytic tasks is so that decision makers do *not* need to scrutinize these details. But since these minutiae matter, any time decision makers solicit input in forming judgments under uncertainty, their reactions to that input depend on the subjective trust that they place in their analysts for the purposes of understanding a specific issue.

instead to place those difficulties into proper theoretical perspective. When foreign policy analysts attempt to assess the uncertainty that surrounds high-stakes
decisions, their judgments should not be viewed as unreliable attempts to estimate frequencies or propensities. Logically speaking, these judgments do not reflect frequencies or propensities at all—even if foreign policy analysts base their
assessments of uncertainty on the output of simulations or statistical analyses,
their conclusions always reflect some measure of subjective belief. The next part
of this section explains how the logic of translating subjective beliefs into probability assessments is entirely different from the manner in which analysts typically interpret output from statistical analyses or mechanical models.

The Subjective Theory of Probability

The subjective theory of probability defines probability assessments with respect to an analyst's personal convictions.[14] The standard way to represent these
convictions is to describe an analyst's willingness to bet. Thus, when you say that
a coin flip has a fifty percent chance of coming up heads, the subjective theory's
interpretation for this statement is that you would be indifferent between betting
on the coin's landing heads versus the coin's landing tails.[15] According to the subjective probability framework, this judgment is considered to be "correct" to the
extent that it accurately characterizes an analyst's personal beliefs.[16]

   The logic of describing an analyst's personal beliefs can sharply diverge from
the logic of describing objective properties of randomness. For example, consider flipping a coin that has an unknown bias. In other words, you know that
this coin is unevenly weighted, but you have no information about whether the
imbalance inclines the coin toward landing heads versus landing tails. Since
you should be indifferent between betting on either outcome, the subjective
theory of probability indicates that you should estimate the probability of this
coin landing heads as fifty percent—even though you know this is the only estimate that does *not* describe the coin's actual, physical properties. The same

---

[14] The Italian economist Bruno de Finetti and the British philosopher Frank P. Ramsey developed
the theory of subjective probability independently. See Frank P. Ramsey, "Truth and Probability,"
in *The Foundations of Mathematics and Other Logical Essays* (New York: Harcourt, Brace, 1931);
and Bruno de Finetti, "Probabilism: A Critical Essay on the Theory of Probability and the Value
of Science," *Logos*, Vol. 14 (1931), pp. 163–219; reprinted in *Erkenntnis*, Vol. 31, Vol. 2/3 (1989),
pp. 169–223. The American mathematician Leonard J. Savage then extended the formal logic behind
this framework in *The Foundations of Statistics* (New York: Wiley, 1954).

[15] And that you would be unwilling to bet on any other outcome, regardless of the payoff. Gillies,
Philosophical Theories of Probability, pp. 55–58, explores conceptual nuances of the comparison of
lotteries (or "betting quotient") method for defining what probability assessments represent.

[16] Frank Lad, *Operational Subjective Statistical Methods* (New York: Wiley, 1996), pp. 8–9.

logic applies to interpreting the "chances" that Osama bin Laden was living at Abbottabad. When President Obama's advisers estimated those chances, their degrees of personal conviction reportedly ranged from thirty percent to ninety-five percent, even though everyone knew that the "real" probability of bin Laden living at Abbottabad was either zero percent or one hundred percent.

Many people find it counterintuitive to equate convictions with probabilities, and laboratory experiments confirm that subjects tend to treat these concepts differently. For example, if given the opportunity to bet on calling the outcome of a fair coin versus calling the outcome of a coin with an unknown bias, most people will choose the first of these gambles. Some people will even pay nontrivial amounts to ensure that they can bet on less-ambiguous probabilities.

This behavior is known as *ambiguity aversion*, and it is easy to demonstrate that ambiguity aversion is misguided.[17] For example, you could simply randomize whether you predict that the coin will land heads or tails. In that case, you would guarantee yourself a fifty percent chance of winning the bet regardless of whether the coin you flip is fair or imbalanced. If anything, it is actually in your interest to flip the coin with an unknown bias, because this would provide potentially valuable information about how that coin is weighted. If you ever have a chance to take this gamble again, you could pick the outcome that you observed from the last time you flipped this coin, and your expected probability of winning the bet would then be greater than fifty percent.[18]

Another source of discomfort with the subjective probability framework is that it conflicts with the desire to base high-stakes choices on objective judgments.[19] Objectivity is in fact a formal requirement in many areas of foreign policy analysis. For example, the very first requirement laid out in the U.S. Intelligence Community's analytic standards is that "analysts must perform their functions with objectivity."[20] U.S. Army planning doctrine similarly revolves

---

[17] The term *ambiguity aversion* was coined by Daniel Ellsberg, the economist who later went on to leak the Pentagon Papers. See Daniel Ellsberg, "Risk, Ambiguity, and the Savage Axioms," *Quarterly Journal of Economics*, Vol. 75, No. 4 (1961) pp. 643–669. In some situations ambiguity can serve as a signal of other decision-relevant factors, but this does not change the fact that ambiguity regarding probability estimates is not, by itself, a component of rational decision making. See Nabil al-Najjar and Jonathan Weinstein, "The Ambiguity Aversion Literature: A Critical Assessment," *Economics and Philosophy*, Vol. 25, No. 3 (2009), pp. 249–284.

[18] Stefan T. Trautmann and Richard Zeckhauser, "Shunning Uncertainty: The Neglect of Learning Opportunities," *Games and Economic Behavior*, Vol. 79 (2013), pp. 44–55.

[19] For a history of debates about rigor, objectivity, and quantification in public policy analysis, see Theodore Porter, *Trust in Numbers: The Pursuit of Objectivity in Science and Public Life* (Princeton, N.J.: Princeton University Press, 1995).

[20] Intelligence Community Directive 203 (ICD-203), *Analytic Standards*, p. 2. U.S. law actually mandates that the Intelligence Community develop institutional mechanisms to "safeguard objectivity." See the 2004 Intelligence Reform and Terrorism Prevention Act, Section 1020A. Recent

around "safeguards to protect objectivity in the assessment process."[21] This is one reason why many scholars and practitioners believe that foreign policy analysts should avoid making their assessments of uncertainty explicit. Thus, in what is arguably the most important contemporary textbook on intelligence studies, Mark Lowenthal writes that numeric probability assessments "run the risk of conveying to the policy client a degree of precision that does not exist. What is the difference between a 6-in-10 chance and a 7-in-10 chance, beyond greater conviction? In reality, the analyst is back to relying on gut feeling."[22]

   Yet leaving assessments of uncertainty vague does not change their conceptual foundations. These judgments do not become subjective once they pass some threshold of specificity. Regardless of how foreign policy analysts express their beliefs about uncertainty, there is no coherent way to say what these beliefs reflect that does not rely on personal conviction. If foreign policy analysts are truly intended to "perform their functions with objectivity," then they would have to reject *all* assessments of uncertainty, not just those expressed using numbers instead of words. The next section explains why this is a position that no foreign policy analyst can accept.

Probability, Confidence, and Analytic Rigor

To say that a judgment is subjective does not mean that it is careless or uninformative. For example, Carl von Clausewitz argued that the key to assessing uncertainty in war lay with cultivating an intuitive "genius" that did not "yield to academic wisdom."[23] In Clausewitz's view, the truly careless move would be to base strategic decisions on a hidebound use of formal logic that left no room to

survey research indicates that intelligence analysts indeed prioritize "objectivity" over ICD-203's other analytic standards: see David R. Mandel and Tonya Hendriks, "ODNI's ICD-203 Standards on Analytic Integrity," Paper presented at the 7th Biannual Meeting of the NATO Systems Analysis and Studies Panel Research Technical Group on the Assessment and Communication of Uncertainty in Intelligence to Support Decision-Making (Madrid, Spain, 2018).

   [21] U.S. Army Field Manual 5-0, *The Operations Process* (2010), p. H-4.

   [22] Mark Lowenthal, *Intelligence: From Secrets to Policy*, 3rd edition (Washington, D.C.: CQ Press, 2006), p. 129. In a similar vein, the former director of national intelligence James Clapper reflected on the debate about the chances that Osama bin Laden was living at Abbottabad, saying: "We put a lot of discussion [into] percentages of confidence, which to me is not particularly meaningful. In the end it's all subjective judgment anyway." CNN, "The Axe Files," Podcast Ep. 247 (31 May 2018).

   [23] Carl von Clausewitz, *On War*, tr. Michael Howard and Peter Paret (Princeton, N.J.: Princeton University Press, 1984); and Clifford J. Rogers, "Clausewitz, Genius, and the Rules," *Journal of Military History*, Vol. 66, No. 4 (2002), pp. 1167–1176.

accommodate a decision maker's personal insight.[24] And in the next chapter, we will also see how fine-grained variations in subjective probability assessments can capture meaningful information about international politics.

It is nevertheless impossible to demonstrate that a single subjective probability assessment is meaningful—in other words, there is no way to demonstrate that an analyst's personal convictions provide a useful guide to assessing uncertainty in any one case.[25] This has led many prominent scholars to question whether subjective probabilities can ever be trusted as a basis for making high-stakes decisions. The philosopher John Stuart Mill expressed this view when he argued that probability estimates "are of no real value" unless analysts derive them from large volumes of reliable data.[26] The economist John Maynard Keynes expressed similar disdain for subjective probabilities, writing that "about these matters, there is no scientific basis on which to form any calculable probability whatsoever. We simply do not know."[27]

Although this position is logically coherent, its consequences are untenable for anyone who seeks to contribute to foreign policy debates. In order to believe that it is possible to distinguish between policies that are acceptable and those that are not, one must implicitly assume that subjective probability assessments are meaningful. For example, consider General Stanley McChrystal's 2009 recommendation that President Obama deploy forty thousand additional troops to Afghanistan. We saw in chapter 1 that General McChrystal argued that a new strategy backed by forty thousand additional troops represented "the best prospect for success in this important mission." Elsewhere in his report, General McChrystal wrote that his proposed troop

---

[24] The rejection of Enlightenment rationality was indeed crucial to Clausewitz's intellectual project. On this point, see Azar Gat, *The Origins of Military Thought: From the Enlightenment to Clausewitz* (Oxford, U.K.: Clarendon Press, 1989). On the distinction between subjectivity and deliberativeness in foreign policy analysis more generally, see Philip E. Tetlock, "Second Thoughts about *Expert Political Judgment*," *Critical Review*, Vol. 22, No. 4 (2010), pp. 467–488. In a similar vein, psychologists have produced a large volume of research showing that unconscious reasoning can improve decision outcomes. See Ap Dijksterhuis et al., "On Making the Right Choice: The Deliberation-Without-Attention Effect," *Science*, Vol. 311 (2006), pp. 1005–1007.

[25] Thus one of the principal critiques of Clausewitz's theory of decision making: if two commanders disagree on the chances that a strategy will succeed, how do we know which one possesses greater "genius"?

[26] John Stuart Mill, *A System of Logic, Ratiocinative and Inductive*, 8th ed. (New York, N.Y.: Harper and Brothers, 1882), p. 539.

[27] John Maynard Keynes, "The General Theory of Employment," *Quarterly Journal of Economics*, Vol. 51, No. 2 (1937), pp. 213–214; see also John Maynard Keynes, *A Treatise on Probability* (London: Macmillan, 1921). For reviews of this argument in international affairs, see Richard K. Betts, "Is Strategy an Illusion?" *International Security*, Vol. 25, No. 2 (2000), pp. 5–50; and Ben Connable, *Embracing the Fog of War* (Santa Monica, Calif.: Rand, 2012).

surge represented "the minimum force levels to accomplish the mission with an acceptable level of risk."

Both statements reflected the premise that sending fewer than forty thousand reinforcements to Afghanistan would produce lower chances of success.[28] It is impossible to believe that General McChrystal could coherently argue for sending additional troops to Afghanistan while also claiming that he had no basis for assessing the chances that the deployment would succeed. If General McChrystal had no basis for assessing those chances, then President Obama would have had no reason to expect that sending forty thousand additional forces to Afghanistan would produce a better outcome than deploying thirty thousand more troops. Iterating this logic, it would become unjustifiable to send any additional soldiers to Afghanistan, or even to keep any remaining U.S. forces in the country at all. Who could have said that withdrawal would lower the chances of defeating the Taliban? What is the purpose of expending lives and resources if there is no basis for believing that this raises the chances of obtaining valuable outcomes?

Few observers would adopt such an extreme viewpoint.[29] Regardless of how complex or subjective a decision might be, it is ultimately necessarily to draw a line somewhere between resource allocations that are acceptable and those that are not. Any deployment of resources thus depends on the notion that it is, in fact, possible to form coherent perceptions of subjective probability.[30]

Of course, this does not mean that anything goes in foreign policy analysis. If a team of subject-matter experts conducts a rigorous, mixed-method analysis to estimate the chances than some event will occur, their judgment clearly deserves

---

[28] This statement also implies that General McChrystal could judge that the *magnitude* of this shift in probability was large enough to justify the additional investment of resources. Similar assumptions are also evident in McChrystal's claim that deploying more than 40,000 additional troops "could achieve low risk, but this would be excessive in the final analysis." Commander, International Security Assistance Force-Afghanistan, *COMISAF Initial Assessment*, August 2009, pp. 2–20 to 2–21.

[29] In fact, if foreign policy analysts cannot make valid probability assessments, then the only ethical move would be to eliminate all defense expenditures. There would be no reason to think that those resources actually make the country safer, and thus the money would be better spent elsewhere (or else returned to taxpayers). As Betts puts it, if there is no hope of predicting the results of military strategy, then "analysts as well as politicians and generals should all quit and go fishing" ("Is Strategy an Illusion," p. 20). See also Robert A. Pape, "The Air Force Strikes Back," *Security Studies*, Vol. 7, No. 2 (1997/98), pp. 191–214.

[30] Note how this discussion inverts the traditional relationship between objectivity and analytic precision. In many areas of public life, scholars and practitioners seek to quantify important parameters as a way of pursuing objective judgment. Yet, when dealing with probability assessments in international politics, many scholars and practitioners seek to *avoid* making precise judgments, on the grounds that these judgments would be excessively subjective. See Porter, *Trust in Numbers*, for more detail on the first of these viewpoints.

more weight than a pundit's off-the-cuff opinion, even if both views reflect subjective probabilities. But how should decision makers determine how much weight these judgments deserve? If objectivity is not the proper standard for assigning credibility to foreign policy analysts' judgments, then what criterion should we use?

Answering these questions requires distinguishing between the concepts of "probability" and "confidence." As mentioned in the introduction, *probability* reflects analysts' beliefs about the chances that a statement is true, while *confidence* reflects the extent to which analysts believe they possess a sound basis for assessing uncertainty. Elsewhere, I have argued for further parsing analytic confidence into at least three components: the reliability of available evidence supporting a judgment, the range of reasonable opinion surrounding a judgment, and the degree to which analysts believe their judgment could change in response to new information. These concepts can vary independently, and each carries distinct implications for high-stakes decision making.[31]

In U.S. criminal trials, for example, jurors are only allowed to convict defendants based on reliable evidence. Inferences based on hearsay, stereotypes, or coerced confessions are barred from jurors' consideration on the grounds that these inferences do not provide a valid basis for revoking defendants' civil liberties. Most criminal trials furthermore require that jurors reach a guilty verdict unanimously, reflecting the premise that a single dissenting view creates enough reasonable doubt to preclude conviction. In this respect, the application of criminal justice is not just a matter of estimating the probability of defendants' guilt. Estimating a high probability of guilt is necessary, but not sufficient, to sustain a guilty verdict.[32]

Controversy over the U.S. invasion of Iraq in 2003 shows how similar factors shape the politics and ethics of foreign policy decision making. As described in chapter 1, most intelligence analysts believed that Iraq was pursuing weapons of mass destruction (WMD), and the Bush administration invoked that belief to justify going to war. However, inferences about Iraq's WMD programs relied heavily on circumstantial evidence and questionable informants. The U.S. State Department had, furthermore, lodged an explicit dissent regarding assessments of Iraq's nuclear program, and the International Atomic Energy Agency had

---

[31] Jeffrey A. Friedman and Richard Zeckhauser, "Analytic Confidence and Political Decision Making: Theoretical Principles and Experimental Evidence from National Security Professionals," *Political Psychology*, Vol. 39, No. 5 (2018), pp. 1069–1087.

[32] On how the standard of "guilt beyond a reasonable doubt" combines assessments of probability and confidence in this way, see Peter Tillers and Jonathan Gottfried, "Case Comment—*United States* v. *Copeland*, 369 F. Supp. 2d 275 (E.D.N.Y. 2005): A Collateral Attack on the Legal Maxim That Proof Beyond a Reasonable Doubt Is Unquantifiable?" *Law, Probability, and Risk*, Vol. 5, No. 2 (2006), pp. 135–157.

warned that there was no factual basis for concluding that the program was op-
erative. Many of the Bush administration's critics argued that the lack of reliable
evidence and the presence of dissenting views undermined the case for war, or
at least justified delaying the invasion in order to gather more reliable information and to build greater consensus.[33] Note that this is distinct from critiquing
how the Bush administration perceived the *probability* that Iraq was pursuing
WMDs. The argument is instead that analysts and decision makers paid insufficient attention to the *confidence* surrounding this judgment.[34]

The degree to which probability assessments might change in response to new
information plays an especially important role when it comes to timing high-
stakes decisions. For example, when the Central Intelligence Agency (CIA) initially approached President Obama with indications that Osama bin Laden might
be living in Abbottabad, Pakistan, Obama decided that the available information
did not yet warrant taking military action. Instead, he asked intelligence analysts to
conduct additional surveillance of the compound. Over the next eight months, the
CIA's collection efforts became increasingly creative. When none of these efforts
produced significant insights, President Obama eventually decided that he could
no longer afford to delay the decision. What swayed Obama's thought process
over time was not that he had gained new insight about the probability that bin
Laden was living in Abbottabad, but rather that it had become increasingly clear
that perceptions of this probability were unlikely to change in response to new
information.[35]

These examples emphasize how assessments of probability provide only
part of what decision makers need to know about the uncertainty surrounding
high-stakes choices. Reliability of available information, range of reasonable
opinion, and responsiveness to new information can also shape decision makers'

---

[33] The lack of direct evidence regarding Iraq's WMD programs was particularly relevant to
judging the Bush administration's attempt to justify the invasion using the doctrine of "preemption," which is generally reserved for cases of clear and present danger. See Michael B. Doyle, *Striking
First: Preemption and Prevention in International Conflict* (Princeton, N.J.: Princeton University Press,
2008). For broader arguments about how the ethics of using force depend on the reliability of the evidence decision makers possess, see Jeff McMahan, *The Ethics of Killing* (New York: Oxford University
Press, 2002); and Michael Walzer, *Just and Unjust Wars*, 4th ed. (New York: Basic Books, 2006).

[34] For expressions of similar views, see Richard K. Betts, *Enemies of Intelligence: Knowledge and
Power in American National Security* (New York: Columbia University Press, 2006), p. 116; Robert
Jervis, "Reports, Politics, and Intelligence Failures: The Case of Iraq," Vol. 29, No. 1 (2006), p. 44;
and Michael Morell, *The Great War of Our Time: the CIA's Fight against Terrorism from Al Qa'ida to
ISIS* (New York: Twelve, 2014), p. 102.

[35] Peter Bergen, *Manhunt: The Ten-Year Search for Bin Laden from 9/11 to Abbottabad*
(New York: Crown 2012); and Mark Bowden, *The Finish: The Killing of Osama bin Laden*
(New York: Atlantic, 2012); Morell, *Great War of Our Time*, ch. 7.

willingness to take risks.[36] These attributes are far more relevant to foreign policy decision making than objectivity—which is, in any case, an impossible standard to apply when assessing uncertainty in international politics. This discussion highlights the importance of drawing clear distinctions between the probability and the confidence that foreign policy analysts assign to their judgments. And in the next section, we will see how foreign policy analysts can always assess probability in clear and structured ways.

Practical Implications of the Subjective Probability Framework

One of the main drawbacks with the frequency and propensity theories of probability assessment is that both frameworks generally preclude analysts from making precise judgments. Strictly speaking, these approaches can only indicate that the correct probability assessment falls within a plausible range of values.[37] And when analysts lack large volumes of well-behaved data, those ranges can be very broad. This is one of the clearest places where the subjective theory of probability departs from alternative frameworks. Conditional on believing that subjective probability assessments convey any insight whatsoever, it is always possible to summarize that insight with respect to a single, numeric point estimate. The subjectivity of these judgments is in fact the very thing that makes it possible to deal with them precisely, as analysts are always in a position to articulate their personal convictions in clear and structured ways.[38]

---

[36] Friedman and Zeckhauser, "Analytic Confidence and Political Decision Making," provide experimental evidence showing that these factors do, in fact, shape the way that national security professionals evaluate risky decisions.

[37] These ranges are often called *confidence intervals* (or credible intervals), but note that this only reflects one of the three elements of analytic confidence described earlier. One reason to shift existing discussions of analytic confidence toward more precise terminology is simply to avoid the confusion that the word "confidence" can generate—including, as we have seen in several places throughout the book, conflating the concepts of confidence and probability.

[38] It is important to note that this logic holds for estimating subjective probabilities, but not for estimating material costs and benefits. The difference stems from the fact that individuals can assign different utilities to these costs and benefits. These utility functions create "risk preferences" that shape the manner in which rational actors resolve ambiguity. For example, a gamble that offers a fifty percent chance of winning $0 and a fifty percent chance of $100 would have an expected monetary value of $50. But the expected *utility* of taking this gamble is not necessarily the utility that gamblers assign to a certain $50 payoff. Risk-averse individuals would value this bet at less than $50, while risk-acceptant individuals would value this bet at more than $50. For more on the contrast between resolving ambiguity about outcomes versus probabilities, see Ellsberg, "Risk, Ambiguity, and the Savage Axioms."

One way to demonstrate this point is with a thought experiment involving the comparison of lotteries. For example, consider the chances that a Republican candidate will win the next U.S. presidential election. Now consider which of the following two gambles you prefer. In the first gamble, you receive $1,000 if a Republican wins the next presidential election, and nothing otherwise. In the second gamble, we will flip a coin at the same time as the election results are announced. If the coin lands heads you will receive $1,000, and if the coin lands tails you will win nothing. If you prefer to bet on the election of a Republican presidential candidate, this indicates that you believe that outcome has a probability of at least fifty percent; otherwise you would have thought that the coin flip was a better bet. If you prefer to bet on the coin flip, it indicates that you believe the chances of a Republican candidate's election are no greater than fifty percent; otherwise you would have bet on that outcome. In principle, we can toggle this comparison of lotteries until you become indifferent between the two gambles. This method will reveal your personal conviction regarding the chances that the next president of the United States will be a Republican.[39]

Rational actors should have just one indifference point when comparing lotteries, or else they can be exploited by a betting strategy known as the Dutch Book. For example, imagine that you believe the chances of a Republican nominee winning the next U.S. presidential election are anywhere between forty and sixty percent, and you are truly indifferent among gambles within this range. This means that you would be willing to offer other gamblers favorable odds that a Republican will be elected, and that you would *also* be willing to offer other gamblers favorable odds that a Republican will *not* be elected. Smart people would take you up on both of these bets, thereby guaranteeing that you will lose money.[40]

Of course, you can always choose to avoid betting on an issue when you think that your probability of success is ambiguous, and thus people are rarely exploited by Dutch Books in real life. But the Dutch Book argument is not necessary for explaining why political analysts can always assess subjective probabilities with a single point estimate. As long as these analysts are willing to scrutinize their own beliefs carefully, it is impossible to be indifferent about what subjective probabilities should entail. For example, imagine that you believe the chances of a Republican candidate winning the next presidential election are somewhere between forty percent and sixty percent, and you believe

---

[39] For a review of similar techniques, see Paul H. Garthwaite, Joseph B. Kadane, and Anthony O'Hagan, "Statistical Methods for Eliciting Probability Distributions," *Journal of the American Statistical Association*, Vol. 100, No. 470 (2005), pp. 680–700.

[40] On the logic of the Dutch Book, see Ken Binmore, *Rational Decisions* (Princeton, N.J.: Princeton University Press, 2009), pp. 123–126.

that all estimates within this range are equally credible. The only sensible way to resolve that kind of ambiguity is to take the range's midpoint of fifty percent. Any estimate higher than fifty percent would implicitly give more weight to possibilities above that value; any estimate lower than fifty percent would implicitly give more weight to possibilities below that value; and either of those options would violate your own personal belief that all estimates within this range are equally credible.

Similar logic allows decision makers to resolve ambiguity when analysts offer diverging views. When analysts study the same information and offer different assessments, a decision maker should consider those assessments' relative credibility.[41] If the available estimates appear equally credible—and this includes situations in which decision makers have no basis for evaluating analysts' credibility at all—then the only reasonable way to resolve the disagreement is to average the available estimates together. Any other approach would violate a decision maker's own assumptions by implicitly assigning some estimates more weight than others. In cases where a decision maker believes that probability assessments are not equally credible, the only logical solution is to take a weighted average.[42]

Viewed in light of the subjective probability framework, seemingly intractable debates about assessing uncertainty become conceptually straightforward, as long as analysts and decision makers are willing to approach these debates in a principled manner. For example, we saw in the book's introduction that President Obama's advisers voiced a broad range of opinions about the chances that Osama bin Laden was living in Abbottabad. Red Teams assigned to draw skeptical conclusions placed these chances around forty percent. CIA Deputy Director Michael Morell offered an estimate of sixty percent. Most advisers placed their judgments around eighty percent, while the leader of the CIA unit assigned to track bin Laden said there was a ninety-five percent chance that he was living in the suspected compound. Multiple sources describe how President Obama found this discussion confusing, and how he concluded that the odds

[41] The weighted averaging approach described here is only valid when analysts base their assessments on the same body of information. When analysts form their estimates based on non-identical information, then resolving their disagreements becomes more complex. See Richard Zeckhauser, "Combining Overlapping Information," *Journal of the American Statistical Association*, Vol. 66, No. 333 (1971), pp. 91–92 and Robert T. Clemen, "Combining Overlapping Information," *Management Science*, Vol. 33, No. 3 (1987), pp. 373–380.

[42] Thus, if one analyst estimates a probability as sixty percent, another analyst estimates that probability as ninety percent, and the latter judgment seems twice as credible, then the only coherent way for a decision maker to resolve the ambiguity is to believe that the probability is eighty percent. For more on the weighted averaging issue, see Jeffrey A. Friedman and Richard Zeckhauser, "Handling and Mishandling Estimative Probability," *Intelligence and National Security*, Vol. 30, No. 1 (2015), pp. 77–99.

were fifty-fifty. "Look guys, this is a flip of the coin," President Obama said according to one account. "I can't base this decision on the notion that we have any greater certainty than that."[43]

Two aspects of President Obama's conclusion are worth noting. First, a fifty-fifty estimate was remarkably conservative given the viewpoints that the president's advisers presented. The simple average of the four estimates described in the previous paragraph is sixty-nine percent. President Obama's coin flip analogy thus implicitly afforded special weight to the lowest estimates he received.[44] Yet it is not at all clear that these were the most credible positions on the table. The Red Teams were developed to offer deliberately pessimistic conclusions, not unbiased reflections of any analysts' actual views. Even Morell indicated that his sixty percent estimate involved intentionally low-balling the issue given how intelligence analysts had overestimated the chances that Iraq was pursuing nuclear weapons a decade earlier.

The point of this discussion is not to second-guess President Obama's judgment, but to show that no matter how much his advisers disagreed over the chances that bin Laden was at Abbottabad, there was no reason to believe that resolving this disagreement represented an intractable problem. As long as analysts are willing to assess uncertainty in transparent ways, and as long as decision makers are willing to consider the relative credibility of those judgments, then it is always possible to reconcile diverging opinions. Greater ambiguity actually makes it easier, not harder, to resolve these disagreements. In the extreme case where a decision maker has no reason to believe that any estimate is more credible than the others, then the only valid approach is simply to average the available assessments together.[45]

This reasoning also implies that any time foreign policy analysts formulate judgments using words of estimative probability, they also possess a coherent basis for converting those judgments into quantitative expressions. Chapter 1, for example, showed how U.S. Intelligence Community standards currently

[43] Bowden, *The Finish*, p. 163.

[44] This estimate may have reflected the well-established "fifty-fifty bias" in which individuals use this phrase to refer to situations in which they feel they have no idea about the right answer and not to indicate that the chances of a particular outcome are actually fifty percent. See Baruch Fischhoff and Wandi Bruine de Bruin, "Fifty-Fifty = 50%?" *Journal of Behavioral Decision Making*, Vol. 12, No. 2 (1999), pp. 149–163.

[45] As mentioned earlier, the weighted averaging approach depends on the assumption that analysts have based their estimates on similar information. This assumption appears safe in most high-level national security debates such as the discussion of whether Osama bin Laden was at Abbottabad. Deputy CIA Director Morell reportedly told President Obama during the meeting: "People don't have differences [in their probability estimates] because they have different intel. . . . We are all looking at the same things." Bowden, *The Finish*, p. 161.

define probabilistic terms with respect to numeric ranges. If analysts have no reason to believe that any value within the range they selected is more credible than others, then the appropriate way to resolve this ambiguity is to state the range's midpoint. If analysts instead believe that estimates toward one end of the relevant range are more plausible, then they can resolve this ambiguity using the logic described earlier in this section.

Though several of the words of estimative probability guidelines shown in chapter 1 entail more ambiguity, it nevertheless remains straightforward to convert these phrases into point estimates. For example, we saw in chapter 1 that the Defense Intelligence Agency currently recommends that analysts express uncertainty by dividing probability assessments into five equally spaced segments. All else being equal, one can assume that each segment spans twenty percentage points. From here, one can employ the previous logic for quantifying ambiguous estimates, interpreting the phrase "highly improbable" as meaning ten percent, "doubtful" as meaning thirty percent, and so forth. Of course, analysts can always shift these interpretations up or down if they believe that other judgments would be more credible on a case-specific basis.

This discussion shows that there is no instance in which foreign policy analysts can coherently offer a qualitative probability estimate but not a quantitative probability estimate. While the search for a middle ground between Sherman Kent's "mathematicians" and "poets" may make sense from an organizational or cultural standpoint, there is no reason to seek this middle ground based on logical principles alone. Scholars, practitioners, and pundits who prefer to leave their assessments of uncertainty vague cannot justify that practice on theoretical grounds. The fact that these probability assessments are subjective is, in fact, exactly what makes it possible to describe those judgments explicitly.

Conclusion

This chapter has argued that aversion to assessing uncertainty in international politics rests, at least in part, on misperceptions of what probabilistic reasoning entails. Much of the existing debate about this subject revolves around the expectation that assessments of uncertainty in international politics should obey the same kind of logic that characterizes statistics or quantum mechanics. Many observers appear to believe that if foreign policy analysts cannot meet those objective standards, then their beliefs cannot provide a credible basis for high-stakes decision making. This emphasis on objectivity is enshrined throughout official analytic standards for intelligence analysis and military planning, and it is often used to justify leaving controversial judgments deliberately vague.

These arguments are misguided. The chapter explained that assessments of
uncertainty in international politics reflect a logic that is distinct from statistical
frequencies or mechanical propensities. We have seen that objectivity is an un-
realistic standard for foreign policy analysis, and that no foreign policy analyst
could ever accept the implications of pursuing that goal. We have seen that even
when assessments of uncertainty are subjective, they can still vary in terms of
credibility, and that explicitly distinguishing between probability and confidence
can help to convey that variation to policymakers.[46] And the chapter explained
that subjectivity is ultimately the main reason why foreign policy analysts can
articulate their assessments of uncrtainty in clear and structured ways. It is, in
fact, the objective theories of probability that usually force analysts to accept
irreducible ambiguity.

Of course, just because some approach makes sense in principle does not
mean that it also works in practice. The remainder of the book will thus explore
a range of psychological and political obstacles that may prevent foreign policy
analysts from implementing the logic that this chapter has described. It is nevertheless important to understand that the only valid objections to pursuing this
approach are empirical, not theoretical. To the extent that scholars, practitioners,
and pundits wish to avoid assessing the uncertainty surrounding foreign policy
debates, it is not enough to say that those assessments are subjective, and it is
wrong to say that those judgments are incoherent.

Moreover, the chapter has argued that understanding the theoretical
foundations of subjective probability can help foreign policy analysts and decision makers to resolve confusion that otherwise seems intractable. The difficulty that President Obama encountered when debating intelligence during the
search for Osama bin Laden is a prime example. Based on the evidence available
at the time, there may have been no "right answer" when it came to estimating
the chances that bin Laden was living in Abbottabad. But there was also no
reason to get stuck addressing this issue. There were, in fact, logically valid and
reasonably straightforward ways for President Obama and his advisers to resolve
the ambiguity surrounding one of their seminal decisions. And in the next two
chapters, we will see how foreign policy analysts and decision makers are remarkably capable of handling this challenge.

[46] Friedman and Zeckhauser, "Analytic Confidence and Political Decision Making," provide
experimental evidence showing that national security professionals interpret and react to these
distinctions in sensible ways.

The Value of Precision
in Probability Assessment[*]

Chapter 2 explored the theoretical foundations of assessing uncertainty in international politics. Yet there is a difference between saying that assessments of uncertainty are theoretically coherent and showing that these judgments are also empirically meaningful.

This is another area in which practical questions about the conduct of foreign policy analysis reflect deeper concerns about the limits of probabilistic reasoning. As noted in the book's introduction, many scholars and practitioners of international politics believe that subjective probabilities are essentially meaningless, or that there is some (low) threshold of precision beyond which assessments of uncertainty provide no relevant insight.[1] In this view, it might be fruitless to argue about whether the chances of a foreign policy decision succeeding are more like sixty percent or ninety percent. Although chapter 1 explained that it is always possible to resolve this ambiguity in principle, there is little point to confronting that challenge in practice if it would only surround foreign policy debates with arbitrary detail.

This chapter thus explores the empirical value of precision when assessing uncertainty in international politics, analyzing a data set that contains nearly one million geopolitical forecasts. We will see that coarsening those forecasts to different degrees of imprecision—including the imprecision

---

[*] Portions of this chapter previously appeared in Jeffrey A. Friedman, Joshua D. Baker, Barbara A. Mellers, Philip E. Tetlock, and Richard Zeckhauser, "The Value of Precision in Probability Assessment: Evidence from a Large-Scale Geopolitical Forecasting Tournament," *International Studies Quarterly*, Vol. 62, No. 2 (2018), pp. 410–422. © published by Oxford University Press, reproduced with permission.

[1] This is the crux of the argument Sherman Kent encountered from intelligence analysts who argued that "the most a writer can achieve when working in a speculative area of human affairs is communication in only the broadest general sense." Sherman Kent, "Words of Estimative Probability," *Studies in Intelligence*, Vol. 8, No. 4 (1964), pp. 49–65.

associated with words of estimative probability, confidence levels, and estimative verbs—systematically sacrifices predictive accuracy. We will also see
that this finding is not driven by easy questions, short time horizons, idiosyncratic topics, nor a small group of "superforecasters" with special cognitive attributes. Instead, the findings presented in this chapter suggest that
the value of precision in probability assessment reflects a generalizable skill
that foreign policy analysts can cultivate through training, effort, and experience. Altogether, this analysis shows that aversion to probabilistic reasoning
does not reflect appropriate analytic humility when assessing international
politics; rather, this practice sells analysts' capabilities short and lowers the
quality of foreign policy discourse.

How Much Precision Does Probability Assessment Allow?

As mentioned in the book's introduction, Aristotle argued that "the educated
person seeks exactness in each area to the extent that the nature of the subject
allows."[2] The goal of this chapter is to determine where the threshold of "allowable exactness" lies when assessing uncertainty in international politics.

Before beginning the analysis, it is important to establish two basic principles.
The first of these principles is that it is only possible to evaluate the accuracy of
probability assessments when analyzing large volumes of data. The second of
these principles is that analytic precision can be meaningful even in cases where
probability assessments contain systematic flaws.

It is notoriously difficult to evaluate the accuracy of a single probability assessment. Consider, for example, how the political analyst Nate Silver predicted
that Donald Trump had a twenty-nine percent chance of defeating Hillary
Clinton in the 2016 presidential election.[3] This forecast was widely criticized,
and in hindsight it seems badly mistaken. Yet Silver did not say that Trump was
guaranteed to lose. By way of comparison, twenty-nine-percent-chance events
occur more frequently than the rate at which the average Major League Baseball
player gets a hit, and no one considers that to be surprising when it happens.[4]

---

[2] Aristotle, *Nicomachean Ethics*, tr. Terence Irwin (Indianapolis, Ind.: Hackett, 1985), p. 1094b.

[3] Nate Silver, "Why *FiveThirtyEight* Gave Trump a Better Chance Than Almost Anyone Else,"
Fivethirtyeight.com, November 11, 2016, https://fivethirtyeight.com/features/why-fivethirtyeight-
gave-trump-a-better-chance-than-almost-anyone-else/.

[4] Among election forecasters, Nate Silver actually assigned one of the highest predicted
probabilities to a Donald Trump victory. David Rothschild, for example, only gave Trump an
eleven percent chance of winning the presidency. But eleven percent chance events should not be

This comparison emphasizes the challenge of distinguishing assessments of uncertainty that are wrong from those that are just unlucky.[5]

The solution to this problem is not to give up on evaluating the accuracy of probabilistic reasoning, but rather to evaluate a large number of judgments at once. For example, if we collect all cases in which election forecasters predicted that a candidate's chances of winning an election were roughly three-in-ten, then we could see whether those candidates actually won their contests thirty percent of the time. If that is what we find, then we would say that this body of judgments is well *calibrated*.[6] If we analyze a large volume of probability assessments, we can also determine the degree to which those judgments effectively *discriminate* between levels of uncertainty. For example, we can examine whether political candidates with an estimated thirty percent chance of success actually win their elections more often than political candidates with an estimated ten percent chance of success. In these ways, the difficulty of evaluating a single probability assessment does not preclude evaluating the accuracy of probabilistic reasoning writ large.

Figure 3.1 presents this kind of analysis for a data set containing nearly 10,000 probability estimates made by more than 300 national security officials at the U.S. National War College.[7] These estimates include responses to such forecasting questions as, "What are the chances that within the next six months, the Iraqi Security Forces will reclaim either Ramadi or Mosul?" as well as factual questions, such as "What are the chances that Pakistan has a larger active-duty military than Iran?" Respondents described their beliefs about these issues using the seven words of estimative probability that we encountered in chapter 1.[8] The

particularly surprising either. An eleven percent chance is roughly equivalent to the probability that a major league *pitcher* gets a hit when batting. Such events are rare, but they do not cause anyone to fundamentally re-evaluate their perceptions of baseball.

[5] Of course, accuracy is just one measure one can use to evaluate assessments of uncertainty. For broader discussions of what "quality" foreign policy analysis entails, see Stephen Marrin, "Evaluating the Quality of Intelligence Analysis: By What (Mis)Measure?" *Intelligence and National Security*, Vol. 27, No. 6 (2012), pp. 896–912; and Kristan J. Wheaton, "Evaluating Intelligence: Answering Questions Asked and Not," *International Journal of Intelligence and CounterIntelligence*, Vol. 22, No. 4 (2009), pp. 614–631.

[6] Steven Rieber, "Intelligence Analysis and Judgmental Calibration," *International Journal of Intelligence and CounterIntelligence*, Vol. 17, No. 1 (2004), pp. 97–112.

[7] I collected these data as part of annual training sessions on assessing uncertainty. The National War College provides mid-career education to an unusually broad cross-section of national security officials, spanning all U.S. military services, civilian national security personnel, and military officers from partner countries. Chapter 4 describes these respondents in more detail: they comprise the subjects from the "qualitative assessment condition" in the second and third experiments that chapter 4 presents.

[8] These words of estimative probability were defined for respondents using the National Intelligence Council's spectrum, which involves seven evenly spaced terms.

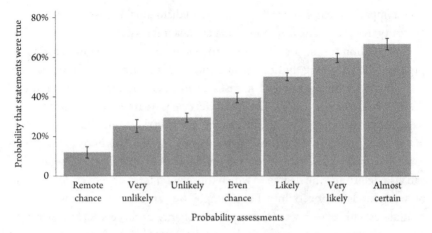

Figure 3.1 Calibration data from a study of U.S. national security officials. The figure shows the relationship (with 95 percent intervals) between estimated probabilities and observed probabilities for 9,480 probability assessments made by 316 students at the U.S. National War College.

horizontal axis on the graph represents the probability respondents assigned to various statements. The vertical axis represents the proportion of the time that those statements turned out to be true.

Figure 3.1 shows that the national security officials who participated in this study were *miscalibrated* in the sense that they tended to attach too much certainty to their judgments.[9] For instance, when these national security officials were "almost certain" that a statement was true, those statements turned out to be true just sixty-seven percent of the time.[10] Participants in the study also appeared to struggle with calibrating judgments of an "even chance," which they applied to statements that were true in just thirty-nine percent of cases.[11] Of course, the data shown in Figure 3.1 reflect intuitive responses to survey

[9] Note that this is another instance in which colloquial uses of the term *confidence* refer to probability assessments themselves, and not to the basis that analysts possess for making those judgments.

[10] Respondents were less overconfident in using the term "remote chance." Just 12 percent of those statements turned out to be true, though this is still at the outer limit of the term's definition according to the National Intelligence Council and more than twice the term's acceptable limit as defined by the director of national intelligence.

[11] This finding may reflect the so-called fifty-fifty bias, where probability assessors conflate "fifty percent" with situations in which they feel they have no basis for rendering a sound judgment. For more on this bias, see Baruch Fischhoff and Wandi Bruine de Bruin, "Fifty-Fifty = 50%?" *Journal of Behavioral Decision Making*, Vol. 12, No. 2 (June 1999), pp. 149–163. For additional evidence that national security officials assign an "even chance" to judgments that are much less likely than fifty percent to be true, see Paul Lehner et al., *Using Inferred Probabilities to Measure the Accuracy of Imprecise Forecasts* (Arlington, Va.: MITRE, 2012), p. 12.

questions rather than the kind of thorough analyses that foreign policy officials use to make high-stakes decisions. It is nevertheless important to understand how intuitive assessments of uncertainty can be miscalibrated, and specifically how these judgments tend to involve excessive levels of certainty.[12]

Yet Figure 3.1 also demonstrates that these national security professionals could reliably *discriminate* among different levels of subjective probability. When study participants said that one set of statements was more likely to be true than another, this consistently proved to be the case.[13] The way in which these officials distinguished between words of estimative probability thus clearly reflected meaningful insight rather than arbitrary detail. And in this respect, the notion that the data in Figure 3.1 reflect intuitive judgments rather than careful analysis only *adds* to the salience of these findings. Here, we see that national security officials can reliably draw distinctions among subjective probabilities, even when they devote limited effort to the task.

Figure 3.1 thus illustrates the difference between estimating the value of precision in probability assessment and examining the accuracy of probabilistic judgments overall. There is no contradiction in accepting that foreign policy analysts' judgments can be flawed *and* in arguing that those analysts can still draw meaningful distinctions among different levels of certainty. Yet the kinds of data shown in Figure 3.1 still provide a limited basis for identifying the threshold of "allowable exactness" in this domain. For one thing, these data leave open the question of whether respondents could have parsed their judgments more precisely than seven words of estimative probability. Moreover, these data ultimately reflect a relatively small number of people answering a relatively small number of questions.

Thus, in order to understand where the threshold of allowable exactness lies when assessing uncertainty in international politics, we need a data set that includes quantitative probability assessments; we need that data set to span a broad range of people and topics; and we need to develop a structured method for estimating the extent to which expressing these judgments more precisely actually changes their predictive value. The next section explains how I teamed up with a group called the Good Judgment Project in order to conduct such a study.

---

[12] The findings in Figure 3.1 resonate with a substantial body of research that documents overconfidence in national security decision making. Chapter 4 presents additional evidence on how judgments involving the highest levels of certainty deserve to be treated with special caution. Dominic D. P. Johnson, *Overconfidence in War: The Havoc and Glory of Positive Illusions* (Cambridge, Mass.: Harvard University Press, 2004).

[13] Differences among these categories were all statistically significant at the $p < 0.001$ level, except for the distinction between judgments that were "unlikely" versus "very unlikely," which was statistically significant at the $p < 0.05$ level.

Measuring the Value of Precision in
Probability Assessment

In 2005, the psychologist Philip Tetlock published a book titled *Expert Political Judgment*.[14] The book examined more than a decade of foreign policy experts' predictions regarding international politics. Tetlock found that the accuracy of these judgments was surprisingly poor. Similar to what we saw in Figure 3.1, Tetlock found that foreign policy experts attached far too much certainty to their forecasts. He also found that many foreign policy experts showed a troubling tendency to disregard or excuse inaccurate predictions in ways that hindered their ability to learn from mistakes.[15]

In response to these findings—and as part of its efforts to prevent the kinds of errors intelligence analysts had made when assessing Iraq's WMD programs— the U.S. Intelligence Community launched a massive research initiative called the Good Judgment Project (GJP).[16] From 2011 to 2015, the GJP recruited thousands of individuals to register predictions about world politics. The study spanned hundreds of topics, such as the likelihood of candidates winning Russia's 2012 presidential election, the probability that China's economy would exceed a certain growth rate in a given quarter, and the chances that North Korea would detonate a nuclear bomb before a particular date. The project was managed by the Intelligence Advanced Research Projects Activity (IARPA), which is the re- search arm of the Office of the Director of National Intelligence. IARPA worked to ensure that the forecasting problems posed to study participants reflected the kinds of issues that confront professional foreign policy analysts.[17] The GJP's

[14] Philip E. Tetlock, *Expert Political Judgment: How Good Is It? How Can We Know?* (Princeton, N.J.: Princeton University Press, 2005).

[15] See also Philip E. Tetlock, "Theory-Driven Reasoning about Plausible Pasts and Probable Futures in World Politics: Are We Prisoners of Our Own Preconceptions?" *American Journal of Political Science*, Vol. 43, No. 2 (1999), pp. 335–366. On broader tendencies for individuals to develop illusory perceptions of effectiveness when assessing uncertainty, see Daniel Kahneman, *Thinking, Fast and Slow* (New York: Farrar, Straus and Giroux, 2011), pp. 199–221, and Robyn Dawes, *Rational Choice in an Uncertain World* (San Diego, Calif.: Harcourt Brace Jovanovich, 1988), pp. 100–120, 256–261.

[16] On the origins of the GJP, see Philip E. Tetlock and Daniel Gardner, *Superforecasting: The Art and Science of Prediction* (New York: Crown, 2015). On the GJP's methodology, see Barbara A. Mellers et al., "Psychological Strategies for Winning a Geopolitical Forecasting Tournament," *Psychological Science*, Vol. 25, No. 5 (May 2014), pp. 1106–1115; Barbara A. Mellers et al., "The Psychology of Intelligence Analysis: Drivers of Prediction Accuracy in World Politics," *Journal of Experimental Psychology: Applied*, Vol. 21, No. 1 (March 2015), pp. 1–14; and Barbara A. Mellers et al., "Improving Probabilistic Predictions by Identifying and Cultivating 'Superforecasters,'" *Perspectives on Psychological Science*, Vol. 10, No. 3 (May 2015), pp. 267–281.

[17] The main exception to ecological validity with respect to IARPA's question list was the require- ment that each question be written precisely enough that the outcomes could be judged clearly after the fact.

forecasters logged predictions online using numeric probabilities. Forecasters could update predictions as often as they liked.

By asking a large and diverse group of people to assign numeric probabilities to a large and diverse range of international events, the GJP collected an unprecedented volume of geopolitical forecasts that is uniquely well-suited to studying the value of precision in probability assessment. To conduct this study, I teamed up with Joshua Baker, Barbara Mellers, Philip Tetlock, and Richard Zeckhauser.[18] The data set we used for our analysis contained 1,832 individuals who registered 888,328 forecasts in response to 380 separate questions.[19]

Given the large number of individuals who participated in this study, it is possible to conduct extensive analysis of the ways in which performance varied across forecasters. These forecasters tended to be males (eighty-three percent) and U.S. citizens (seventy-four percent). Their average age was forty. Sixty-four percent of respondents had a bachelor's degree, and fifty-seven percent had completed postgraduate training.[20]

The Good Judgment Project randomly assigned forecasters to work alone or in collaborative teams. Another random subset of forecasters received a one-hour online training module that covered various techniques for effective forecasting.[21] Thus in addition to analyzing variations across demographic categories, we can examine *untrained individuals* (whom we might expect to exhibit relatively low-quality performance), as well as *trained groups* (whom we would expect to more closely resemble national security professionals). We will see that training and groupwork exerted a consistent, positive impact on the value of precision in probability assessment.

The chapter will also analyze a group of respondents called *superforecasters*, who include the top two percent of performers in any given year of the forecasting competition. One of the GJP's most important findings was that the superforecasters' predictions remained superior to those of other respondents

---

[18] Jeffrey A. Friedman, Joshua D. Baker, Barbara A. Mellers, Philip E. Tetlock, and Richard Zeckhauser, "The Value of Precision in Probability Assessment: Evidence from a Large-Scale Geopolitical Forecasting Tournament," *International Studies Quarterly*, Vol. 62, No. 2 (2018), pp. 410–422.

[19] The GJP also administered a prediction market, but because those data involve respondents making buy/sell decisions as opposed to registered probability assessments, the prediction market is less relevant to the analysis presented in this chapter.

[20] In order to exclude less serious participants from our study, we limited our analysts to forecasters who made at least twenty-five predictions in a given year.

[21] Topics included defining base rates, avoiding cognitive biases, and extrapolating trends from data. For a discussion of these methods, see Welton Chang, Eva Chen, Barbara Mellers, and Philip Tetlock, "Developing Expert Political Judgment: The Impact of Training and Practice on Judgmental Accuracy in Geopolitical Forecasting Tournaments," *Judgment and Decision Making*, Vol. 11, No. 5 (2016), pp. 509–526.

as the study continued. This finding suggests that geopolitical forecasting is a stable skill, contrary to expectations that high performers had succeeded by force of sheer luck.[22] As one might expect, the superforecasters captured the largest returns to precision when assessing uncertainty, and the penalties associated with coarsening their judgments are especially high.

Measuring the Value of Precision

Measuring the "value of precision" across these data was a nontrivial task. Since my colleagues and I were unaware of any previous study to this effect, we had to develop our own methodology for addressing the subject. The method we developed involved three steps. We started by evaluating the accuracy of the forecasts in our data set; we coarsened those forecasts to different degrees of imprecision; and we recorded the extent to which these coarsened forecasts were more or less accurate than the originals. The remainder of this section provides some more information on what each of these steps entailed. Readers who are interested in a greater level of technical detail will find a formal description of our methodology in the appendix.

We evaluated the accuracy of respondents' probability assessments using a metric called the Brier score. The Brier score measures the square of the difference between an analyst's estimates of the chances that statements are true and the estimates an analyst could have made had she known the future in advance. Thus, if you say that some event has a sixty percent chance of occurring, and that event does indeed occur, then your Brier score for that estimate would be 0.16.[23] If you assign a sixty percent probability to an event that does *not* happen, then your Brier score for that estimate would be 0.36.[24] We can think of the Brier score as measuring the "error" or the "distance" that distinguishes analysts' judgments from perfect foresight. Of course, analysts should seek to make those errors or

---

[22] The GJP team analyzed the superforecasters in extensive detail. Broadly speaking, they found that superforecasters were not experts in particular subjects or methodologies. Instead, superforecasters typically shared a willingness to address each forecasting problem in a flexible way and to draw on an eclectic range of inputs rather than any particular theoretical or methodological framework. See Mellers et al., "Psychological Strategies for Winning a Geopolitical Forecasting Tournament"; Mellers et al., "The Psychology of Intelligence Analysis"; and Mellers et al., "Improving Probabilistic Predictions by Identifying and Cultivating 'Superforecasters.'"

[23] Someone who knew the future would have given a probability estimate of one hundred percent, the difference between sixty percent and one hundred percent is 0.40, and 0.40 squared is 0.16. See appendix section 1a for a more formal description of the Brier score.

[24] Someone who knew the future would have provided a probability estimate of zero percent, the difference between sixty percent and zero percent is 0.60, and 0.60 squared is 0.36.

that distance as small as possible. All else being equal, lower Brier scores thus represent more accurate judgments.

The Brier score is what decision theorists call a *strictly proper scoring rule.* This means that there is no way to cheat the Brier score when reporting probability estimates. Analysts should always expect to receive their best Brier scores by honestly reporting their beliefs about the chances that a statement is true.[25] The Brier score is the most common method scholars use to evaluate the accuracy of probability assessments, which is why my colleagues and I chose to make it the main metric for our study. But to make sure that our findings were not driven by the specific properties of the Brier score, we replicated our results using another evaluation technique called *logarithmic scoring.* The appendix explains what logarithmic scoring entails and shows that it does not meaningfully impact the empirical analysis presented here.[26]

The second step in our analysis involved coarsening the forecasts in our data set. There are many ways one can do this. For example, we saw in chapter 1 that the DNI's current analytic standards divide probability estimates into seven bins. The middle of these bins, labeled "even chance," spans probabilities between forty-five and fifty-five percent. Chapter 2 then explained that, absent additional information, assessing a range of probabilities is equivalent to stating its midpoint.[27] We can thus say that every probability estimate in our data set that falls between forty-five and fifty-five percent corresponds to the DNI's definition of "even chance," and we can assume that the word "even chance" implies a probability estimate of fifty percent.[28] Coarsening probability assessments according to the DNI standards thus results in rounding all of forecasts in our data set to seven possible values.[29]

We can generalize this approach by dividing the number line into *bins* of any shapes and sizes that we like. Chapter 1, for example, showed how the National Intelligence Council (NIC) divides words of estimative probability into seven equally spaced categories. Rounding probability estimates to the midpoint of these segments will thus coarsen forecasts to another set of seven possible values. In other cases, national security analysts assess uncertainty by ascribing "low confidence," "moderate confidence," or "high confidence" to

[25] Chapter 5 provides additional discussion of strictly proper scoring rules.

[26] See appendix section 1b.

[27] We also experimented with an alternative rounding method in which we replaced each observation with the *mean* forecast that fell within each bin on each question. This allows the meaning of each qualitative expression to vary by context, and it did not meaningfully change our results.

[28] Chapter 2 noted that it is often useful to explain the ambiguity surrounding a probability estimate, but this is part of assessing analytic confidence, not estimating probability per se.

[29] When forecasts fell on the boundaries between bins, we randomized the direction of rounding.

their judgments—this essentially divides the number line into three bins.[30] The vaguest way that we have seen foreign policy analysts express uncertainty is by using estimative verbs, such as "we assess" or "we judge." Estimative verbs essentially divide probability estimates into two bins: statements that analysts think are likely to be true and those they do not think are likely to be true.

The final step in our methodology involved comparing the accuracy of forecasts between their original and coarsened values. For instance, if the original forecast had a Brier score of 0.20 and the coarsened forecast had a Brier score of 0.22, that would represent a ten percent degradation in predictive accuracy. We call these relative comparisons *rounding errors*. Rounding errors indicate the loss of accuracy that forecasts suffered when we rounded these judgments to different degrees of (im)precision. These rounding errors provide our main metric for estimating the value of precision across nearly one million geopolitical forecasts.

Caveats

To my knowledge, this analysis represents the first systematic attempt to understand the value of precision when assessing subjective probability. It is certainly the first attempt to estimate the threshold of "allowable exactness" when assessing uncertainty in international politics—a notable fact given the strong views many scholars, practitioners, and pundits appear to hold on the issue. And the Good Judgment Project's data are uniquely positioned to assess the value of precision in probability assessment given the sheer volume of forecasts that the GJP collected, the range of individuals that the project involved, and the efforts of IARPA to ensure that forecasters addressed questions that were relevant to policymakers' concerns. Nevertheless, any research design has drawbacks, four of which are worth addressing up front.

---

[30] As chapters 1 and 2 explained, assessments of confidence are technically distinct from assessments of probability, but foreign policy analysts regularly conflate confidence and probability when expressing their judgments. For example, a controversial 2007 NIE titled *Iran: Nuclear Intentions and Capabilities* presented twenty-six key judgments. Fourteen of them assessed uncertainty using confidence levels without also offering words of estimative probability. The document thus stated: "We assess with high confidence that until fall 2003, Iranian military entities were working under government direction to develop nuclear weapons" and "We judge with moderate confidence that Tehran had not restarted its nuclear weapons program as of mid-2007." Readers could reasonably assume that a statement made with "high confidence" was more likely to be true than a statement made with "moderate confidence" or "low confidence." In this way, the use of confidence levels to assess uncertainty effectively divides the number line into three segments, in a manner that is more precise than estimative verbs but less precise than words of estimative probability.

First, the GJP only asked respondents to make predictions that could be resolved within a feasible time frame. An average of seventy-six days (standard deviation, eighty days) elapsed between the time when a forecast was registered and the time when that forecast's outcome became known. Yet most foreign policy analysis tends to focus on relatively short-term issues, too.[31] We will also see that the value of precision across GJP forecasts held relatively consistent across time spans. At the very least, it is possible to show that our assessments of analysts' capabilities in this area are not driven by the shortest-term forecasts in the data set.

A second caveat for interpreting these data is that the GJP only asked respondents to assess the probability of future events, whereas we saw in chapter 2 that foreign policy analysts must also assess uncertainty about factual matters, such as Osama bin Laden's location or Saddam Hussein's weapons of mass destruction programs. Yet forecasting should generally be more difficult than assessing uncertainty about the current state of the world—in addition to grappling with imperfect information, forecasters must also account for the possibility that this information may change in the future. If making predictions is indeed harder than assessing uncertainty about the present and past, then the findings presented in the rest of the chapter should actually understate the value of precision when assessing probability in international politics.

Because the participants in the Good Judgment Project volunteered their time and effort, it would be a mistake to claim that these individuals are a representative sample of foreign policy analysts. One particular concern is that the individuals who self-selected into the competition might be unusually capable at probabilistic reasoning. Selection bias is a concern in nearly all survey-based research, and I will address that challenge in two ways. First, I will show that returns to precision correlate with individual attributes such as education, numeracy, and cognitive style. Then, in chapter 4, I will compare how national security professionals and non-elite respondents perform on similar probability assessment tasks. Neither of these analyses provides any indication that the book's main findings depend on survey respondents possessing special backgrounds.

Finally, even though the GJP data set contains nearly one million forecasts, those forecasts are correlated with each other, in the sense that the GJP gathered large numbers of responses to each question that it posed, and because forecasters could update their forecasts over time. It would therefore be inappropriate to treat all forecasts in the data set as representing independent observations. My colleagues and I accounted for this issue by treating forecasting questions as our

[31] David Mandel and Alan Barnes, "Geopolitical Forecasting Skill in Strategic Intelligence," *Journal of Behavioral Decision Making*, Vol. 31, No. 1 (2018), pp. 127–137.

unit of analysis. As the appendix describes in more detail, we took all forecasts in the data set that corresponded to a given question; we calculated Brier scores across all of those forecasts simultaneously; and then we examined how much coarsening forecasts changed their predictive accuracy.[32] This was an extremely conservative approach to conducting statistical analysis, because it reduced our effective sample size from 888,328 forecasts to 380 forecasting questions. The next section nevertheless uses this method to demonstrate that the value of precision in probability assessment is larger and more consistent than what the conventional wisdom expects.

Primary Results

To recap, the goal of this chapter is to estimate where the threshold of "allowable exactness" lies when it comes to assessing uncertainty in international politics. If such a threshold exists, it would reflect a fundamental constraint on the conduct of foreign policy analysis. Yet to date, there has been virtually no systematic empirical study of where this threshold might lie. The analysis in the remainder of this section suggests that this threshold—if it exists at all—is much more permissive than the conventional wisdom expects.

Table 3.1 summarizes the main results from this analysis, showing that coarsening forecasts to different degrees of imprecision consistently reduced their predictive accuracy. For example, the top-right corner of the table shows that the Brier scores associated with GJP forecasts became 31 percent worse, on average, when we transformed numeric probabilities into estimative verbs. Outliers did not drive this difference, as the median rounding error across all forecasts in the data set was 22 percent.[33] Even the worst-performing group of forecasters in the data set—untrained individuals who worked alone—incurred an average rounding error of 15 percent when we rounded their forecasts into two bins. Figure 3.1 also shows substantial penalties from coarsening GJP forecasts into "confidence levels." On average, this level of imprecision degraded forecast accuracy by more than ten percent, and far more than that for the higher-performing analysts. These findings provide unambiguous evidence of how the vague language foreign policy analysts typically use to assess uncertainty systematically sacrifices meaningful information.

Translating forecasts into seven-step words of estimative probability recovered some, but not all, of these losses. Despite the extremely conservative

---

[32] See appendix section 1a.

[33] We estimated statistical significance using standard two-way t-tests when comparing means, and using Wilcoxon signed-rank tests when comparing medians.

Table 3.1. **Analytic Precision and Predictive Accuracy: Main Results**

Reference Class		Brier scores for numeric forecasts	Rounding Errors			
			Words of estimative probability (DNI version)	Words of estimative probability (NIC version)	Confidence levels (3 bins)	Estimative verbs (2 bins)
All forecasters	Mean:	0.153	0.7%	1.9%[+]	11.8%	31.4%
	Median:	0.121	0.9%	1.2%	7.3%	22.1%
Untrained individuals	Mean:	0.189	0.5%	0.5%	5.9%	15.0%
	Median:	0.162	0.6%	0.2%	3.6%	9.9%
Trained groups	Mean:	0.136	0.8%	3.3%[^]	17.8%	48.6%
	Median:	0.100	0.9%	2.4%	11.0%	30.1%
Superforecasters	Mean:	0.093	6.1%	40.4%	236.1%	562.0%
	Median:	0.032	1.7%	10.2%	54.7%	141.7%

Note: the table describes the extent to which coarsening probability assessment using different systems of expression reduced the judgmental accuracy of the Good Judgment Project (GJP) forecasts. For example, rounding superforecasters' estimates into the seven equal bins recommended by the National Intelligence Council degraded Brier scores by an average of 40%.

Unless otherwise noted, all estimates are statistically distinct from zero at the $p < 0.001$ level. GJP = Good Judgment Project; DNI = Director of National Intelligence; NIC = National Intelligence Council.

[^]This estimate is statistically distinct from zero at the $p < 0.05$ level.

[+]This is the only estimate that is not statistically distinct from zero at the $p < 0.05$ level.

approach my colleagues and I took to estimating statistical significance, every subgroup of respondents encountered consistent losses of predictive accuracy when we coarsened their forecasts according to the analytic standards currently recommended by the U.S. director of national intelligence (DNI). The National Intelligence Council (NIC) standards, which divide probability assessments into seven equal bins, induce greater variance: rounding errors here proved to be larger but less consistent.[34]

As one might expect, the superforecasters suffered the harshest penalties when we coarsened their judgments. And while that fact alone is unsurprising, the scale of the penalties was remarkable. For example, rounding superforecasters' estimates into confidence levels caused a 55 percent increase in Brier scores at the median, while more than doubling Brier scores at the mean. The NIC's words-of-estimative-probability spectrum degraded the superforecasters' median judgment by more than ten percent. In general, Table 3.1 shows that coarsening probability assessments sacrifices information disproportionately from the sources that produce the most informative judgments.

These results strike a sharp contrast to the pessimistic views that many scholars and practitioners offer regarding the prospects for improving assessments of uncertainty in foreign policy analysis. Mark Lowenthal, a scholar with three decades of experience in the U.S. Intelligence Community, thus observes: "No one has yet come up with any methodologies, machines or thought processes that will appreciably raise the Intelligence Community's [performance]."[35] Thomas Fingar, formerly the U.S. Intelligence Community's top analyst, writes: "By and large, analysts do not have an empirical basis for using or eschewing particular methods."[36] By contrast, the results presented in Table 3.1 indicate that forming and communicating clearer assessments of uncertainty could bring wide-ranging improvements to foreign policy discourse. Even if these judgments are subjective, there is a real cost to leaving them vague.

[34] The DNI spectrum compensates for tightening the "remote" and "almost certain" bins by widening the "likely" and "unlikely" bins. This makes a majority of forecasts worse (and the difference in means more statistically significant) even as average rounding errors decline.

[35] Mark Lowenthal, "Towards a Reasonable Standard for Analysis: How Right, How Often on Which Issues?" *Intelligence and National Security*, Vol, 23, No. 3 (2008), p. 314.

[36] Thomas Fingar, *Reducing Uncertainty: Intelligence Analysis and National Security* (Stanford, Calif.: Stanford Security Studies, 2011), pp. 34, 130.

Examining Variation across Questions

The findings summarized in Table 3.1 reflect nearly one million judgments spanning roughly four hundred separate topics. Nevertheless, skeptics might assume that these findings are driven by specific subsets of easy questions. If that were the case, then it would be a mistake to use general patterns across those data to draw inferences about foreign policy analysts' broader capabilities for assessing international politics.

There are three ways to address this concern. One indicator of a question's ease is the degree of certainty that analysts assign to their judgments, on the assumption that forecasters should possess higher degrees of certainty when answering easier questions. A second indicator of a question's difficulty is its time horizon, on the assumption that nearer-term events should be easier to predict. It is also possible that some kinds of subject matter simply lend themselves to analytic precision more than others. But as this section shows, none of these factors appears to play a major role in shaping the value of precision in probability assessment.

Returns to Precision across the Number Line

Table 3.2 shows that GJP analysts could meaningfully discriminate among a wide range of probabilities, and not just in cases where they felt they could form conclusions with near certainty. To demonstrate this point, my colleagues and I divided GJP forecasts into seven bins according to National Intelligence Council guidelines. We separately examined the forecasts falling within the seven bins that these guidelines contain. We found that coarsening superforecasters' estimates in this way consistently sacrificed information within all seven segments of the number line.[37]

We found mixed results from rounding other forecasters' most extreme estimates. When those estimated probabilities fell within the highest or lowest bins, we found that coarsened judgments were more accurate at the median but less accurate on average. This is not a contradiction. Coarsening these forecasts tended to shift them closer to certainty.[38] This shift improved the accuracy of

---

[37] These results are symmetrical (e.g., the results of rounding forecasts to the terms "likely" and "unlikely" create identical rounding errors) because any forecast automatically implies its complement. In other words, stating that an outcome has a ten percent chance of occurrence is equivalent to estimating a ninety percent chance of *non*-occurrence, and we score both judgments simultaneously.

[38] For instance, the average forecast falling in the "remote chance" segment of the number line was ten percent. The midpoint of the "remote chance" bin is seven percent. Coarsening forecasts thus tended to shift judgments in this part of the number line a bit closer toward certainty.

Table 3.2. **Returns to Precision across the Number Line**

Group		Remote (.00–.14)	Very unlikely (.15–.28)	Unlikely (.29–.42)	Even chance (.43–.56)	Likely (.57–.71)	Very likely (.72–.85)	Almost certain (.86–1.0)
All Forecasters	Mean:	3.4%	4.3%	2.3%	1.3%	2.3%	4.3%	3.4%
	Median:	-0.5%	3.7%	2.2%	1.1%	2.2%	3.7%	-0.5%
Superforecasters	Mean:	85.8%	16.2%	7.0%	1.8%	7.0%	16.2%	85.8%
	Median:	32.2%	12.1%	4.1%	1.0%	4.1%	12.1%	32.2%

Note: The table examines how rounding probability estimates into seven equal bins influences the accuracy of forecasts within different segments of the number line. For example, coarsening the probability estimates that fell between 72% and 85% into the phrase "very likely" degraded forecasters' Brier scores by an average of 4.3%. All estimates in this table are statistically distinct from zero at the *p* < 0.001 level.

forecasts more often than not (hence the improvement in the median Brier score), but when analysts' judgments proved to be mistaken, making forecasts more extreme caused analysts to suffer large penalties (hence the degradation in the average Brier score). In any case, these findings demonstrate that the value of precision across GJP forecasts did not depend on nearly certain responses to especially easy questions.

Returns to Precision across Time Horizons

The GJP data also make it possible to examine how returns to precision in probability assessment vary across time horizons.[39] We divided the forecasts into four categories for this purpose.

First, we identified forecasts as *Lay-Ups* if they were made with no more than five percent probability or no less than ninety-five percent probability, and if they were also registered within two weeks of the date when a forecasting problem's outcome became known. We expected to see special returns to precision on these highly certain, near-term estimates. We divided all other forecasts into three groups with equal numbers of observations.[40] *Short-term* forecasts were made within thirty-six days of a question's closing date; *medium-term* forecasts were made between thirty-seven and ninety-six days of a question's closing date; and *long-term* forecasts were registered more than ninety-six days from a question's closing date.[41]

The appendix shows that the main findings presented in Table 3.1 hold constant across all four of these subsets.[42] In each case, we see statistically significant losses of accuracy from coarsening probability assessments into estimative verbs, confidence levels, or words of estimative probability. This analysis shows that the value of precision in probability assessment is not conditional on making judgments about the near-term future.

[39] As previously mentioned, forecasters were allowed to register and update their predictions whenever they liked over the course of the competition. The average forecast was registered seventy-six days before the outcome of that forecast became known, but there is substantial variation on that metric (standard deviation, eighty days).

[40] There were 109,240 Lay-Ups in our data, leaving 259,696 forecasts in each of the other three categories.

[41] The average duration of a long-term forecast was 177 days (standard deviation, 77 days).

[42] See appendix section 1c.

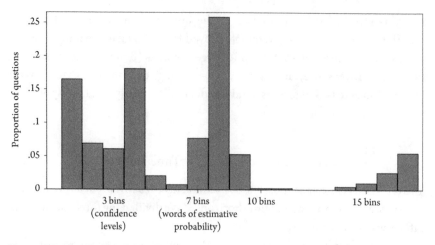

Figure 3.2 Thresholds of estimative precision across the Good Judgment Project questions.

Returns to Precision across Question Content

As a final way of examining the extent to which the value of precision in probability assessment varied across topics in our data set, my colleagues and I examined the individual questions that the Good Judgment Project posed to its forecasters. We defined each question's *threshold of estimative precision* as the smallest number of bins where the median rounding error was statistically indistinguishable from zero.[43] Because we set these thresholds at the lowest possible value where we could not reject the hypothesis that coarsening did not make forecasts less accurate, and because we tested this hypothesis by comparing median rounding errors instead of mean rounding errors, this represents another highly conservative approach to statistical analysis.

Figure 3.2 shows how these thresholds were distributed.[44] The first column of the graph indicates that, for 17 percent of questions in the data set, there was no cost to treating the number line as a single "bin" (that is, to rounding all forecasts to fifty percent). These were the cases where most forecasters were surprised by an outcome: where an event they expected to happen did not take place, or

---

[43] Thus, we began by coarsening all forecasts into one bin (that is, we rounded all judgments to fifty percent). If this degraded the accuracy of the median forecast, then we coarsened all forecasts into two bins: that is, we rounded all judgments to either twenty-five percent or seventy-five percent. We continued this procedure until we no longer found that coarsening judgments generated statistically significant rounding errors. We estimated statistical significance for these purposes using a comparison of medians, based on a one-sided, paired-sample Wilcoxon signed rank test with a 0.05 significance threshold.

[44] The average threshold is 6.1 bins, with a standard deviation of 4.4.

where an event they thought was unlikely did in fact occur. In another 7 percent of cases, we observed no systematic costs to rounding analysts' judgments into "estimative verbs."

Yet we found that foreign policy analysts could generally do better than this. Coarsening judgments into estimative verbs systematically sacrificed predictive accuracy for 77 percent of questions in the data set. Rounding these judgments into confidence levels degraded respondents' Brier scores 70 percent of the time. Coarsening forecasts into seven-step words of estimative probability systematically sacrificed information for 42 percent of the questions we examined. And for 9 percent of these questions, we found that respondents could reliably parse their judgments more finely than intervals of ten percentage points. In other words, we found that the U.S. Intelligence Community's official analytic standards for assessing uncertainty systematically sacrificed information on nearly half of the forecasting problems in our data set, and that there was a nontrivial proportion of topics where even rough *numeric* expressions were insufficient to capture all the insight foreign policy analysts could reliably provide.

Nevertheless, it could still be the case that returns to precision in probability assessment are concentrated in particular sectors of foreign policy analysis. To test this hypothesis, we classified questions as corresponding to eleven regions (e.g., Western Europe, Sub-Saharan Africa) and fifteen topics (e.g., domestic conflict, trade).[45] We found that this information captured almost no systematic variation in returns to precision across questions in the GJP data set.[46] This finding—or, more accurately, this lack of consistent variation in returns to precision across substantive domains—further supports the argument that the value of precision in probability assessment extends across a broad range of foreign policy issues.

"Mathematicians and Poets" Revisited: Examining Variation across Individuals

The previous section demonstrated that there is no clear threshold of "allowable exactness" when it comes to assessing uncertainty in international politics, and that this finding is not driven by easy questions, short time horizons, or idiosyncratic topics. This section examines how the value of precision in probability

---

[45] These categories were not mutually exclusive.

[46] When we combined all 26 variables into a model predicting thresholds of estimative precision across questions—a method that biases statistical analysis toward "overfitting" the data based on spurious correlations—this model had an R^2 value of just 0.16. See Friedman et al., "The Value of Precision in Probability Assessment," for more details on this analysis.

assessment varies across individuals, and shows that this capability does not depend on special levels of numeracy, high degrees of educational achievement, or particular cognitive profiles.

In addition to extending the robustness of the chapter's empirical results, this analysis speaks to long-standing concerns about the divide between "mathematicians" and "poets" in foreign policy analysis. As we saw in chapter 1, descriptions of this divide date back to the writings of Sherman Kent, who found that many intelligence officials were extremely uncomfortable with the idea of treating subjective judgments through the lens of rationalist logic.[47] If this discomfort maps onto aptitudes for assessing uncertainty—that is, if the so-called mathematicians are the only analysts who can draw meaningful distinctions among their probability estimates—that would undermine the generalizability of the findings presented in this chapter.

This concern resonates with a large body of research that examines the relationship between numeracy and political knowledge.[48] In many areas of public policy, it appears that only a small fraction of the population can grasp politically relevant numbers. One prominent example is that most voters possess wildly inaccurate perceptions of how much money the U.S. government spends in different policy areas.[49] A majority of American voters cannot estimate the size of the budget deficit within an order of magnitude, let alone command the array of figures necessary to understand the federal budget in a serious way.[50] These findings are disheartening, but they are not particularly surprising. Most voters are not naturally exposed to information about the federal budget as part of their daily lives, and there is virtually no other domain in which one encounters dollar values so enormous. As a result, few people are positioned to develop an

[47] For contemporary descriptions of this controversy, see Ben Connable, *Embracing the Fog of War* (Santa Monica, Calif.: Rand, 2012); and Rob Johnston, *Analytic Culture in the U.S. Intelligence Community* (Washington, D.C.: Center for the Study of Intelligence, 2005). Discomfort with scientific approaches to national security analysis dates back to Clausewitz. See Azar Gat, *The Origins of Military Thought: From the Enlightenment to Clausewitz* (Oxford, U.K.: Clarendon Press, 1989).

[48] See, for example, Ellen Peters et al. "Numeracy and Decision Making," *Psychological Science*, Vol. 17, No. 5 (2006), pp. 407–413; and Michael Delli Carpini and Scott Keeter, *What Americans Know about Politics and Why It Matters* (New Haven, Conn.: Yale University Press, 1996).

[49] See, for example, Martin Gilens, "Political Ignorance and Collective Policy Preferences," *American Political Science Review*, Vol. 95, No. 2 (2001), pp. 379–396; James H. Kuklinksi et al., "Misinformation and the Currency of Democratic Citizenship," *Journal of Politics*, Vol. 62, No. 3 (2000), pp. 790–816; Steven Kull, *Americans and Foreign Aid: A Study of American Public Attitudes* (College Park, Md.: Program on International Policy Attitudes, 1995).

[50] On the broader cognitive challenges that many people face in dealing with money, see Dan Ariely and Jeff Kriesler, *Dollars and Sense: How We Misthink Money and How to Spend Smarter* (New York: HarperCollins, 2017).

intuitive sense about what it means for the federal government to spend a "small" or a "large" amount of money on any policy issue, let alone to calibrate their perceptions of the federal budget in a systematic way.

Yet there are two main reasons why these findings may not extend into the realm of probability assessment. The first of these reasons is that probability estimates fall along a scale that is easy to understand. All probabilities are bounded between zero and one hundred percent. Virtually everyone knows that a ten percent chance is quite small, that a ninety percent chance is quite large, and that fifty-percent chance events occur as often as not. Thus, even though probability is an abstract concept, it is reasonable to expect that most people will find those numbers to be more intuitive than federal expenditures or other numbers that citizens often struggle to comprehend.

Furthermore, most people naturally encounter probabilities throughout a broad range of activities in daily life. Obvious examples involve weather forecasts, sports statistics such as batting averages or free-throw percentages, and assigning betting odds . This does not mean that we should expect everyone to possess identical skill in assessing uncertainty. But the everyday nature of probabilistic judgment is another reason to expect that fluency in this domain will be distributed more broadly than capabilities for dealing with other kinds of politically relevant numbers.

Consistent with this argument, the remainder of the section will demonstrate that the value of precision in probability assessment does not appear to depend on numeracy, education, or cognitive style. Instead, the data suggest that the ability to draw meaningful distinctions among probability assessments is a generalizable skill that foreign policy analysts can cultivate through training, effort, and experience. And if that is the case, then the data presented in this chapter may actually underestimate the value of precision in probability assessment among professional foreign policy analysts, who can devote far more time and effort to political forecasting than the individuals who participated in the Good Judgment Project.

Targets for Cultivation versus Targets for Selection

The dependent variable for this analysis is each GJP forecaster's threshold of estimative precision. As previously explained, this variable reflects the smallest number of bins that does not cause a statistically significant loss of accuracy when we coarsen respondents' forecasts.[51] The goal of this section is to understand

---

[51] This variable had a mean of 4.36, standard deviation 8.02. Note that the mean threshold of estimative precision at the individual level is thus lower than the mean threshold of estimative precision at the question level. This is because the average forecaster registered 85 predictions throughout the

how these thresholds varied across the 1,832 forecasters who participated in the Good Judgment Project.

My colleagues and I divided independent variables into two categories. The first of these categories captures skill, training, effort, experience, and collaboration. We can call these factors *Targets for Cultivation*, because organizations and individuals have feasible opportunities to develop these attributes. The second category of predictors in this analysis captures information on numeracy, education, and cognitive style. If these prove to be the primary source of returns to precision, then this finding would bolster the notion that the ability to assess uncertainty with meaningful detail belongs to people with special backgrounds. We can call these attributes *Targets for Selection*, because such findings would suggest that improving returns to precision in foreign policy analysis is mainly a matter of recruiting the right analysts for the job. This would also lend credence to the idea that individuals who self-identify as "poets" could justifiably conclude that they would be incapable of assessing subjective probabilities with meaningful detail.

The appendix provides more information on each of these attributes, but here is a short description of what those variables entailed.[52] We measured forecasting skill by calculating respondents' median Brier scores. Though we expected to see that higher-quality forecasters would incur greater penalties from having their forecasts coarsened, it is important to note that this relationship is not tautological. It is possible for a forecaster to be excellent at discriminating events that are unlikely from those that are likely, even if she is not especially good at calibrating fine-grained distinctions within each category. This is, indeed, the hypothesis implied by recommendations that foreign policy analysts express their judgments using coarse language like estimative verbs or confidence levels.[53]

We used five additional variables to capture effort, training, experience, and collaboration. We counted the number of questions each forecaster answered across all the years of the competition, and we counted the average number of times each forecaster revised those predictions. Each variable proxies for the effort respondents expended in engaging with the competition and for their experience responding to forecasting questions. We also included a measure of the granularity of respondents' forecasts, which captures the proportion of the

---

GJP, whereas each question received more than 1,000 individual forecasts. Larger volumes of data make it possible to detect smaller statistical changes: hence the higher thresholds of estimative precision when aggregating the data by questions relative to individuals.

[52] See appendix section 1d.

[53] An analyst who is excellent at discrimination yet overconfident in her estimates could even see her estimates *improve* on account of rounding schemes that shift her most extreme judgments away from certainty.

time that forecasters registered probability assessments that were not multiples of ten percentages points. Finally, we recorded which GJP respondents received training in probabilistic reasoning as part of participating in the study, and which forecasters were assigned to teams with whom they could collaborate before making their judgments. Since the GJP assigned respondents to these conditions at random, these data provide a unique opportunity to study how training and group work improve probabilistic reasoning.

Our analysis spanned six Targets for Selection. We measured respondents' education in terms of the highest academic degree they had obtained. We measured respondents' numeracy using a standard battery of word problems that psychologists use to capture mathematical fluency. We also examined four batteries of questions that GJP forecasters completed to establish a cognitive profile: Raven's Progressive Matrices, which is an index that captures reasoning ability; the expanded Cognitive Reflection Test, which reflects an individual's propensity to suppress misleading intuitive reactions in favor of more accurate, deliberative answers; a Fox-Hedgehog index that captures respondents' self-assessed tendency to rely on ad hoc reasoning versus simplifying frameworks; and Need for Cognition, a scale that reflects respondents' self-assessed preference for addressing complex problems.[54]

Results

To summarize, this portion of the analysis aims to provide insight into why foreign policy analysts vary in their ability to draw meaningful distinctions among subjective probabilities. From a conceptual standpoint, we can divide these sources of variation into two groups: Targets for Cultivation and Targets for Selection. My colleagues and I collected data on six separate factors that fell into each category. The appendix presents a full statistical analysis of how these variables predict returns to precision across individuals.[55] Here, I will summarize the main findings from that analysis.

We found that the Targets for Cultivation variables consistently predicted returns across forecasters. Across nearly two thousand people who participated in the Good Judgment Project, forecasters demonstrated a greater ability to draw meaningful distinctions among probabilities when they had better forecasting skill, when they responded to more questions, when they revised their forecasts more often, when they received training in probabilistic

---

[54] In addition to measuring respondents' cognitive style using these indices, we also included control variables for age, gender, and whether a respondent was designated as a superforecaster in any tournament year. See appendix section 1e.

[55] See appendix section 1e.

reasoning, and when they worked together in groups.[56] Granularity was the only Target for Cultivation variable that did not prove to be a statistically significant predictor of returns to precision. In other words, we found that coarsening probability assessments systematically sacrificed predictive accuracy, even among forecasters who were naturally inclined to express their judgments in terms of round numbers.

By contrast, we found that the Targets for Selection variables had almost no ability to predict returns to precision in probability assessment. None of our measures for education, numeracy, or cognitive style proved to be statistically significant predictors of why some respondents demonstrated higher returns to precision than others. We thus found no evidence that returns to precision belong primarily to "mathematicians" versus "poets," nor that the ability to make subjective probability assessments belongs to people who possess special cognitive skills. Instead, we found that when a broad range of foreign policy analysts took the time and effort to assess uncertainty in clear and structured ways, that consistently improved the accuracy of their judgments.

These findings provide a heartening basis for generalizing on the basis of the chapter's empirical results. For example, collaboration tends to be much denser among foreign policy professionals than it was among GJP groups who worked together sporadically and online. Government agencies can train professional analysts much more extensively than the simple, one-hour training modules that GJP respondents received. Many foreign policy analysts assess uncertainty on a regular basis over many years, which affords them far more experience than the respondents who participated in the GJP competition. And most practitioners have far more opportunity and incentive to refine and revise their forecasts in light of new information.[57] All these factors correlate with higher returns to precision across the GJP data set. It is thus reasonable to

---

[56] It is not surprising that Number of Questions predicted returns to precision among GJP respondents. Forecasters who registered more predictions were not only more experienced and more engaged in the competition, but they also provided more statistical power for calculating thresholds for estimative precision, such that smaller rounding errors would register as being statistically significant. The analysis presented here cannot isolate how much of this correlation resulted from sample size versus gains from experience. Yet either interpretation has the same practical implication: the more forecasts analysts make, the more likely it becomes that coarsening those estimates will systematically sacrifice information. Given the vast quantity of judgments that national security officials make, along with the vast numbers of interviews and essays that make up the marketplace of ideas, the relationship we observe between Number of Questions and returns to precision further emphasizes how the GJP data may understate the degree to which vague probability assessments sacrifice information from foreign policy discourse.

[57] GJP respondents revised their forecasts, on average, less than twice per question.

expect that the findings presented here understate the degree to which placing greater emphasis on probability assessment could improve the quality of foreign policy discourse.

Reconsidering the Agnostic View of Assessing Uncertainty

Chapters 2 and 3 have refuted what the book has called the "agnostic" view of assessing uncertainty in international politics. The agnostics' thesis holds that probabilistic reasoning is too subjective to be useful when debating foreign policy issues. Part of this critique rests on the theoretical claim that "gut instincts" do not provide a coherent basis for evaluating high-stakes choices. Other agnostics base their skepticism of subjective probability on empirical grounds, arguing that international politics is too complex to permit assessing uncertainty with any meaningful detail. These beliefs are widespread among scholars, practitioners, and pundits, and they are relevant to the conduct of virtually any foreign policy debate.

The last two chapters have also shown that these views do not withstand scrutiny. We saw in chapter 2 that, even though assessments of probability in international politics are inherently subjective, it is still possible to form and communicate those judgments in clear and structured ways. Indeed, we saw that subjectivity is the very thing that makes it possible to debate such judgments directly, because analysts are always in a position to describe their personal beliefs as precisely as they like. This chapter then demonstrated how assessments of subjective probability reflect meaningful insight rather than arbitrary detail. Foreign policy analysts' capacity to generate this insight does not appear to depend on easy questions, short time horizons, idiosyncratic topics, or special cognitive profiles. Instead, the analysis presented in this chapter suggests that the value of assessing uncertainty in international politics is greater and more generalizable than many skeptics suspect.

Chapters 4 and 5 move on to tackle what the book has called the "rejectionist" objection to assessing uncertainty in international politics. As described in the book's introduction, the rejectionists argue that even if foreign policy analysts could make meaningful assessments of uncertainty in principle, it could still be counterproductive to place too much emphasis on those judgments in practice. Chapter 4 describes the psychological dimensions of this argument, including the common notion that transparent probabilistic reasoning could surround subjective judgments with illusions of rigor. Chapter 5 then addresses concerns about the politics of probabilistic reasoning, evaluating the argument that assessing uncertainty in clear and structured ways could expose foreign policy analysts to excessive criticism.

These arguments are important because they suggest another set of fundamental obstacles that foreign policy analysts face when it comes to assessing uncertainty. Yet chapters 4 and 5 will explain that the theoretical and empirical foundations of these arguments are much weaker than the conventional wisdom suggests. Here, too, we will see that common objections to assessing uncertainty in international politics reflect basic misperceptions about the nature and limits of probabilistic reasoning.

4

Dispelling Illusions of Rigor*

The book's previous chapters explained how foreign policy analysts can assess uncertainty in a manner that is theoretically coherent and empirically meaningful, even when they are dealing with complex, unique phenomena. But are those judgments actually useful for policymaking? In this chapter, we will encounter two main sources of skepticism to that effect. The first is that foreign policy decision makers are largely uninterested in probabilistic reasoning, preferring that analysts "make the call" on tough questions. The second concern is that debating assessments of uncertainty in clear and structured ways could surround subjective judgments with illusions of rigor that warp high-stakes choices.[1] The illusions-of-rigor argument plays an especially prominent role in what the book calls the "rejectionist" objection to probabilistic reasoning—the idea that assessing uncertainty can be actively counterproductive in shaping foreign policy debates.

The rejectionists' concerns are worth taking seriously in light of the growing body of scholarship that shows how cognitive constraints hinder foreign policy decision making.[2] Yet while psychologists generally believe that decision makers can mitigate their cognitive shortcomings by analyzing high-stakes issues in clear and structured ways, the rejectionist viewpoint suggests that clarity and structure can backfire when it comes to assessing uncertainty, activating psychological distortions that create major problems of their own. At best, the

---

* Portions of this chapter previously appeared in Jeffrey A. Friedman, Jennifer S. Lerner, and Richard Zeckhauser, "Behavioral Consequences of Probabilistic Precision: Experimental Evidence from National Security Professionals," *International Organization*, Vol. 71, No. 4 (2017), pp. 803–826. ©, published by Cambridge University Press, reproduced with permission.

[1] Of course, these arguments cannot simultaneously be true: the first posits that foreign policy officials ignore assessments of uncertainty, and the second posits that foreign policy officials care too much about such judgments. Ironically, we will see that both arguments are widespread in scholarship on foreign policy decision making and intelligence analysis.

[2] Rose McDermott, *Risk-Taking in International Politics* (Ann Arbor, Mich.: University of Michigan Press, 1998); Daniel Kahneman and Jonathan Renshon, "Why Hawks Win," *Foreign Policy*,

rejectionists believe that debating subjective probabilities can divert attention from other factors that actually help decision makers to evaluate tough foreign policy choices. At worst, placing greater emphasis on subjective assessments of uncertainty might undermine those choices. The rejectionists' objections to subjective probability thus posit a basic conflict between the demands of analytic rigor and the limits of human cognition.

Yet to date, these concerns have relied mainly on speculation. We will see that in some cases it is not even clear that the rejectionists have articulated their arguments in a falsifiable manner, let alone bolstered those claims with systematic empirical evidence. To help fill this gap, the chapter presents four survey experiments that examine how more than six hundred national security officials and more than three thousand non-elite respondents assess and interpret subjective probability.

These data refute the argument that foreign policy decision makers are unable or unwilling to engage in probabilistic reasoning. We will see that small changes in probability assessments triggered substantial shifts in the way that respondents evaluated risky actions. The findings presented in this chapter also run contrary to the notion that transparent probabilistic reasoning creates illusions of rigor. Instead, the experiments described in the following sections indicate that decision makers confronted with clearer assessments of uncertainty became more cautious when taking risks and more willing to gather additional information before making high-stakes choices.

These findings do not imply that foreign policy officials are rational actors who are free from cognitive constraints. Indeed, the second half of the chapter shows that encouraging foreign policy analysts to provide explicit probability assessments can exacerbate a tendency for some analysts to attach too much certainty to their judgments. But we will also see that this behavior appears primarily among low-quality assessors and that brief (two-minute) training sessions can mitigate the problem. Thus, while the experiments presented in this chapter hardly exhaust debate about the psychological obstacles that hinder foreign policy analysts from assessing uncertainty in clear and structured ways, the chapter hones a broad list of concerns about this topic into a specific and previously undocumented bias that training can presumably correct.

Do Foreign Policy Decision Makers Really Care about Probabilities?

In 1975, the psychologists Daniel Kahneman and Zvi Lanir led an effort to train Israeli intelligence analysts in the principles of decision analysis. Kahneman and Lanir placed special emphasis on improving assessments of uncertainty, given Israeli analysts' perceived failure to warn political leaders about the 1973 Arab invasion. Yet Kahneman and Lanir found that Israeli decision makers demonstrated a "conspicuous lack of interest" in the probability assessments that intelligence analysts provided. Kahneman later reflected on how this experience "greatly reduced his faith in the applicability of decision analysis" to the foreign policy realm. The authors concluded that they had been "naively enthusiastic about what they saw as a chance to improve the rationality of decision-making on truly important issues."[3]

Similar impressions appear throughout the literature on foreign policy analysis and intelligence reform. A CIA study reviewing the impact of Sherman Kent's research on words of estimative probability found that Kent's arguments had "not struck a very responsive chord" with readers of intelligence reports.[4] An important article by James Marchio chronicles how several subsequent attempts to improve probability assessments in U.S. intelligence analysis faltered as a result of decision makers' apparent disinterest.[5] Former Chairman of the National Intelligence Council Greg Treverton channeled similar concerns in summing up the impact of recent efforts to improve analytic standards for assessing uncertainty, writing, "I doubt if policy officials ever notice."[6]

While interviewing intelligence analysts as part of the background research for this book, I found that many of them had drawn similar lessons from their interactions with high-ranking officials. Assessments of uncertainty may be

No. 158 (2007), pp. 34–38; Jack S. Levy, "Psychology and Foreign Policy Decision-Making," in Leonie Huddy, David O. Sears, and Jack S. Levy, eds., *The Oxford Handbook of Political Psychology*, 2nd ed. (New York: Oxford University Press, 2013); and Emilie M. Hafner-Burton et al., "The Behavioral Revolution and the Study of International Relations," *International Organization*, Vol. 71, No. S1 (2017), pp. S1–S31.

[3] Zvi Lanir and Daniel Kahneman, "An Experiment in Decision Analysis in Israel in 1975," *Studies in Intelligence*, Vol. 50, No. 4 (2006). Available at https://www.cia.gov/library/center-for-the-study-of-intelligence/csi-publications/csi-studies/studies/vol50no4/an-experiment-in-decision-analysis-in-israel-in-1975.html.

[4] Center for the Study of Intelligence, *National Estimates: An Assessment of the Product and Process* (Central Intelligence Agency, 1977), p. 34.

[5] James Marchio, "The Intelligence Community's Struggle to Express Analytic Certainty in the 1970s," *Studies in Intelligence*, Vol. 58, No. 4 (2015), pp. 31–42.

[6] Gregory F. Treverton, "Theory and Practice," *Intelligence and National Security*, Vol. 33, No. 4 (2018), p. 476. On how foreign policy decision makers often pressure analysts to "make the call" rather than offering uncertain judgments, see Mark M. Lowenthal, *Intelligence: From Secrets to Policy*, 3rd ed. (Washington, D.C.: CQ Press, 2006); Richard K. Betts, *Enemies of Intelligence: Knowledge and Power in American National Security* (New York: Columbia University Press, 2007); and Thomas Fingar, *Reducing Uncertainty: Intelligence Analysis and National Security* (Stanford, Calif.: Stanford Security Studies, 2011).

crucial to the logic of foreign policy decision making. But the analysts' job is to provide foreign policy decision makers with useful information. If decision makers do not find assessments of uncertainty to be useful, then analysts might reasonably choose to spend their time and effort elsewhere.[7]

At the same time, one of the central lessons of behavioral psychology is that decision makers respond to a vast range of stimuli, knowingly or otherwise. Just as no one would conclude that decision makers are free from confirmation bias or the sunk-cost fallacy simply because they say so, there is no reason to conclude that assessments of uncertainty are irrelevant to foreign policy decision making just because policymakers seem disinterested in the subject.

Indeed, decision makers' apparent ambivalence toward assessments of uncertainty might signal discomfort instead of apathy. As we saw in chapters 1 and 2, many foreign policy officials are reluctant to accept the fact that high-stakes choices depend on subjective judgments. If reasonable people can disagree about what those judgments entail, then it can be genuinely difficult to say how that information should inform rigorous decisions.[8] Decision makers may thus prefer to steer policy debates toward information that is more concrete and less arguable. Such behavior might resemble the "conspicuous disinterest" in assessments of uncertainty that Kahneman and other scholars have described—but this does not mean that foreign policy decision makers literally ignore those judgments.

If scholars want to understand how probability assessments shape foreign policy decisions, it is therefore important to study the topic systematically, and not simply to infer what decision makers might or might not be thinking based on outward appearances. The ideal research design for this purpose would compare how foreign policy decision makers respond to scenarios that are identical in all respects, save for the manner in which analysts assess uncertainty. Needless to say, it is impossible to conduct such a study from archival records, given how foreign policy decisions vary on so many dimensions, and given how foreign policy analysts tend to assess uncertainty in such vague and idiosyncratic ways. A second-best, but far more feasible, research design is to employ

---

[7] This concern resonates with a broad range of international relations scholarship that argues that foreign policy decision makers can be insensitive to nuance when assessing uncertainty, preferring instead to base their actions on gut instincts, salient cues, or simple analogies. Prominent examples include Robert Jervis, *Perception and Misperception in International Politics* (Princeton, N.J.: Princeton University Press, 1976); Keren Yarhi-Milo, *Knowing the Adversary: Leaders, Intelligence, and Assessment of Intentions in International Relations* (Princeton, N.J.: Princeton University Press, 2014); Aaron Rapport, *Waging War, Planning Peace: U.S. Noncombat Operations and Major Wars* (Ithaca, N.Y.: Cornell University Press, 2015); and Yuen Foong Khong, *Analogies at War: Korea, Munich, Dien Bien Phu, and the Vietnam Decisions of 1965* (Princeton, N.J.: Princeton University Press, 1992).

[8] Chapter 6 explores the theoretical basis for addressing this challenge.

the experimental method, presenting respondents with decision scenarios that involve randomly varying assessments of risk. The remainder of the chapter presents four such experiments.[9]

The experimental method has several known drawbacks.[10] One of these drawbacks is that respondents' reactions to hypothetical scenarios can never replicate the complexity or intensity that real foreign policy decisions entail. The experimental method is thus properly viewed as a tool for probing respondents' basic intuitions—a "rough draft" of how individuals might approach actual high-stakes choices. Yet if anything, this attribute of the experimental method should favor confirming the rejectionists' claims. If decision makers are truly disinterested in assessments of uncertainty, or if they are truly incapable of processing such information effectively, then we would expect their intuitive reactions to be relatively *in*sensitive to subtle differences in probabilistic reasoning. And if probability assessments create illusions of rigor, then we would expect those problems to be the most pronounced when measuring decision makers' immediate reactions, before they are able to notice or correct their cognitive biases.[11]

Another common drawback with the experimental method is that study participants may not reflect populations of interest. This problem is particularly acute in attempting to understand the psychology of foreign policy decision making. There are many ways in which foreign policy officials differ from the college students or other "non-elite" participants who provide the subject pools for most psychological research.[12] This is another concern that I have

---

[9] Portions of experiments 2 and 3 appeared in Jeffrey A. Friedman, Jennifer S. Lerner, and Richard Zeckhauser, "Behavioral Consequences of Probabilistic Precision: Experimental Evidence from National Security Professionals," *International Organization*, Vol. 71, No. 4 (2017), pp. 803–826. The analysis of experiments 1 and 4 are new to this chapter.

[10] See, for example, Jason Barabas and Jennifer Jerit, "Are Survey Experiments Externally Valid?" *American Political Science Review*, Vol. 104, No. 2 (2010), pp. 226–284. For evidence that survey experiments nevertheless provide reliable benchmarks for some kinds of political behavior, see Jens Hainmueller, Dominik Hangartner, and Teppei Yamamoto, "Validating Vignette and Conjoint Survey Experiments against Real-World Behavior," *PNAS*, Vol. 112, No. 8 (2015), pp. 2395–2400.

[11] The notion that immediate, intuitive reactions to decision scenarios are particularly susceptible to cognitive biases is the central message of Daniel Kahneman, *Thinking, Fast and Slow* (New York: Farrar, Straus and Giroux, 2011).

[12] On the relationship between survey research on non-elite samples and practical concerns in international relations, see Emilie Hafner-Burton, Alex Hughes, and David G. Victor, "The Cognitive Revolution and the Political Psychology of Elite Decision Making, *Perspectives on Politics*, Vol. 11, No. 2 (2013), pp. 368–386; Susan D. Hyde, "Experiments in International Relations: Lab, Survey, and Field," *Annual Review of Political Science*, Vol. 18 (2015), pp. 403–424; and Jonathan Renshon, "Losing Face and Sinking Costs: Experimental Evidence on the Judgment of Political and Military Leaders," *International Organization*, Vol. 69, No. 3 (2015), pp. 659–695.

often encountered when discussing the decision sciences with foreign policy professionals. Even if some academic finding is well-established in studies of undergraduate sophomores, this does not mean we should necessarily see the same behavior among practitioners of international politics.

To guard against this problem, I administered all four of the survey experiments described in this chapter to cross-sections of actual foreign policy officials, as well as to larger samples of non-elites. This "paired sample" approach offers unique insight into the extent to which foreign policy professionals and non-elites differ in how they assess and interpret subjective probabilities. In general, we will see that these differences turn out to be relatively small, and that all of the chapter's substantive findings hold across both samples. This comparison helps to reinforce the chapter's empirical results, while refuting concerns about how foreign policy elites possess some kind of peculiar psychology that should make them unusually incapable or unwilling to engage in probabilistic reasoning.

Experiment 1: Assessing the "Disinterest Hypothesis"

The first empirical question the chapter examines is the extent to which decision makers actually incorporate probability assessments into their evaluations of high-stakes decisions. If decision makers are truly disinterested in assessments of uncertainty, then there would be little purpose in having foreign policy analysts devote time and effort toward that end. To examine this issue, I designed a survey experiment that presented respondents with three decision-making scenarios.[13] These involved a proposed hostage-rescue mission in Syria, a proposed drone strike in Yemen, and a choice of whether or not to support a group of local security forces in Afghanistan. Figure 4.1 presents an example of the hostage-rescue scenario. The book's appendix contains the other two vignettes, which followed a similar structure.[14]

Each scenario began by summarizing the decision that respondents were asked to consider. Respondents then read a series of statements describing various elements of uncertainty surrounding this choice. For example, the hostage-rescue scenario described the chances that the hostages were in the suspected location, the chances that U.S. Special Forces could safely retrieve the hostages, and the chances that innocent civilians would be harmed during this process. Each scenario was designed as though it were describing the key judgments section of an intelligence report, and each scenario concluded with

---

[13] The scenarios appeared in random order.
[14] See appendix section 2b.

ISIS is holding three American aid workers hostage. The U.S. Intelligence Community has used human intelligence and communications intercepts to trace these hostages to a compound in Manbij, Syria.

Intelligence analysts stress that their judgments are subjective and that they are based on incomplete information. However, after reviewing all available information, they estimate that it is likely that the hostages are at the Manbij compound. U.S. Special Forces have designed and rehearsed a hostage rescue mission. Based on their track record and on the specific details of this plan, military officials assess that if the hostages are in this location, it is very likely that Special Forces can retrieve the hostages alive.

This mission entails several risks. Analysts believe there is an even chance that ISIS will wound or kill U.S. soldiers on this mission. They believe that it is possible, though unlikely, that the mission would inadvertently wound or kill a small number of innocent civilians living near the suspected compound. They also warn that if the raid fails (including if the aid workers are not being held in the Manbij location), ISIS will almost certainly execute the hostages.

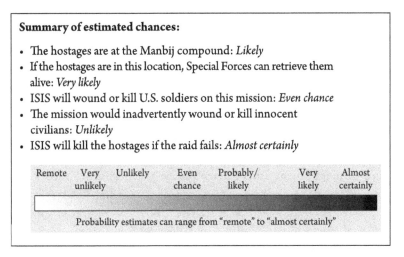

Summary of estimated chances:

- The hostages are at the Manbij compound: *Likely*
- If the hostages are in this location, Special Forces can retrieve them alive: *Very likely*
- ISIS will wound or kill U.S. soldiers on this mission: *Even chance*
- The mission would inadvertently wound or kill innocent civilians: *Unlikely*
- ISIS will kill the hostages if the raid fails: *Almost certainly*

| Remote | Very unlikely | Unlikely | Even chance | Probably/ likely | Very likely | Almost certainly |

Probability estimates can range from "remote" to "almost certainly"

Figure 4.1 Hostage-rescue scenario.

a text box summarizing what those key judgments entailed.[15] After reading each scenario, respondents reported how much they supported or opposed taking the proposed action.[16] Respondents were also asked to say how much they supported or opposed delaying that choice in order to gather more information.

[15] Some of these estimates were represented in terms of words of estimative probability shown in Figure 4.1, and others were represented in terms of numeric percentages. This variation provides the basis for evaluating the illusions-of-rigor thesis in the next section.

[16] Respondents provided those assessments on a seven-point scale. For simplicity, the chapter will present information only on the proportion of respondents who supported or opposed taking

The latter question will be relevant to evaluating the illusions-of-rigor thesis later in the chapter.

The key manipulation in this experiment involved randomizing the probability assessments each scenario contained. A "neutral" version of each scenario was designed to make the costs and benefits of taking action appear roughly equivalent.[17] A "pessimistic" version of each scenario entailed altering those probability assessments in a manner that increased the potential costs and reduced the potential benefits of taking risky action. An "optimistic" version of each scenario entailed shifting probability assessments in the opposite direction. These changes were made as subtly as possible, involving just a single step along the National Intelligence Council's recommended words-of-estimative-probability spectrum. Thus, while the neutral version of the hostage-rescue mission said it was "very likely" that Special Forces could retrieve the hostages alive, the pessimistic version said just that this possibility was "likely," and the optimistic version said that this outcome was "almost certain."[18] Each respondent evaluated one randomly selected version of each scenario.

I administered this experiment to a cross-section of 208 national security officials enrolled at the U.S. National War College. The National War College provides advanced education to military officers who gain appointments to the rank of colonel or commander, and draws students from each branch of the U.S. military. The student body also includes active-duty officials of similar rank from civilian agencies and from other countries' militaries. Twenty-five percent of respondents were professionals from the Department of State, the Intelligence Community, or other foreign policy organizations. Thirteen percent were military officers from countries besides the United States. National War College students thus provide a relatively broad cross-section of relatively high-ranking national security personnel. Response rates among this sample are also extremely high—in this case, ninety-five percent—thereby mitigating concerns about response bias that are common to elite-level survey experiments.

---

action. All results are substantively similar (and indeed more statistically significant) when treatment effects are measured using the full seven-point measures.

[17] Though such cost-benefit comparisons are inherently subjective, they proved to be relatively predictable. The national security officials who participated in this study supported taking action in these scenarios 45 percent of the time and opposed taking these actions 49 percent of the time, with 6 percent saying that they neither supported nor opposed these choices.

[18] See appendix section 2c.

I also administered this experiment to 1,458 respondents recruited from Amazon Mechanical Turk (AMT). AMT is an online platform on which respondents complete surveys in exchange for compensation. Although AMT "workers" are not a representative sample of the U.S. population,[19] the chapter does not seek to draw inferences about the public writ large. As mentioned earlier, the primary purpose of recruiting the AMT respondents is to understand the extent to which "elite" and "non-elite" respondents might react differently to assessments of uncertainty.

Results and Discussion

If the respondents who participated in this study did not find assessments of uncertainty to be meaningful, then changing those judgments should not have systematically altered the way that respondents evaluated national security decisions. Instead, Figure 4.2 shows how small changes in probability estimates substantially altered national security officials' willingness to support risky actions. The national security officials who participated in this study supported taking action in 45 percent of the neutral scenarios; however, that figure fell to just 17 percent in the pessimistic scenarios, and it rose to 61 percent in the optimistic scenarios.[20]

Keep in mind that the difference between the pessimistic, neutral, and optimistic versions of each scenario were subtle, differing by the smallest amounts that words-of-estimative-probability spectrums allow. Nevertheless, support for risky action nearly *tripled* between the pessimistic and neutral scenario versions, and it nearly *quadrupled* between the pessimistic and optimistic scenario versions. These results provide unambiguous evidence that national security officials find probability assessments to be meaningful, and that these judgments shape the way that decision makers intuitively evaluate high-stakes choices.

Figure 4.2 also shows that there was little apparent difference between how elites and non-elites reacted to this experiment. With far more respondents in

[19] The workers who participated in this study were 52 percent female and 80 percent white; 61 percent reported that they held a college degree; and the median age was 35.

[20] These differences are apparent not just when pooling data from the three scenarios together, but also when comparing responses to each scenario individually. When examining different versions of individual scenarios, there was only one of nine instances in which shifting probability assessments did *not* cause a statistically significant shift in respondents' willingness to support risky actions. As mentioned above, all results are similar—and indeed statistically stronger—when measuring treatment effects in terms of seven-point scales.

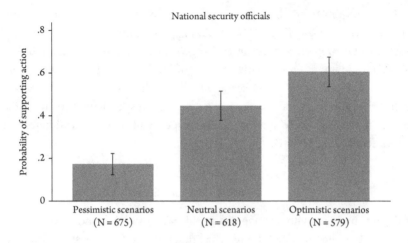

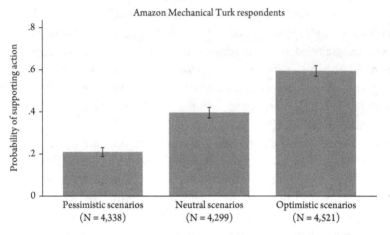

Figure 4.2 How small changes in probability assessments shape support for risky actions. The graphs shows how small variations in probability assessments substantially altered respondents' support for proposed actions. The bars in the graphs represent mean levels of support for proposed actions (plotted with 95 percent intervals). All differences are statistically significant at the p = 0.001 level or below.

the latter sample, the reliability of statistical estimates becomes greater, hence the smaller confidence intervals surrounding the bars in the graph. But the substantive effects of manipulating probability assessments across subjects was essentially the same among participants recruited through AMT as it was for national security officials enrolled at the National War College. The similarity of responses across these samples helps to refute the notion that national security professionals are, for whatever reason, unusually unwilling or particularly unable to engage in probabilistic reasoning.

These findings are consistent with a similar set of experiments that Richard Zeckhauser and I conducted with another cross-section of national security professionals.[21] That experiment involved presenting a different cohort of National War College students with decision-making scenarios in which we randomly varied probability assessments by small amounts. In this case, we varied probability assessments by intervals of 15 percentage points—roughly the same width of a standard word of estimative probability, and thus a level of detail that most qualitative expressions conceal. We also presented decision makers with randomly varying assessments of analytic confidence as enumerated in chapter 2: reliability of available evidence, range of reasonable opinion, and responsiveness to new information. We presented all four of these judgments in a single paragraph, using a format that was deliberately designed to magnify any conceptual confusion that national security officials might encounter when interpreting these judgments (and would thus presumably underestimate their ability to employ this information when evaluating high-stakes choices). The data we gathered showed that all four elements of uncertainty simultaneously shaped national security officials' support for risky actions.

These results indicate that it is mistake to believe that foreign policy analysts need to "dumb down" their assessments of uncertainty (or avoid these assessments altogether) in order to make their judgments meaningful to decision makers. Foreign policy officials might find it uncomfortable to engage with these judgments, and they might prefer to steer policy debates away from considerations of subjective probability. But this does not imply that these judgments are actually unimportant or that decision makers truly ignore them. Indeed, if scholars, practitioners, and pundits are uncomfortable scrutinizing key assumptions directly, then that is exactly why one should support developing norms and procedures that encourage careful discussions of controversial issues.

Illusions of Rigor and Foreign Policy Decision Making

Of course, decision makers who react to probability assessments may not actually process that information effectively. Indeed, a different objection to assessing uncertainty in clear and structured ways is the fear that decision makers might care *too much* about these judgments. As described at the start of the chapter, the

[21] Jeffrey A. Friedman and Richard Zeckhauser, "Analytic Confidence and Political Decision Making: Theoretical Principles and Experimental Evidence from National Security Professionals," *Political Psychology*, Vol. 39, No. 5 (2018), pp. 1069–1087.

basis for this view is the notion that providing clear estimates of subjective probability create illusions of rigor, leading decision makers to see these judgments
as being sounder or more informative than they really are.

These concerns appear throughout public policy analysis and the social
sciences.[22] The political theorist Isaiah Berlin thus cautioned: "To demand or
preach mechanical precision, even in principle, in a field incapable of it is to be
blind and to mislead others."[23] The governing board on risk assessment of the
National Research Council captured a similar sentiment when it warned: While
quantitative risk assessment facilitates comparison, such comparison may be illusory or misleading if the use of precise numbers is unjustified."[24] And when the
National Intelligence Council incorporated words of estimative probability into
its analytic standards, it explained that this might be the outer limit of allowable
detail, since "assigning precise numerical ratings to such judgments would imply
more rigor than we intend."[25]

The illusions-of-rigor thesis presents an especially direct challenge to the
arguments presented in this book. Previous chapters have explained how
marginalizing assessments of uncertainty can enable unsound choices. But the
illusions-of-rigor thesis suggests that efforts to *clarify* probabilistic reasoning
can have harmful effects, too. Instead of emphasizing uncertainty and encouraging careful reasoning about the ambiguity that surrounds major decisions, the
illusions-of-rigor thesis suggests that analytic clarity can drive decision makers
toward overconfidence and premature cognitive closure.

Yet, while this is another plausible reason for skepticism regarding probability
assessment in international politics, I am unaware of any previous scholarship

[22] See David V. Budescu and Thomas S. Wallsten, "Subjective Estimation of Vague and Precise
Uncertainties," in George Wright and Peter Ayton, eds., *Judgmental Forecasting* (Chichester: Wiley,
1987), pp. 63–82; Theodore Porter, *Trust in Numbers: The Pursuit of Objectivity in Science and Public
Life* (Princeton, N.J.: Princeton University Press, 1995).

[23] Isaiah Berlin, "On Political Judgment," *New York Review of Books*, October 3, 1996. Note that
Berlin's concern goes beyond the arguments made by such scholars as Keynes and Mill that subjective probability assessments are meaningless (see chapter 2). Berlin argues that analytic precision is
not just meaningless, but that it can also be actively misleading.

[24] National Research Council, *The Handling of Risk Assessments in NRC Reports* (Washington,
D.C.: National Academy Press, 1981), p. 15. See also Frank Ackerman and Lisa Heinzerling,
Priceless: On Knowing the Price of Everything and the Value of Nothing (New York: New Press, 2004).

[25] National Intelligence Council, *Prospects for Iraq's Stability: A Challenging Road Ahead* (January
2007), available at https://fas.org/irp/dni/iraq020207.pdf. For similar arguments, see Charles
Weiss, "Communicating Uncertainty in Intelligence and Other Professions," *International Journal
of Intelligence and CounterIntelligence*, Vol. 21, No. 1 (2008), pp. 57–85; Kristan J. Wheaton, "The
Revolution Begins on Page Five: The Changing Nature of NIEs," *International Journal of Intelligence
and CounterIntelligence*," Vol. 25, No. 2 (March 2012), pp. 330–349; and James Marchio, "'If the
Weatherman Can...': The Intelligence Community's Struggle to Express Analytic Uncertainty in the
1970s," *Studies in Intelligence*, Vol. 58, No. 4 (2014), pp. 31–42.

that has systematically examined that subject. Indeed, given how foreign policy analysts tend to leave their probability assessments so vague, it is hard to know how concerns about illusions of rigor have emerged, and on what basis skeptics have become so convinced that assessing uncertainty in clear and structured ways would warp high-stakes choices.[26]

It is also unclear what form these illusions of rigor would actually take should they exist. Consider what might have happened, for example, if General McChrystal had told President Obama that sending forty thousand additional troops to Afghanistan would raise the U.S. military's chances of success from ten percent to forty percent (whereas we saw in chapter 1 that General McChrystal justified by Afghan Surge by saying only that sending more troops was "best prospect for success in this important mission"). Assume for the sake of argument that providing a clearer assessment of uncertainty would have surrounded General McChrystal's recommendation with an unjustified illusion of rigor. Would that illusion of rigor have made General McChrystal's recommendation seem more defensible? Or would it have highlighted the prospect of failure and thereby made President Obama likely to have approved the Afghan Surge? I know of no existing studies that attempt to answer these questions. Testing the illusions-of-rigor thesis is thus not simply a matter of gathering empirical evidence—it also requires conducting the basic conceptual legwork of specifying falsifiable claims about what the illusions-of-rigor problem entails.

This problem could take at least three forms. First, illusions of rigor could cause decision makers to become more willing to put lives and resources at risk. This argument builds from the premise that foreign policy officials may be uncomfortable about the prospect of basing life-and-death decisions on subjective judgments. Just as criminal courts forbid convicting defendants without concrete evidence of their guilt, there are clear political and ethical concerns that mediate against using lethal force based on arguable assumptions.[27] If illusions

---

[26] This argument became particularly prominent given the failure of Secretary McNamara's Whiz Kids during the Vietnam War. The orthodox narrative is that the Whiz Kids' use of quantitative analysis lent undeserved credibility to their arguments. Critics of structured analytic techniques for military planning almost always invoke this case as a cautionary tale. We saw in chapter 1, however, how the orthodox narrative gives the Whiz Kids too much credit for their analytic ambitions. Though McNamara's team constructed an unprecedentedly complex system for evaluating tactical outcomes in Vietnam, McNamara himself admitted that he devoted virtually no effort to analyzing the chances that U.S. strategy would ultimately succeed. In this sense, what appeared to be rigorous analysis on the part of McNamara's Defense Department actually ignored the most important elements of uncertainty surrounding escalation in Vietnam.

[27] Prior to the invasion of Iraq, for example, public officials created the impression that the United States possessed reliable intelligence indicating that Saddam Hussein was developing WMDs, whereas those judgments actually depended on circumstantial evidence and questionable informants. If the speculative nature of these judgments had been clearer, then even if senior officials

of rigor lead decision makers to believe they possess a stronger evidentiary basis for evaluating choices under uncertainty, it could increase their willingness to take military action.

A second way to specify the illusions-of-rigor thesis is to say that analytic precision does not necessarily bias decision makers toward supporting or opposing risky actions, but that these illusions amplify the weight decision makers assign to analysts' judgments.[28] When analysts express probabilities more precisely, decision makers may believe that those judgments are more credible. Under this interpretation, clarifying a seemingly *favorable* probability assessment (such as a high chance that a hostage-rescue mission will succeed) could increase decision makers' support for taking action. By contrast, clarifying a seemingly *unfavorable* assessment of uncertainty (such as a high chance that a drone strike will cause collateral damage) could increase decision makers' opposition to taking action.

A third way that illusions of rigor could impair decision making is by reducing decision makers' willingness to gather additional information. This is perhaps the most straightforward implication of the idea that clear probability estimates seem more reliable than they really are. When dealing with uncertainty, decision makers frequently confront a trade-off between acting immediately versus conducting additional analysis. Because conducting additional analysis carries costs—both the direct costs of gathering more information and the opportunity costs of delay—rational decision makers must consider the potential benefits that gathering this additional information might bring. If illusions of rigor lead decision makers to believe that assessments of uncertainty are more reliable than they really are, then this could also cause decision makers to undervalue the benefits of delaying high-stakes choices, thereby encouraging a potentially harmful rush to judgment.

There are thus three distinct ways in which illusions of rigor can potentially degrade the quality of foreign policy decision making. Before we move on to test these claims, however, it worth noting that each of these arguments relies on an

---

in Congress or the Executive Branch still believed that it was likely that Iraq was pursuing WMDs, they might have found it harder to justify pursuing regime change. On how these concerns appear in many areas of political decision making (and on how they form a rational basis for "ambiguity aversion"), see Friedman and Zeckhauser, "Analytic Confidence and Political Decision Making."

[28] For psychological research supporting this perspective in other areas of decision making, see Ido Erev, Gary Bornstein, and Thomas S. Wallsten, "The Negative Effect of Probability Assessments on Decision Quality," *Organizational Behavior and Human Decision Making*, Vol. 55, No. 1 (1993), pp. 78–94; Claudia C. Gonzalez-Vallejo, Ido Erev, and Thomas S. Wallsten, "Do Decision Quality and Preference Order Depend on Whether Probabilities Are Verbal or Numerical?" *American Journal of Psychology*, Vol. 107, No. 2 (1994), pp. 157–172; and Nathan F. Dieckmann, Paul Slovic, and Ellen M. Peters, "The Use of Narrative Evidence and Explicit Likelihood by Decisionmakers Varying in Numeracy," *Risk Analysis*, Vol. 29, No. 10 (2009), pp. 1473–1488.

extremely pessimistic view of the cognitive abilities of foreign policy decision makers. The illusions-of-rigor thesis assumes that foreign policy decision makers can lose sight of the subjectivity that surrounds key assumptions simply as a result of the manner in which advisers express their judgments. It is only possible to confirm or refute this position based on empirical evidence, but it seems hard to believe that serious public servants could so easily misinterpret contentious foreign policy issues.

This is an area where there may in fact be substantial differences between foreign policy and other areas of high-stakes decision making. Much of the existing research on the psychology of assessing uncertainty examines such domains as medicine and sports betting.[29] In these fields, it is often possible to make reasonably scientific judgments on the basis of analyzing large data sets. Thus, when a doctor warns a patient about the potential side effects of undergoing a major procedure, the patient might interpret a numerically precise probability estimate as a signal that the doctor's judgment does, in fact, reflect rigorous research. By contrast, when foreign policy officials debate the chances of success in war, the odds that a drone strike will cause collateral damage, or any other high-stakes issue, it is hard to believe that anyone truly questions the subjectivity of those beliefs. It is thus possible that foreign policy decision making represents a domain in which the illusions-of-rigor problem could be relatively muted. That is indeed what the experimental evidence presented in the remainder of this section suggests.

Experiment 2: Testing the Illusions-of-Rigor Thesis

The key to testing the illusions-of-rigor thesis is to present foreign policy officials with probability assessments that are identical in all ways except for their analytic precision. To conduct such a study, I teamed up with Jennifer Lerner and Richard Zeckhauser. We designed an experiment that presented respondents with the same decision-making scenarios described in the previous section. The key variation across these scenarios was that some of them presented assessments of uncertainty using the National Intelligence Council's words-of-estimative-probability spectrum (see Figure 4.1) and others presented assessments of uncertainty using equivalent numeric percentages.[30]

---

[29] For a review of fundamental research in this field, see Thomas Wallsten, "Costs and Benefits of Vague Information," in *Insights in Decision Making*, ed. Robin Hogarth (Chicago, Ill.: University of Chicago Press, 1990), pp. 28–43.

[30] We translated words of estimative probability into numeric percentages in terms of the round number (multiples of 5 percentage points) that was closest to the midpoint of the range that each word of estimative probability represented. Thus, given that the word "unlikely" spans probabilities from 29 percent to 43 percent, according to National Intelligence Council guidelines, we translated this term into an estimate of 35 percent for the experiment's numeric condition. Of course, there

We administered the experiment to the same group of national security officials from the National War College and non-elite respondents from Amazon Mechanical Turk who participated in experiment 1. Since we anticipated that this study might produce null results—particularly in the neutral scenarios, where we did not expect respondents to have strong reactions to whether the costs of risky actions outweighed the prospective benefits—we also administered the neutral hostage vignette to a separate sample of 199 national security officials recruited from a different National War College cohort.[31] Altogether, we searched for evidence to support the illusions-of-rigor thesis across 407 national security professionals and 1,458 non-elite respondents, who evaluated a total of 5,209 scenarios.

As noted earlier in this section, the first way of specifying the illusions-of-rigor thesis is to hypothesize that making assessments of uncertainty more precise will increase decision makers' willingness to support risky actions. Figure 4.3 shows that the opposite was true across our experiments. All else being equal, we found that survey respondents were *less* likely to support actions whose risks were described using numeric probabilities. This effect was not driven by particularly strong reactions to any given decision problem. If we divide the data into all nine possible vignettes (three separate versions of three distinct scenarios), there is not a single case in which quantifying probability assessments consistently increased support for risky action.[32]

The next way of specifying the illusions-of-rigor critique is to say that clearer probabilistic reasoning should amplify the weight decision makers assign to these cues. If that were true, then we should observe two main findings. First, we should see that clearer probability assessments depress respondents' support for proposed actions most extensively in pessimistic scenarios, which would be consistent with the notion that explicit judgments make bad options seem worse. Second, we should see that clearer probability assessments increase respondents' support for proposed actions in optimistic scenarios, indicating that analytic precision amplifies positive cues.

are many other ways we could have chosen to vary the precision that these judgments entailed. Chapter 1, for example, described how national security analysts often express their beliefs in terms of confidence levels or estimative verbs. However, we expected that any problems associated with illusions of rigor would likely be the most pronounced when comparing the way respondents reacted to the difference between qualitative and quantitative judgments, and so that is where we chose to put our main focus.

[31] Appendix section 2a provides more details on respondent demographics for all four experiments presented in this chapter.

[32] This is also true if we examine the two samples of national security official separately. The findings presented in Figures 4.3 and 4.4 hold in multivariate regression as well. See Friedman, Lerner, and Zeckhauser, "Behavioral Consequences of Probabilistic Precision."

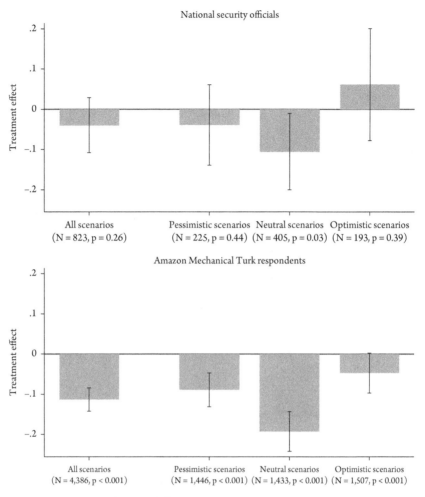

Figure 4.3 How quantifying probability assessments shapes support for risky actions. The figure shows the "treatment effect" associated with providing respondents with probability assessments expressed using numbers instead of words. The bars represent the change in the proportion of respondents who support taking action (with 95 percent intervals).

Figure 4.3 shows that the experimental data refuted both of these predictions. Quantifying probability assessments actually had its strongest impact when it came to reducing support for risky actions in the *neutral* scenarios, and it did not increase support for risky action in the optimistic scenarios. These results show that decision makers do not simply assign greater weight to explicit probability assessments. Instead, we see that clearer probabilistic reasoning caused decision makers to be more careful about taking risks where the evidence was most ambiguous. This is consistent with the idea that assessing uncertainty in clearer and more structured ways makes leaders more sensitive to the risks that

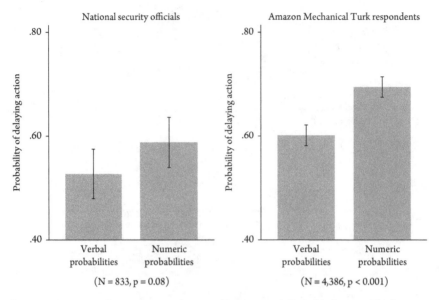

Figure 4.4 How analytic precision shapes willingness to delay risky choices. The figure compares the proportion of respondents who support delaying risky choices to gather more information, based on whether those respondents were provided with probability assessments expressed in verbal versus numeric form. Data shown with 95 percent intervals. AMT = Amazon Mechanical Turk.

high-stakes decisions entail—and it is the opposite of what the illusions-of-rigor thesis would anticipate.

The third way of specifying the illusions-of-rigor thesis is to say that clearer probability assessments should make decision makers less willing to delay action in order to gather additional information. Once again, our experimental data refuted this hypothesis. Figure 4.4 shows that respondents presented with explicit probability assessments were, in fact, *more* interested in gathering additional information before determining whether or not to take risky actions.[33] Concerned with the possibility that such a finding might simply reflect decision makers' confusion in interpreting quantitative assessments, we also asked respondents to rate the level of confidence they had in making their choices. All else being equal, we found that respondents were slightly *more* confident in their ability to make judgments under uncertainty when they were presented with

---

[33] This finding falls just outside the standard $p = 0.05$ threshold for statistical significance in the national security officials sample. Yet this is partly because collapsing survey respondents into binary categories (i.e., whether or not they support delay) sacrifices information. If we instead measure treatment effects using the full seven-point scale respondents used to provide their answers, then the treatment effect for national security officials is statistically significant at $p = 0.002$.

numeric probabilities, though this effect was statistically insignificant among both the national security officials and the non-elite respondents.

To summarize, the first two experiments described in this chapter involved more than 400 national security professionals and nearly 1,500 non-elite respondents. These experiments showed that both elite and non-elite subjects consistently drew upon subjective probability estimates in order to evaluate risky decisions; that even minor changes in assessments of uncertainty had substantively and statistically significant effects on decision makers' willingness to act; that expressing these judgments more precisely did not appear to create harmful illusions of rigor; and that, if anything, clearer assessments of uncertainty made decision makers more sensitive to risk. Each of these findings refutes widespread (but previously untested) skepticism about the extent to which foreign policy decision makers are capable of using subjective probabilities to inform major choices.

Experiment 3: Balancing Calibration and Discrimination

At the same time as we examined how decision makers react to assessments of uncertainty when evaluating foreign policy choices, my colleagues and I conducted a third experiment that explored how analytic precision affects the content of foreign policy analysis itself. To do this, we asked 208 national security professionals and 1,561 AMT respondents to make 35 assessments of uncertainty about international politics.[34] Some of these questions had factual, yes-or-no answers, such as "what are the chances that Russia's economy grew in 2014?" Other questions required making predictions, such as "what are the chances that within the next six months, Syrian president Bashar al-Assad will be killed or no longer living in Syria?"[35] We randomly assigned respondents to estimate these chances using either numeric percentages or the seven-step words-of-estimative-probability spectrum used by the National Intelligence Council.[36]

---

[34] Elite respondents completed a survey containing both this experiment and the decision scenarios from experiment 2 (in random order). This sample of AMT respondents was recruited specifically for this study. See appendix section 2a for more detail on respondent demographics.

[35] The experiment's full question list is in appendix section 2e. All findings in this section are robust to examining forecasts or non-forecasts independently.

[36] Together, these surveys produced a total of 61,901 probability estimates (excepting 14 estimates that were greater than 100 percent, presumably due to typographical errors).

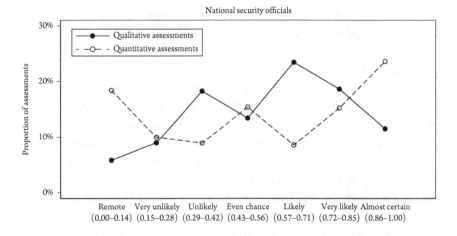

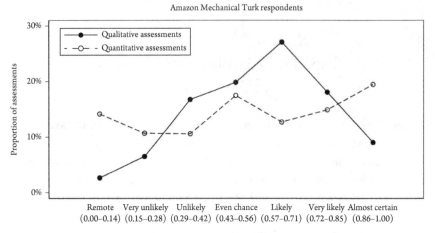

Figure 4.5 Comparing distributions of qualitative and quantitative assessments. The graphs display the frequency with which respondents estimated probabilities with different levels of certitude, depending on whether respondents provided those estimates using numbers versus words.

When we analyzed the data from this experiment, we found that the numeric probabilities respondents provided were not just more precise than the verbal judgments. Instead, we found that the two sets of judgments were distributed in entirely different ways. Figure 4.5 describes this pattern. The black circles in the figure show the frequency with which qualitative assessors employed each word of estimative probability. The graphs show that respondents were most likely to employ terms near the middle of the probability spectrum. The hollow circles in Figure 4.5 plot the frequency with which respondents provided numeric estimates that corresponded to each word of estimative probability. The distribution of these judgments is almost exactly the opposite of what the qualitative assessors reported: those judgments tended to cluster near the edges of the probability spectrum, not the middle.[37]

The remainder of this section explains how these data indicate that foreign policy analysts face a trade-off between discrimination and calibration when assessing uncertainty. As described in chapter 3, *discrimination* reflects the ability to distinguish which outcomes are more likely than others, whereas *calibration* reflects the congruence between probability estimates and observed frequencies. For example, a weather forecaster who always predicts a ten percent chance of rain in an area where it rains on ten percent of the days would demonstrate excellent calibration but no discrimination. If a different weather forecaster said there was a sixty percent chance of precipitation every time it rained and a forty percent chance of precipitation every day it was sunny, then this would reflect perfect discrimination but poor calibration.

We saw in chapter 3 that foreign policy analysts are remarkably effective at discriminating among subjective probabilities. Indeed, chapter 3 showed that foreign policy analysts were so effective at this task that even rough *quantitative* expressions could not capture the distinctions that analysts could reliably draw when assessing uncertainty in international politics. Yet the data shown in Figure 4.5 indicate that providing this level of detail can come at the expense of calibration. This pattern does not appear to reflect a quirk in the data: it is highly statistically significant; it appears in both elite and non-elite samples; and a later part of this section will replicate that finding in another experiment that employed a separate question list.

The discrimination-calibration trade-off is arguably the most important drawback to transparent probabilistic reasoning that we will encounter in this book. And it is important to know what that trade-off entails—in particular, the data presented in this section indicate that verbal and numeric probabilities should not be seen as equivalent expressions, but rather as entirely separate languages for assessing uncertainty. Yet the remainder of this section will show that the discrimination-calibration trade-off mainly appears among low-quality analysts; that mere minutes of feedback can mitigate the problem; and that foreign policy decision makers who are forced to choose between conducting debates in a language that is either highly discriminating or well calibrated should generally prefer the former.

The Discrimination-Calibration Trade-off

In principle, foreign policy analysts should not face a trade-off between discrimination and calibration. The main purpose of developing words-of-estimative-

---

[37] All differences in proportions between qualitative and quantitative assessors in Figure 4.5 are statistically significant at the $p < 0.01$ level.

probability spectrums is to ensure that there are no major discrepancies between qualitative and quantitative judgments. This is why intelligence agencies put so much effort into distributing guidelines that affix words of estimative probability to segments of the number line. If foreign policy analysts actually followed these instructions, then it should be impossible to observe the kinds of patterns presented in Figure 4.5: the only difference between qualitative and quantitative probability estimates is that the latter would be more precise.

Yet, when I interviewed intelligence analysts and other foreign policy officials in the course of researching this book, many of them told me that they made virtually no attempt to ensure that they were using qualitative expressions of uncertainty in the way the relevant guidelines intended. Instead, the analysts said that they tended to translate their beliefs about uncertainty directly into verbal language, without ever attempting to peg this language to numeric reference points. Many could not recall how words of estimative probability were officially defined. Several even rejected the idea that one *can* draw connections between words of estimative probability and numeric probabilities (even though, as we saw in chapter 2, it is always possible to do so).

These reactions suggest that verbal and numeric expressions of uncertainty may not be as closely related in practice as they appear to be on paper.[38] It may instead be more accurate to see these terms as reflecting entirely separate languages for conveying perceptions of uncertainty. And if foreign policy analysts are more comfortable describing their beliefs using a qualitative language, then they might also be better able to calibrate their judgments in that medium. That is why my colleagues and I designed the experiment presented earlier in this section. The data in Figure 4.5 confirmed that these suspicions were correct.[39]

The logic behind the discrimination-calibration trade-off is not unique to foreign policy analysis. For instance, if you have ever taken a political survey during the run-up to a presidential election, you were presumably asked to describe the chances that you would vote. Few pollsters will ask you to answer this question by providing a numeric percentage. Instead, pre-election surveys generally ask respondents to state the probability that they will vote by selecting among a handful of qualitative phrases (e.g., "likely," "almost certainly," and so forth).

---

[38] On persistent discrepancies between the intended and actual definitions of verbal probability estimates, see David V. Budescu, Han-Hui Por, Stephen B. Broomell, and Michael Smithson, "Improving Communication of Uncertainty in the Report of the Intergovernmental Panel on Climate Change," *Psychological Science*, Vol. 20, No. 3 (2009), pp. 299–308.

[39] Friedman, Lerner, and Zeckhauser, "Behavioral Consequences of Probabilistic Precision," refer to this as the "numbers as a second language" problem. For similar ideas in other disciplines, see Wallsten, "Costs and Benefits of Vague Information"; and Alf C. Zimmer, "Verbal vs. Numerical Processing of Subjective Probabilities," in R. W. Scholtz ed., *Decision Making under Uncertainty* (Amsterdam: North-Holland, 1983).

Even though this information is less precise than providing a numeric estimate of the chances that you will head to the polls, survey researchers generally believe that qualitative response scales are less confusing and more reliable.

The broader practice of eliciting survey responses using "feeling thermometers," "rating scales," or other non-numeric tools is usually justified on similar grounds. In each of these areas, scholars deliberately sacrifice their ability to observe fine-grained detail (that is, they sacrifice *discrimination*) because they worry that the act of providing such detail might warp the content of what survey respondents say (and would thus sacrifice *calibration*). Figure 4.5 indicates that a version of this trade-off also appears when researchers are eliciting subjective probability estimates. Specifically, Figure 4.5 shows that foreign policy analysts who express subjective probabilities using numbers instead of words also tend to make those estimates more extreme.

The most plausible explanation for this behavior is that respondents relied on the cut-points between words of estimative probability as anchors for calibrating their judgments. Thus, if a foreign policy analyst thinks that a statement is more probable than not but still far from certain, then she would presumably express this judgment as being "likely" or "very likely" according to the standard words-of-estimative-probability spectrum that we used in our experiment. This analyst's response would thus turn on her perception of whether her judgment falls above or below the boundary between two terms. If she wishes to be cautious, then our analyst might say that her judgment is, simply, "likely." But if we ask her to express that same judgment using numeric percentages, then she would not have a natural benchmark to use when calibrating her judgment. This analyst might say that a judgment that is more probable than not but still far from certain is something like eighty percent. That estimate actually lies beyond the range of values that the word "likely" could plausibly take according to the guidelines that we used in our experiment. This is the sense in which the boundaries between words of estimative probability can provide anchors for restraining the natural inclinations of foreign policy analysts to make their judgments too extreme.

The tendency of foreign policy analysts to attach extra certainty to numeric judgments appears to exact a toll on judgmental accuracy. When we measured judgmental accuracy in terms of each respondent's overall Brier score, then national security officials who assessed uncertainty using words of estimative probability instead of percentages performed 14 percent better than their counterparts (0.230 versus 0.265).[40] Among the AMT respondents, the gap in

---

[40] The appendix describes this methodology in more detail, and explains how these findings are robust to a range of alternative approaches for comparing the accuracy of qualitative and quantitative judgments. The appendix also provides more detail on the relationship between certitude and judgmental accuracy in this experiment.

performance was 11 percent (0.276 versus 0.310). Both findings were statistically significant at the $p < 0.001$ level (that is, the chances that the data would
produce these distinctions through random chance are less than one in a thousand). These patterns hold regardless of respondents' numeracy, gender, language, nationality, age, education, or military experience.[41]

One group of respondents, however, drove these patterns more than others.
In particular, the gap in performance between qualitative and quantitative
assessors in this experiment was almost entirely associated with the worst-
performing analysts in the study. For instance, if we exclude respondents whose
average Brier scores fell into the bottom quartile of their respective samples, then
this eliminates roughly two-thirds of the gap in performance between qualitative
and quantitative assessors.[42] And if we limit the analysis to respondents whose
Brier scores were better than the median within their respective samples, then
there is no longer any statistically significant difference between the Brier scores
associated with qualitative and quantitative assessors.[43] This finding suggests
that, even if some foreign policy analysts face a trade-off between discrimination and calibration when assessing uncertainty, it may not take much talent or
effort to overcome that problem. The next section presents additional data that
supports this view.

Experiment 4: Cultivating Fluency
with Numeric Expressions

The last section showed that verbal and numeric expressions of uncertainty
should not be seen as equivalent to one other, and certainly not as equivalent as
many foreign policy agencies intend. I argued that one should instead conceive
of qualitative and quantitative probabilities as separate languages, and I showed
that some people appear to be more comfortable calibrating their judgments in
the first of these languages over the second. Yet this only raises the question of
how hard it might be to cultivate fluency with the language of subjective probability. To examine that question, I designed a fourth survey experiment that

[41] See Friedman, Lerner, and Zeckhauser, "Behavioral Consequences of Probabilistic Precision,"
for multivariate analysis.

[42] Among national security professionals, dropping the bottom quartile of responses narrows the
gap in Brier scores from 14 percent ($p < 0.001$) to 5 percent ($p < 0.05$). Dropping the bottom quartile
of AMT respondents narrows the gap in performance from 11 percent to 3 percent (both $p < 0.001$).

[43] Non-elite assessors in the quantitative assessment condition returned slightly better Brier
scores ($p = 0.41$). The degradation in performance among numerical assessors in the elite sample is
not statistically significant ($p = 0.31$).

I administered to 183 national security professionals recruited from the National War College and to 1,208 individuals recruited via Amazon Mechanical Turk.[44]

This survey was identical to experiment 3, save for two key differences. First, I gave respondents a new list of questions to answer, so as to replicate the discrimination-calibration trade-off in a different setting.[45] Second, I gave half of the respondents brief training in how to calibrate their assessments of uncertainty.[46] The appendix provides the text of this training material, along with the text of a "placebo treatment" of similar length than was shown to the remainder of the study's respondents.[47] The crucial portion of the training text was just four sentences long:

> In previous experiments, we have found that most people are substantially overconfident when they provide these answers. For example, when respondents have said that they think it is 90% likely that a statement is true, we have found that those statements are actually true about 65% of the time. When respondents have said that they think a statement has a 0% chance of being true, we have found that those statements are actually true about 25% of the time. Overall, we found that 99 out of every 100 respondents would have given more accurate judgments by making those judgments more cautious (that is, by making their estimates closer to 50%).

This information amounted to little more than warning respondents that most previous survey takers had provided overconfident answers. (These data accurately reflected performance in the previous survey experiment.[48]) And since I conducted this experiment using an online survey platform, it was possible to measure exactly how long respondents dwelled on this portion of the survey. On average, respondents were exposed to the full training module for less than two minutes apiece.

Nevertheless, even this brief feedback noticeably impacted respondents' performance. Among the national security professionals who took the survey, respondents who received calibration training received Brier scores that were

---

[44] The elite respondents surveyed in this experiment came from a second cohort at the National War College, surveyed a year after the survey experiments described in prior sections of this chapter. See appendix section 2a for demographic details.

[45] See appendix section 2e for the question list.

[46] The other half of respondents received placebo text of similar length that did not include performance-related feedback. See appendix section 2h.

[47] See appendix section 2h.

[48] Respondents in the qualitative assessment condition received equivalent information, as documented in appendix section 2h.

6 percent better, on average, than those of the respondents who received the placebo treatment. That improvement amounted to roughly one-third of a standard deviation in respondent Brier scores, and it fell just outside the standard threshold for statistical significance ($p = 0.06$). Among the 1,208 AMT respondents who participated in the same experiment, individuals who received calibration feedback provided assessments of uncertainty with Brier scores that were 5 percent better, on average, than their counterparts. This improvement also reflected roughly one-third of a standard deviation in overall performance, and with a much larger amount of data to draw on, this finding was highly statistically-significant ($p < 0.001$).

Figures 4.6 and 4.7 show that this brief training also narrowed the divergence between qualitative and quantitative judgments. Figure 4.7 shows how

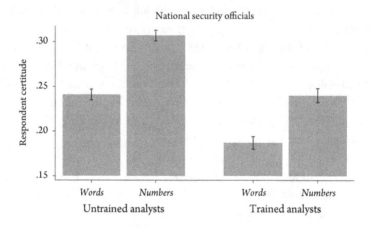

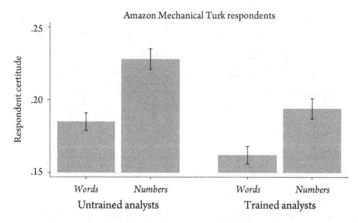

Figure 4.6 How brief calibration training influenced respondent certitude. The graphs display the average levels of certitude (with standard deviations) that respondents attached to their judgments, based on whether or not they assessed uncertainty using words versus numbers, and on whether or not they received brief calibration training.

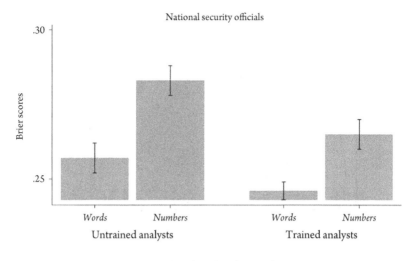

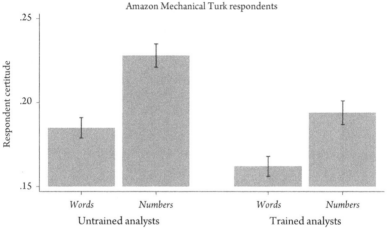

Figure 4.7 How brief calibration training influenced response accuracy. The graphs display respondents' average Brier scores (with standard deviations), based on whether or not they assessed uncertainty using words versus numbers, and on whether or not they received brief calibration training.

respondents who received calibration feedback attached far less certainty to their judgments.[49] Figure 4.8 then shows how this adjustment helped to narrow the performance gap between qualitative and quantitative assessors. Among national security professionals, those two minutes of training closed roughly one-quarter

[49] Among national security officials in the placebo condition, numeric assessors attached an average of 6.6 extra percentage points of certainty to numeric judgments (0.307 versus 0.241, $p <$ 0.001); among national security officials in the training condition, numeric assessments attached an average of 5.2 extra percentage points of certainty to their judgments (0.240 versus 0.187, $p < 0.001$).

Experiment	Participants	Research design	Main findings
Experiment 1:			
How decision makers respond to probability assessments	208 National security officials 1,458 AMT respondents	Vary probability assessments across otherwise-identical decision scenarios	Small variations in subjective probabilities shape DMs' willingness to take risky actions
Experiment 2:			
Do explicit probability assessments create illusions of rigor?	407 National security officials 1,458 AMT respondents	Vary whether DMs receive probability expressed using numbers versus words	Clearer probability assessments make DMs less likely to approve risky actions, especially in close-call scenarios
			Clearer probability assessments make DMs more likely to seek additional information before making risky choices
			No evidence that clearer probability assessments amplify reactions to risk
Experiment 3:			
Discrimination-calibration tradeoff	208 National security officials 1,561 AMT respondents	Vary whether analysts assess probabilities using numbers versus words	Numeric expression exacerbates overconfidence among low-quality assessors
Experiment 4:			
Cultivating fluency with the language of subjective probability	183 National security officials 1,208 AMT respondents	Provide some analysts with 2 minutes of calibration feedback	Brief training substantially mitigates the discrimination-calibration problem

Figure 4.8 Summary of experiments and results. AMT = Amazon Mechanical Turk; DM = decision maker.

of the gap in Brier scores between analysts who assessed probabilities using numbers versus words. Among AMT respondents, the training eliminated this gap almost entirely, with the difference in mean Brier scores between qualitative and quantitative assessors becoming trivial (0.281 versus 0.282) and no longer approaching statistical significance ($p = 0.63$).[50]

Practical Implications of the Discrimination-Calibration Trade-off

Of course, mitigating the discrimination-calibration trade-off is not the same thing as making it go away. And even if brief training could eliminate that trade-off entirely, this would still require effort on the part of foreign policy analysts or organizations. The fact remains that some people are better able to calibrate their assessments of uncertainty in international politics using verbal language. To my knowledge, this is a novel finding. That finding appears to deserve more attention than concerns about illusions of rigor—a widespread argument that received no discernible support from this chapter's experimental data.

There are, nevertheless, three reasons why the discrimination-calibration trade-off does not appear to reflect a major barrier to foreign policy discourse. The first reason is that the discrimination-calibration trade-off appeared mainly among low-quality analysts, particularly those in the bottom quartile of overall performance. These respondents may have shown that they were not intuitively equipped to translate their assessments of uncertainty into numbers, but their performance hardly indicates that serious, talented foreign policy analysts could not manage this challenge if they set their minds to doing so.

We then saw that small amounts of effort indeed make a substantial dent in the discrimination-calibration trade-off. Just two minutes of training significantly mitigated this trade-off among national security officials and entirely eliminated the problem among non-elite respondents. We also saw that brief feedback yielded across-the-board benefits for improving judgmental accuracy.[51]

Among non-elite respondents, the gap in certitude declined from 4.4 percentage points in the placebo condition (0.228 versus 0.185, $p < 0.001$) to 3.3 percentage points in the training condition (0.194 versus 0.161, $p < 0.001$).

[50] See appendix section 2i for full results.

[51] This finding is consistent with research from the Good Judgment Project (GJP). As described in chapter 3, the GJP demonstrated that just one hour of online training in probability assessment produced substantial improvements in forecasting performance that persisted throughout four separate, year-long study periods. See Welton Chang, Eva Chen, Barbara Mellers, and Philip Tetlock, "Developing Expert Political Judgment: The Impact of Training and Practice on Judgmental Accuracy in Geopolitical Forecasting Tournaments," *Judgment and Decision Making*, Vol. 11, No. 5 (2016), pp. 509–526.

Thus, even if providing brief calibration training requires some systematic effort, that effort is surely worth the investment, especially relative to other methods for improving the quality of foreign policy analysis. In previous decades, the U.S. government has repeatedly conducted large-scale organizational overhauls of its Intelligence Community despite ambiguous theoretical and empirical justifications for doing so.[52] If such costly measures are justified on such a contested basis, then it should also be worthwhile to provide analysts with mere minutes or hours of training that have been consistently shown to improve the accuracy of analysts' judgments.

Finally, even if analysts and decision makers *were* ultimately stuck making a trade-off between discrimination and calibration in foreign policy analysis, it would generally be worth privileging the first of these attributes over the second. To see why this is the case, return to the two weather forecasters described earlier. Recall that the first forecaster always predicts a ten percent chance of rain in an area where it actually rains on ten percent of the days. This forecaster is flawlessly calibrated, but she provides no useful information. Because this forecaster always says the same thing—that is, she makes no attempt to discriminate among different probabilities—her advice never helps anyone predict how one day's weather might differ from another's.

The second weather forecaster said that there was a sixty percent chance of precipitation every time it rained and predicted a forty percent chance of precipitation every time it was sunny. These predictions may be poorly calibrated, but they are still extremely useful. In fact, the moment you become aware of this forecaster's tendencies, then her judgments are as good as perfect. Every time this forecaster predicts a sixty percent chance of rain, you know to leave home with an umbrella, and every time she predicts a forty percent chance of rain, you know to leave your umbrella behind.

This is the sense in which consistent discrimination is far more important than consistent calibration when it comes to assessing uncertainty. Discrimination is the hard part: it takes genuine insight to determine which outcomes are more likely than others, especially in domains that are as complex as international politics. Calibration, by contrast, is relatively easy to cultivate. It takes just a few minutes to collect, analyze, and distribute data that describes individual biases

[52] For skepticism regarding the theoretical and empirical basis for organizational intelligence reforms, see Richard A. Posner, *Preventing Surprise Attacks: Intelligence Reform in the Wake of 9/11* (Lanham, Md.: Rowman and Littlefield, 2005); Uri Bar-Joseph and Rose McDermott, "Change the Analyst and Not the System: A Different Approach to Intelligence Reform," *Foreign Policy Analysis*, Vol. 4, No. 2 (April 2008), pp. 127–145; Paul Pillar, *Intelligence and U.S. Foreign Policy: Iraq, 9/11 and Misguided Reform* (New York: Columbia University Press, 2011); and Betts, *Enemies of Intelligence*.

when assessing uncertainty.[53] Thus, while the discrimination-calibration trade-off is real and worth noting, the evidence presented in this chapter suggests that this trade-off should not be viewed as a fundamental cognitive constraint on the quality of foreign policy analysis, but rather as a technical problem that can be dispelled with feasible effort.

Conclusion

We have seen throughout the book how many scholars and practitioners believe that probabilistic reasoning in international politics is either meaningless, counterproductive, or both. Yet chapter 3 demonstrated that foreign policy analysts are, in fact, capable of assessing subjective probabilities with remarkable levels of detail. The evidence presented in this chapter then showed that clear assessments of uncertainty do not appear to mislead decision makers in the manner that conventional wisdom suggests.

After administering four survey experiments to more than six hundred national security officials and over three thousand non-elite respondents, I found no evidence to support the common view that clear assessments of uncertainty in international politics create harmful illusions of rigor. These experiments also refuted concerns that foreign policy decision makers are somehow unable or unwilling to grapple with subjective probabilities when they evaluate risky choices. Instead, the chapter showed that subtle differences in probability estimates convey information that national security officials use to evaluate high-stakes decisions, and that expressing these distinctions more clearly causes decision makers to become more cautious about placing lives and resources at risk. The chapter then showed that, even though some people face a trade-off between discrimination and calibration when assessing uncertainty, this problem appeared mainly among low-quality analysts, and it can be mitigated with mere minutes of effort.

Figure 4.8 summarizes the design, results, and implications of these experiments. In addition to testing specific hypotheses about the psychology of assessing uncertainty in international politics, these studies offer three broad messages.

The first of these messages relates to the state of existing scholarship on the psychology of foreign policy analysis. Throughout the chapter, we have encountered a broad range of arguments about the cognitive constraints that

---

[53] On methods for collecting and evaluating calibration data across foreign policy organization writ large, see Jeffrey A. Friedman and Richard Zeckhauser, "Why Evaluating Estimative Accuracy Is Feasible and Desirable," *Intelligence and National Security*, Vol. 31, No. 2 (2016), pp. 178–200.

hinder probabilistic reasoning in international affairs. These concerns are not just academic matters: questions about proper methods for assessing uncertainty surround nearly every judgment about world politics. Yet we have also seen that scholars and practitioners have generally taken these concerns at face value, without testing the validity of these arguments in systematic ways.

Moreover, it does not take much scrutiny to realize that these arguments are problematic. For instance, we saw at the beginning of the chapter how skeptics often worry that there is no point in assessing subjective probabilities because foreign policy decision makers will simply ignore those judgments. But then we saw how other skeptics worry that decision makers would care *too much* about subjective probabilities, placing excessive weight on assessments of uncertainty that are surrounded by illusions of rigor.

The fact is that, even though uncertainty surrounds nearly any kind of foreign policy analysis and decision making, scholars still know relatively little about the strengths and weaknesses of different methods for addressing this challenge. Widespread views of this issue amount to little more than speculation.[54] Evaluating these claims requires performing substantial theoretical and empirical legwork that the existing literature has not yet provided. One of the primary goals of this chapter has been to supply these debates with stronger conceptual and experimental foundations.

A second overarching message from the chapter is that it is important to distinguish between whether assessing uncertainty is uncomfortable and whether that discomfort actually harms the quality of foreign policy analyses and decisions. Probabilistic reasoning *should* be uncomfortable in foreign policy discourse—it is genuinely unsettling to think that foreign policy decisions require placing lives and resources at risk on the basis on subjective judgments. But this does not mean that foreign policy decision makers literally ignore assessments of uncertainty, or that they cannot comprehend what subjective probabilities mean.

Similarly, even though the chapter has shown that some foreign policy analysts are not automatically comfortable expressing their insights in the language of subjective probability, we have also seen that cultivating fluency in that language is not especially difficult. If anything, the fact that many people are uncomfortable debating assessments of uncertainty is exactly why it is important to develop norms and standard operating procedures that prevent analysts and decision makers from avoiding this challenge. The book's concluding chapter will say more about what these norms and procedures might entail.

---

[54] For more on how widespread assumptions about assessing uncertainty in international politics lack rigorous foundations, see Philip Tetlock, "Second Thoughts about *Expert Political Judgment*," *Critical Review*, Vol. 22, No. 4 (2010), pp. 467–488.

Finally, and most importantly, the findings presented in this chapter rebut common notions that human cognition is somehow unequipped to assess subjective probability in international politics. No one should pretend that this challenge is easy or uncontroversial. But that is true of virtually any element of high-stakes decision making. For practical purposes, the key question is not just how good we are at assessing uncertainty in general, but how we can approach this challenge as effectively as possible. The experiments presented in this chapter have honed wide-ranging concerns about this topic to a specific and previously undocumented trade-off that training can apparently correct. These findings support the book's broader argument that foreign policy analysts and decision makers do best when they confront the challenge of assessing uncertainty head-on, particularly if they are willing to put minimal effort into calibrating their views.

5

The Politics of Uncertainty and Blame

In March 2009, a series of seismic tremors shook the city of L'Aquila, Italy. Italy's National Commission for the Forecast and Prevention of Major Risks met on March 31. The commission observed that low-level tremors generally do not predict the onset of major earthquakes, and concluded that there was no cause for alarm. Within a week, a 6.3-magnitude earthquake struck L'Aquila, killing more than three hundred people. Seven members of the risk commission were subsequently convicted of manslaughter.

Scientists swiftly condemned this verdict. Earthquakes are rare, it is essentially impossible to predict them, and it is true that low-level tremors do not consistently predate major shocks. Punishing analysts for saying as much could encourage them to give inflated warnings, to keep their judgments deliberately vague, or to avoid addressing controversial subjects. Many scientists thus argued that the L'Aquila convictions were not only unfair to the risk commission itself, but that this episode would also discourage experts from assisting with public policy matters moving forward.

Yet the judge who issued the L'Aquila verdict explained that his decision was not, in fact, based on the scientists' inability to predict natural disasters. Instead, he argued that the risk commission had been negligent in offering "vague, generic, and ineffective" information.[1] For example, the official in charge of the commission had said in a press conference that "the scientific community tells me there is no danger," which was not the same thing as saying that small-scale tremors do not reliably signal larger shocks. "I'm not crazy," said the prosecutor in the case—"I know they can't predict earthquakes." The basis for the charges, he insisted, was that the risk commission had overstepped the evidence in appearing to conclusively reject the possibility of an impending crisis.[2]

[1] Liza Davies, "L'Aquila Quake: Italian Judge Explains Why He Jailed Scientists over Disaster," *The Guardian*, January 18, 2013.

[2] Michael Lucibella, "Communication Breakdown Played Role in Scientists' Convictions," *American Physical Society News*, Vol. 21, No. 1 (2012), pp. 1–6.

Of course, Italy's risk commission would surely have come under fire no matter how it had communicated its findings to the public. In the aftermath of crises like the L'Aquila earthquake, the public naturally searches for scapegoats. But that is different from saying that the prospect of criticism prevents public officials from making clear and honest assessments of uncertainty. In the L'Aquila case, the risk commission received special scrutiny for appearing to ignore the uncertainty that surrounded their predictions.

This chapter explains how similar dynamics surround foreign policy analysis. The politics of foreign policy are notoriously adversarial, with critics poised to claim that unpleasant surprises reflect analytic malfeasance. It is widely observed that there are only two kinds of outcomes in international affairs: policy successes and intelligence failures.[3] Many scholars and practitioners thus believe that foreign policy analysts face a trade-off between providing useful assessments of uncertainty and minimizing their exposure to criticism.[4] As a shorthand, the chapter refers to this logic as the *politics of uncertainty and blame.*

It is important to note that concerns about the politics of uncertainty and blame are not purely self-serving. Foreign policy analysts cannot have much influence unless they are perceived to be credible. And analysts who come under fire for making errors can lose their credibility, regardless of whether or not this criticism is deserved. As a former deputy director of national intelligence, Thomas Fingar, puts it, "Criticism has a badly corrosive effect on the confidence in—and the confidence of—the analytic community."[5] Scholars, practitioners, and pundits thus have legitimate reasons to worry about how their errors will be perceived by potential critics.

---

[3] As intelligence scholar John Hedley puts it, "Anything that catches the U.S. by surprise and is bad news is deemed an intelligence failure." Hedley, "Learning from Intelligence Failures," *International Journal of Intelligence and CounterIntelligence,* Vol. 18, No. 3 (2005), pp. 436. See also Paul R. Pillar, *Intelligence and U.S. Foreign Policy* (New York: Columbia University Press, 2011), pp. 175–201; and Philip E. Tetlock and Barbara A. Mellers, "Intelligent Management of Intelligence Agencies: Beyond Accountability Ping-Pong," *American Psychologist,* Vol. 66, No. 6 (2011), pp. 542–554.

[4] On this point, see Philip E. Tetlock and Daniel Gardner, *Superforecasting: The Art and Science of Prediction* (New York: Crown, 2015); John Mueller and Mark G. Stewart, *Chasing Ghosts: The Policing of Terrorism* (New York: Oxford University Press, 2016); and Nate Silver, *The Signal and the Noise: Why Most Predictions Fail—but Some Don't* (New York: Penguin, 2012).

[5] Thomas Fingar, *Reducing Uncertainty: Intelligence Analysis and National Security* (Stanford, Calif.: Stanford Security Studies, 2011), p. 35. This statement holds for professional foreign policy analysts as well as for public intellectuals who seek to inform the marketplace of ideas. Increasing political polarization throughout Western democracies is thus widely seen as driving a so-called death of expertise, as voters lose faith in intellectual elites and become increasingly attached to beliefs having little basis in fact. See, for example, Tom Nichols, "How America Lost Faith in Expertise," *Foreign Affairs,* Vol. 96, No. 2 (2017), pp. 60–73; and Matthew Motta, "The Dynamics and Political Implications of Anti-intellectualism in the United States," *American Politics Research,* Vol. 46, No. 3 (2018), pp. 465–498.

Yet, in principle, this is exactly the kind of problem that transparent probabilistic reasoning should solve. The purpose of assessing uncertainty is to explain what analysts do *not* know, and to emphasize how decision makers *cannot* count on assumptions being true. As we have seen in previous chapters, there is virtually no way to conclude that a single probability assessment is "wrong." And when analysts express probabilities more clearly, they leave less room for critics to misperceive their views.

Moreover, we will see throughout the chapter how the conventional wisdom regarding the politics of uncertainty and blame contains basic contradictions. For instance, if foreign policy analysts were truly judged on the basis of policy outcomes, then they would have no incentive to conceal or to distort their views.[6] The notion that analysts benefit from leaving their judgments vague assumes that adversarial critics are willing to grant analysts the benefit of the doubt when it comes to interpreting what those judgments mean. And in order to believe that foreign policy analysts have an incentive to draw excessively cautious conclusions, one must assume that critics actually care about the nuances of how analysts express uncertainty—which, of course, contradicts the premise that critics automatically treat all unpleasant surprises as analytic failures. The chapter thus explains that the conventional wisdom about the politics of uncertainty and blame is more tenuous than it seems and may in fact get its subject exactly backward: if foreign policy analysts are truly worried about making errors or having their judgments distorted, their best move might be to embrace probabilistic reasoning, rather than to avoid it.

The chapter backs this argument with a combination of qualitative and quantitative evidence. The qualitative evidence explores the historical record of perceived intelligence failures in the United States. With just one clear exception (assessments of the Soviet Union's development of nuclear weapons), we will see that intelligence analysts did not come under fire in these cases as a result of making clear and honest assessments of uncertainty. Quite the opposite, the judgments analysts offered in these cases tended to be to be extraordinarily vague or to avoid important elements of uncertainty entirely. Yet we will see that these practices did not shield analysts from blame in the manner that the conventional wisdom expects. Instead, critics tended to exploit the gaps and ambiguities in intelligence reporting in order to make the Intelligence Community appear more complacent or more mistaken than it really was.

The chapter then replicates this finding through a survey experiment designed to understand why critics evaluate some assessments of uncertainty

---

[6] On how outcome-based evaluations do not necessarily distort analysts' incentives, see Mehmet Y. Gurdal, Joshua B. Miller, and Aldo Rustichini, "Why Blame?" *Journal of Political Economy*, Vol. 121, No. 6 (2013), pp. 1205–1247.

more harshly than others. The data from this experiment revealed that analysts were judged less on the basis of judgmental accuracy than on policy outcomes. Since those outcomes lie outside analysts' control, this is a clear sense in which criticism can be unfair. But we will also see little evidence that this criticism gives analysts any incentive to distort or conceal their judgments. Criticism directed toward foreign policy analysts in this experiment was systematically *lower*, on average, when analysts framed their judgments with explicit probabilities. These data complement the chapter's historical evidence in suggesting that transparent probabilistic reasoning not only improves the quality of foreign policy discourse, but also protects the interests of foreign policy analysts themselves.

Uncertainty and Accountability in Foreign Policy Analysis

It is important in any profession to develop systems of accountability that in-centivize good performance. Yet when incentive structures are poorly designed, they can create more problems than they solve.[7] This dilemma has generated a large body of important research spanning government, medicine, economics, and other disciplines.[8] Within the domain of international politics specifically, major research programs examine how foreign policy officials make choices based on a desire to minimize criticism, to avoid losing elections, or to escape a variety of other personal and political sanctions.[9]

In the decision sciences, the key concept for incentivizing accurate assessments of uncertainty is the *strictly proper scoring rule*. A strictly proper scoring rule rewards analysts for making more accurate assessments and also gives them incentives to report their true beliefs. Chapter 3 explained how scoring rules

---

[7] For a review of foundational literature on this subject, see Jennifer S. Lerner and Philip E. Tetlock, "Accounting for the Effects of Accountability," *Psychological Bulletin*, Vol. 125, No. 2 (1999), pp. 255–275.

[8] On blame avoidance in politics, see R. Kent Weaver, "The Politics of Blame Avoidance," *Journal of Public Policy*, Vol. 6, No. 4 (1986), pp. 371–398, and Christopher Hood, *The Blame Game: Spin, Bureaucracy, and Self-Preservation in Government* (Princeton, N.J.: Princeton University Press, 2011). On defensive decision making in other professions, see Gerd Gigerenzer, *Risk Savvy: How to Make Good Decisions* (New York: Viking, 2014).

[9] On how attempts to sanction leaders for poor performance can end up corrupting incentives, see George W. Downs and David M. Rocke, *Optimal Imperfection?* (Princeton, N.J.: Princeton University Press, 1995); and H. E. Goemans, *War and Punishment* (Princeton, N.J.: Princeton University Press, 2000). On the challenges of oversight in national security analysis and decision making specifically, see Amy B. Zegart, *Eyes on Spies* (Stanford, Calif.: Hoover Institution Press, 2011); Loch Johnson, *Spy Watching* (New York: Oxford University Press, 2017); and Tetlock and Mellers, "Intelligent Management of Intelligence Agencies."

measure accuracy based on *judgmental error*, which is the difference between a probability estimate, and what that analyst would have said had she known the right answer with certainty.[10] Chapter 3 also introduces the Brier score, a strictly proper scoring rule which is based on the square of judgmental error.[11] Since Brier scores measure judgmental error, lower scores are more desirable.

The Brier score can be unfair. For example, consider two analysts who are predicting the outcome of a coin flip. Analyst A states that the coin has a fifty percent chance of turning up heads; Analyst B is certain that heads will be the result. If the coin does indeed turn up heads, then Analyst B would receive a perfect Brier score of zero, and Analyst A would receive the mediocre Brier score of 0.25, even though everyone knows that Analyst A made a more sensible bet.

Yet, even though the Brier score can be unfair, it does not distort anyone's incentives. In the long run, analysts who are evaluated using the Brier score will achieve their best results by reporting their true beliefs. Analyst B may sometimes get lucky by making wild guesses on a coin flip, but when she gets these guesses wrong, she will suffer large penalties. Over the course of many trials, an analyst who continually guesses the outcomes of coin flips with certainty will end up with an expected Brier score of 0.50, which is far worse than Analyst A's expected Brier score of 0.25. Analyst A might thus be justifiably annoyed any time that her counterpart is rewarded for making judgments that are obviously flawed. But Analyst A has no incentive to do anything besides report her true beliefs so long as her performance is being evaluated using the Brier score.

One of the most important takeaways from the study of strictly proper scoring rules is the idea that evaluating assessments of uncertainty requires calibrating criticism in a nuanced manner. If we evaluate probability estimates using a measure that penalizes analysts more harshly than the Brier score does (for example, by taking the cube rather than the square of judgmental error), then this would give analysts incentives to make their estimates excessively cautious, so that they could avoid extreme penalties. If we evaluate probability estimates using a method that is more lenient than the Brier score (for example, by measuring judgmental error itself), then analysts would have incentives to express their estimates with undue

---

[10] If an analyst says that an event has a thirty percent probability and the event does not happen, then her judgmental error for that estimate is 0.30; if the event does take place, then her judgmental error for that estimate is 0.70.

[11] If an analyst says that an event has a thirty percent probability and the event does not happen, then her judgmental error for that estimate is 0.30 and her Brier score is 0.09; if the event does take place, then her judgmental error for that estimate is 0.70 and her Brier score is 0.49.

certainty, so as to reap the highest rewards when their judgments are correct.[12] Of course, it seems hard to believe that critics can strike this kind of balance when it comes to evaluating assessments of uncertainty in foreign policy discourse. Yet the remainder of this section explains how scholars cannot agree on what these distortions actually entail, and how they sometimes offer contradictory views of how these factors shape the politics of uncertainty and blame.

Elastic Redefinition, Intentional Vagueness, and Strategic Caution

There are at least two widespread arguments about how the politics of uncertainty and blame distort foreign policy analysts' incentives. The first of these arguments is that foreign policy analysts can protect themselves from excessive criticism by keeping their assessments of uncertainty intentionally vague. Intentional vagueness supposedly gives analysts the freedom to reinterpret their judgments after the fact. This property is known as *elastic redefinition*.

Consider a case in which analysts are trying to predict whether or not the global price of oil will rise over the next year. If an analyst says that there is an eighty percent chance the global price of oil will be higher a year from now, then it will be easy to determine how much judgmental error this prediction entailed. If the analyst uses vaguer language, such as stating that "the price of oil is liable to increase," then there will always be room to argue about the quality of that statement. If the price of oil goes up, then the analyst can claim credit for making the right call. If the price of oil declines, then the analyst can plead guilty to lesser charges: she might say that her original prediction was more of a fifty-one/forty-nine proposition, or that the word "liable" simply indicated that it was *possible* for oil prices to rise, not that this outcome was ever particularly likely.[13]

Many scholars believe that foreign policy analysts avoid assessing uncertainty in clear and structured ways so that they can preserve elastic redefinition. Mark Lowenthal thus criticizes intelligence officials for filling their reports with

[12] Glenn W. Brier, "Verification of Forecasts Express in Terms of Probability," *Monthly Weather Review*, Vol. 78, No. 1 (1950), pp. 1–3; Edgar C. Merkle and Mark Steyvers, "Choosing a Strictly Proper Scoring Rule," *Decision Analysis*, Vol. 10, No. 4 (2013), pp. 292–304.

[13] M. David Piercey, "Motivated Reasoning and Verbal vs. Numerical Probability Assessment: Evidence from an Accounting Context," *Organizational Behavior and Human Decision Processes*, Vol. 108, No. 2 (2009), pp. 330–341; Andrew Mauboissin and Michael Mauboissin, "If You Say Something Is 'Likely,' How Likely Do People Think It Is?" *Harvard Business Review* (July 2018), available at https://hbr.org/2018/07/if-you-say-something-is-likely-how-likely-do-people-think-it-is, accessed August 2018. Hood, *Blame Game*, provides a broader discussion of "abstinence," when public officials deliberately withhold information or services that could expose them to criticism after the fact.

"weasel words" that reflect "analytical pusillanimity" rather than efforts to provide useful information.[14] Philip Tetlock argues that this problem undermines the quality of foreign policy discourse, both in government and throughout the broader public sphere. "Both private- and public sector prognosticators," he writes,

> must master the same tightrope-walking act. They know they need to sound as though they are offering bold, fresh insights into the future not readily available off the street. And they know they cannot afford to be linked to flat-out mistakes. Accordingly, they have to appear to be going out on a limb without actually going out on one. That is why [foreign policy analysts] so uniformly appear to dislike affixing 'artificially precise' subjective probability estimates to possible outcomes. . . . It is much safer to retreat into the vague language of possibilities and plausibilities."[15]

Another common argument about the politics of uncertainty and blame involves incentives for *strategic caution*. The idea behind strategic caution is that foreign policy analysts can reduce expected criticism by shifting their probability assessments away from certainty. Thus, if an analyst believes there is only a ten percent chance that one country will attack another (or that this outcome is "very unlikely"), she might instead say that this outcome has a thirty percent chance of taking place (or report that this event is simply "unlikely"). That will make her judgment less honest, but it may also help to guard against extreme criticism in the event of surprise.

Many scholars and practitioners believe that this kind of behavior is also widespread throughout foreign policy analysis. John Hedley argues, for example, that "analysts laboring under a barrage of allegations will become more and more disinclined to make judgments that go beyond ironclad evidence."[16] Former National Intelligence Council Chairman Gregory Treverton channels similar concerns in reviewing recent efforts to improve the communication

---

[14] Mark Lowenthal, *Intelligence: From Secrets to Policy*, 3rd ed. (Washington, D.C.: CQ Press, 2006), p. 129. Alan Barnes similarly describes how Canadian intelligence analysts were only willing to participate in a study that involved quantifying probability estimates if researchers ensured that their judgments would only be used for academic purposes, and not for professional evaluations. See Alan Barnes, "Making Intelligence Analysis More Intelligent: Using Numeric Probabilities," *Intelligence and National Security*, Vol. 31, No. 1 (2016), pp. 327–344. On foreign policy analysts' general reticence to provide assessments of uncertainty in a form that could be evaluated objectively, see Jeffrey A. Friedman and Richard Zeckhauser, "Why Assessing Estimative Accuracy Is Feasible and Desirable," *Intelligence and National Security*, Vol. 31, No. 2 (2016), pp. 178–200.

[15] Philip E. Tetlock, "Reading Tarot on K Street," *The National Interest*, No. 103 (2009), p. 67.

[16] Hedley, "Learning from Intelligence Failures," p. 447.

of uncertainty in intelligence analysis. Although these reforms may have encouraged analysts to become more disciplined about sourcing and language, Treverton writes, those gains may have come "at the price, I fear, of making a risk-averse analytic community even more so."[17] This insight captures the core concern surrounding the politics of uncertainty and blame: the notion that well-intentioned attempts to improve assessments of uncertainty can backfire if they expose analysts to excessive criticism.

Questioning the Conventional Wisdom about the Politics of Uncertainty and Blame

Many scholars and practitioners appear to take it for granted that vagueness and strategic caution can shield foreign policy analysts from blame. Yet I am unaware of any study that actually demonstrates these claims systematically. Moreover, the logic behind this conventional wisdom is not as straightforward as it seems at first blush.

Consider, for example, how vague probability assessments allow analysts flexibility for interpreting their own statements after the fact.[18] Although analysts may seek to use this flexibility in favorable ways, it is unclear why critics should accept those interpretations at face value. In order to believe that elastic redefinition shields analysts from blame, it is thus necessary to assume that critics systematically defer to analysts' interpretations of ambiguous statements. That is inconsistent with the notion that critics tend to be reflexively adversarial, which is the main reason why many scholars and practitioners believe that foreign policy analysts seek to avail themselves of elastic redefinition in the first place.

Indeed, if foreign policy discourse is truly as adversarial as many observers believe, then one should expect critics to exploit elastic redefinition, too, by actively portraying analysts' judgments as being worse than they really were. Leaving assessments of uncertainty vague would thus *increase* blame exposure. And even if critics deferred to analyst's interpretations more often than not, the mere prospect of having vague judgments exploited could encourage risk-averse analysts to foreclose that option. The logic of elastic redefinition thus depends not just on the idea that critics generally grant analysts benefit of the doubt, but

---

[17] Gregory F. Treverton, "Theory and Practice," *Intelligence and National Security*, Vol. 33, No. 4 (2018), p. 477.

[18] For evidence that foreign policy analysts naturally avail themselves of this opportunity, and do so in ways that hamper effective learning, see Philip E. Tetlock, "Theory-Driven Reasoning about Plausible Pasts and Probable Futures in World Politics: Are We Prisoners of Our Preconceptions?" *American Journal of Political Science*, Vol. 43, No. 2 (1999), pp. 335–366.

that they do this consistently enough to outweigh the risks of adversarial exploi-tation.[19] The next two sections present historical and experimental evidence that contradicts this claim.

The logic of strategic caution also presumes a substantial degree of for-giveness on the part of supposedly adversarial critics. This logic asserts that critics are willing and able to calibrate political attacks based on semantic nuance. For analysts to have an incentive to say that outcomes are "likely" instead of "very likely" (or that a probability is thirty percent instead of ten percent), they must believe that critics will actually afford greater leniency to judgments that convey less certainty. But why would adversarial critics do that? This perspective is, once again, inconsistent with the notion that critics automatically characterize unpleasant foreign policy surprises as analytic failures.

The logic of strategic caution actually relies on the assumption that critics are *overly* sensitive to nuance when evaluating assessments of uncertainty. As we have seen, strictly proper scoring rules should penalize analysts more harshly for assessments that entail greater degrees of judgmental error, because this is the only way to give analysts an incentive to report their honest beliefs. The Brier score, which is based on the square of judgmental error, is a prime example. In order to assume that the prospect of criticism gives analysts incentives for stra-tegic caution, it is necessary to believe that critics are so sensitive to nuances in probabilistic reasoning that their "penalty function"—the relationship between judgmental error and assigned criticism—accelerates more sharply than the Brier score. This is an extremely specific and nonintuitive claim that no scholar, to my knowledge, has ever tested directly.

Summary and Empirical Agenda

None of the arguments presented in this section refutes the idea that foreign policy analysts receive unfair criticism. The point, instead, is that unfair criticism does not necessarily distort foreign policy analysts' incentives to make clear and honest assessments of uncertainty. At the very least, this section has explained why the politics of uncertainty and blame are much less straightforward than the conventional wisdom suggests. In order to believe that analysts are better-off leaving their assessments of uncertainty intentionally cautious or deliberately

---

[19] In this way, making explicit assessments of uncertainty can be compared to buying insurance against the risk of adversarial exploitation. As with other forms of insurance, risk-averse individuals should be willing to pay costs in order to avoid bad outcomes. The historical review presented in the section shows that analysts can indeed suffer extreme criticism when they leave their assessments of uncertainty vague.

vague, it is necessary to make counterintuitive assumptions about how critics are overly sensitive to nuance and generally willing to grant analysts the benefit of the doubt.

The remainder of the chapter tests those assumptions using qualitative and quantitative evidence. I begin by explaining how the historical record of perceived intelligence failures in the United States is inconsistent with the notion that foreign policy analysts can avoid criticism by making vague assessments of uncertainty. Then I present a survey experiment designed to understand why critics evaluate some probability estimates more harshly than others. Both bodies of evidence suggest that the conventional wisdom exaggerates the obstacles to assessing uncertainty in international politics. If anything, it appears as though foreign policy analysts' aversion to assessing uncertainty in clear and structured ways generally leaves them worse-off, exacerbating unfair criticism instead of providing a bulwark against political attacks.

Uncertainty, Blame, and Perceived Intelligence Failures

This section explores perceived intelligence failures in the United States since World War II. We will see that these perceived failures have almost never involved intelligence analysts making judgments that were overly precise. With just one clear exception (assessments of the Soviet Union's development of nuclear weapons), the assessments that drew criticism were extremely cautious and extraordinarily vague. This section explains how critics have generally exploited this vagueness to make intelligence analysts seem more mistaken than they really were.

Of course, there are clear limitations to analyzing the historical record in this way. We cannot replay events to know what exactly would have changed if intelligence analysts had offered clearer assessments of uncertainty in these cases. And even if clearer assessments of uncertainty would have deflected criticism in these cases, that practice might have triggered blowback elsewhere.

This analysis nevertheless shows that there is remarkably little historical evidence to support the conventional wisdom about the politics of uncertainty and blame. If offering clear and honest assessments of uncertainty exposes analysts to accusations of major failure, then one would expect to see at least *some* consistent evidence of the problem. Yet the remainder of this section shows that the opposite is true. The experimental evidence presented later in the chapter will replicate this claim in a setting that allows for more precise causal analysis.

Absences of Warning

To structure a historical review of the politics of uncertainty and blame, I gathered a list of cases that have been labeled as "intelligence failures" in multiple, peer-reviewed sources.[20] I identified nineteen such cases, which are listed in Figure 5.1. Broadly speaking, we can divide these cases into two groups. The first group can be labeled *absences of warning*. These are episodes in which intelligence analysts were criticized because they did not appear to anticipate strategic problems. Prominent absences of warning include Pearl Harbor, the terrorist attacks of September 11, 2001, and the Arab Spring. The second category of perceived intelligence failures can be labeled *flawed assessments*. These are episodes in which intelligence analysts were criticized for making judgments that later appeared to be inaccurate. Prominent examples of flawed assessments include intelligence reports concerning the October War, the Iranian Revolution, and Iraq's presumed WMD programs.

According to the conventional wisdom surrounding the politics of uncertainty and blame, foreign policy analysts can deflect criticism by leaving their assessments of uncertainty vague. Almost by definition, none of the perceived intelligence failures in the absence of warning category fits this logic. Quite the opposite: if analysts had explicitly assessed the probability of events like Pearl Harbor, 9/11, or the Arab Spring, then there would have been no basis for arguing that the Intelligence Community had failed to consider alternative viewpoints, or that analysts had lacked the imagination to anticipate strategic surprise.[21]

Even if analysts had assigned a low probability to these events—say, just five or ten percent—then it would be much more plausible to characterize these cases as policy failures instead of intelligence failures. For instance, one reason

[20] I compiled this list by conducting searches for the term "intelligence failure" in JSTOR, Google Scholar, and the journals *Intelligence and National Security* and *International Journal of Intelligence and CounterIntelligence*. This section takes no stance as to whether any of these cases truly deserved to be called a "failure," as opposed to the sort of surprises that are inevitable when assessing uncertainty in world politics. On the importance and the difficulty of drawing this distinction, see Richard K. Betts, *Enemies of Intelligence: Knowledge and Power in American National Security* (New York: Columbia University Press, 2007).

[21] These are, respectively, the central argument of Roberta Wohlstetter's criticism of intelligence analysis regarding Pearl Harbor, and one of the main conclusions of the 9/11 Commission's report. See Roberta Wohlstetter, *Pearl Harbor: Warning and Decision* (Stanford, Calif.: Stanford University Press, 1964); and National Commission on Terrorist Attacks Upon the United States [9/11 Commission], *Final Report* (Washington, D.C.: U.S. Government Printing Office, 2004).

Absences of warning: *Cases in which analysts were criticized for not anticipating strategic problems*

Pearl Harbor, 1941: Analysts do not warn that Japan would attack U.S. soil.

Sputnik, 1957: Analysts do not warn that the USSR is preparing to launch a satellite, and are surprised to learn that the Soviets possess the capability to do so.

Tet Offensive, 1968: Analysts do not warn that the Communists will conduct a major offensive in Vietnam, and are surprised to learn that they possess the resources to conduct this attack.

Fall of the USSR, 1989-1991: Analysts do not warn that the Soviet Union faces collapse.

Indian nuclear test, 1998: Analysts do not warn of an impending Indian nuclear test.

Belgrade, 1999: An airstrike inadvertently targets China's embassy.

September 11, 2001: Analysts do not anticipate that al Qaeda will use airplanes as missiles.

Arab Spring, 2011: Analysts do not foresee a wave of uprisings that will topple several regimes.

Flawed assessments: *Cases in which analysts were criticized for making judgments that later appeared to be inaccurate*

Soviet nuclear test, 1949: Analysts believe the USSR is still years from testing a nuclear bomb.

Korean War, 1950: Analysts do not warn that North Korea will invade South Korea.

Chinese intervention in Korea, 1950: Analysts discount warnings that China will intervene in the conflict.

Bay of Pigs, 1961: Analysts downplay the risks of a military operation to topple Fidel Castro.

Cuba, 1962: Analysts believe it is unlikely that the USSR will place nuclear missiles in Cuba.

Czechoslovakia, 1968: Analysts could have provided clearer warning of Soviet invasion.

October War, 1973: Analysts believe it is unlikely that Egypt will invade Israel.

Afghanistan, 1979: Analysts believe the Soviet Union is unlikely to conduct direct military intervention.

Iran, 1979: Analysts believe that popular uprisings pose little threat to the Shah's rule.

Kuwait, 1990: Analysts believe that Saddam Hussein is bluffing in his threats to invade Kuwait.

Iraq, 2002: Analysts mistakenly judge that Iraq is pursuing weapons of mass destruction.

Figure 5.1 Perceived U.S. intelligence failures, 1949–2016.

why Japan's attack on Pearl Harbor was so destructive was that U.S. forces had taken few defensive precautions. U.S. aircraft were parked wingtip-to-wingtip, presenting easy targets for Japanese bombers. Meanwhile, many of the ships stationed at Pearl Harbor sustained damage because their hatches were open on the morning of the attack.[22] If U.S. commanders had been warned before the fact that there was even a small chance of attack, then they could not have later argued that their lack of preparation resulted from having no awareness of the potential threat.

Similar dynamics surround the politics of blame regarding the terrorist attacks of September 11, 2001. In the months leading up to the attacks, the Intelligence Community was well aware that al Qaeda was determined to strike within the United States. The Central Intelligence Agency even wrote an August 2001 briefing for President George W. Bush to that effect. But intelligence analysts did not warn decision makers that al Qaeda might turn airplanes into missiles in order to cause unprecedented damage.

The Intelligence Community's harshest critics argue that it should have been possible to warn the White House about this vulnerability. For example, a Federal Bureau of Investigation (FBI) agent stationed in Phoenix had sent a memorandum to headquarters in July 2001 advising of the "possibility of a co-ordinated effort by Usama bin Ladin" to send al Qaeda operatives to U.S. flight schools. In August, the FBI's Minnesota field office opened an investigation into Zacarias Moussaoui, an extremist who had raised alarm bells when he sought to learn how to fly a Boeing 747 despite lacking the usual qualifications for flight training.[23] Though CIA Director George Tenet was briefed about Moussaoui's suspicious behavior, neither he nor the FBI shared this information with the White House, and the FBI did not grant special priority to these investigations until after the 9/11 attacks had transpired.[24]

Other observers defend the Intelligence Community's performance prior to 9/11 by arguing that signals of airborne terrorism remained ambiguous; that intelligence officials did not have sufficient evidence to prioritize these investigations over countless other threats to national security; and that even if the Intelligence Community had briefed President Bush about al Qaeda's interest in flight training, it would have been politically impossible to take effective

---

[22] Uri Bar-Joseph and Rose McDermott, "Pearl Harbor and Midway: The Decisive Influence of Two Men on the Outcomes," *Intelligence and National Security*, Vol. 31, No. 7 (2016), p. 954.

[23] Moussaoui was in fact working with al Qaeda, and 9/11 pilots Mohamed Atta and Marwan al-Shehhi had visited the same flight school.

[24] 9/11 Commission, *Final Report*, pp. 272–276. For more detail on how the Intelligence Community might have anticipated the 9/11 attacks, see Amy Zegart, *Spying Blind: The CIA, the FBI, and the Origins of 9/11* (Princeton, N.J.: Princeton University Press, 2007).

countermeasures at the time.[25] Yet simply passing along this warning—even with the caveat that it reflected a low-probability threat—would have allowed the Intelligence Community to counter the criticism that its analysts had overlooked the issue, or that they had failed to envision a major strategic vulnerability.

Of course, intelligence analysts cannot ring alarm bells about every possible threat to national security. Analysts who continually predict the occurrence of threats that do not materialize could develop a reputation for "crying wolf" that would undermine their credibility. Yet that is exactly the kind of problem that transparent probabilistic reasoning prevents. Assessing the probability of some event is different from saying that the event will occur (and, in fact, explicitly indicates that the event is *not* guaranteed to take place). If decision makers then determine that these probabilities are not large enough to warrant preventive action, they cannot later claim they had no reason to believe that these threats could materialize.

Assessing Nuclear Weapons Programs in the Soviet Union and Iraq

If there is historical evidence to support the conventional wisdom regarding the politics of uncertainty and blame, it would have to appear in the cases that Figure 5.1 labels flawed assessments: episodes when foreign policy analysts directly addressed some issue on which they later appeared to be mistaken. Intelligence assessments leading up to the 1949 Soviet nuclear test provide one clear example of this dynamic. In 1946, the CIA's Office of Reports and Estimates (ORE) wrote, "It is probable that the capability of the USSR to develop weapons based on atomic energy will be limited . . . [to] sometime between 1950 and 1953."[26] A 1947 interdepartmental intelligence study further argued: "It is doubtful that the Russians can produce a bomb before 1953 and almost certain they cannot produce one before 1951."[27] On August 25, 1949—just five days before the actual bomb test—the CIA's Office of Scientific Intelligence wrote that mid-1950 was the "earliest possible date" and that 1953 was the "most probable date" for that event.[28] After the fact, it is clear that these judgments were well off the

[25] See, for example, Richard Posner, *Preventing Surprise Attacks: Intelligence Reform in the Wake of 9/11* (Lanham, Md.: Rowman and Littlefield, 2005); Pillar, *Intelligence and U.S. Foreign Policy,* pp. 233–280; and Betts, *Enemies of Intelligence,* pp. 104–116.

[26] ORE 3/1, "Soviet Capabilities for the Development and Production of Certain Types of Weapons and Equipment," October 31, 1946.

[27] Interdepartmental Intelligence Study, "Status of the Russian Atomic Energy Product," December 15, 1947.

[28] ISO/SR-10/49/1, "Status of the USSR Atomic Energy Project," August 25, 1949. For discussion of this report and other contemporary analyses, see Donald P. Steury, "How the CIA Missed Stalin's Bomb," *Studies in Intelligence,* Vol. 49, No. 1 (2005).

mark. Intelligence analysts could surely have reduced their exposure to criticism in this case by making their judgments more cautious or by leaving their reasoning vague.

At the same time, we have already seen how vague assessments of uncertainty led to far greater levels of criticism regarding the Intelligence Community's assessments of nuclear weapons programs in Iraq. The 2002 NIE on this subject is often criticized for presenting a "slam dunk" conclusion that Saddam Hussein was pursuing nuclear weapons. This assessment played a major role in public debates about the 2003 invasion of Iraq, and it is now widely seen as one of the most consequential intelligence failures in U.S. history.[29]

It is, however, important to note that intelligence analysts did not actually say that Saddam Hussein was pursuing nuclear weapons. The NIE's crucial judgment said, "We judge that Iraq has continued its weapons of mass destruction programs in defiance of UN resolutions and restrictions." As we saw in chapter 1, the estimative verb, "we judge," is technically supposed to *highlight* the presence of uncertainty—it is the logical opposite of saying that this conclusion was a "slam dunk."[30] The NIE then contained an explicit dissent from the U.S. State Department, highlighting concerns about the lack of concrete evidence to support the claim that Saddam Hussein was building nuclear weapons.

A literal reading of this document would thus grant intelligence analysts a wide berth to explain exactly what they believed. According to the conventional wisdom about the politics of uncertainty and blame, this vagueness should have shielded the Intelligence Community from criticism. Of course, that is not what happened. Most critics of the Iraq NIE simply ignored analysts' use of estimative verbs and pilloried the Intelligence Community for implying false certainty.

This is not to absolve the Intelligence Community for its conclusions regarding Iraq's non-existent WMD programs. Most intelligence agencies—both in the United States and in other countries—believed that Saddam Hussein was building nuclear weapons in 2002.[31] If the NIE's authors had committed their views to paper explicitly, they would surely have assigned this hypothesis a high probability, and their judgment would surely have been criticized after the fact. But even if the NIE's authors had assessed these chances to be as high

---

[29] For an overview of debates surrounding the Iraq NIE, see Jervis, *Why Intelligence Fails*, pp. 123–155; and Fingar, *Reducing Uncertainty*, pp. 89–115.

[30] The "slam dunk" phrase originated when CIA Director George Tenet told President Bush that he could provide enough evidence to convince the American public that Iraq was pursuing weapons of mass destruction. Thus, the "slam dunk" phrase referred to political messaging, not to levels of certainty surrounding intelligence analyses themselves. See George Tenet, *At the Center of the Storm: My Years at the CIA* (New York: HarperCollins, 2007), p. 62.

[31] Robert Jervis, "Reports, Politics, and Intelligence Failures: The Case of Iraq," *Journal of Strategic Studies*, Vol. 29, No. 1 (2006), p. 18.

as eighty or ninety percent, they could not have been accused of concealing the fact that they lacked conclusive evidence.[32] The notion that analysts argued this judgment was a "slam dunk" was always mistaken. The fact that this perception spread so widely throughout public discourse serves as a prime example of how critics can exploit ambiguous language in ways that harm analysts' credibility. The remainder of this section will show how similar dynamics surround several other perceived intelligence failures.

The Bay of Pigs Invasion

The Bay of Pigs invasion is widely seen as one of the worst U.S. foreign policy blunders of the Cold War. This case is also frequently described as an intelligence failure because President Kennedy's advisers failed to provide him with a clearer warning about the invasion plan's flaws. President Kennedy was particularly upset that the Joint Chiefs of Staff had not given him better advice on how to evaluate this decision. Two months after the Bay of Pigs operation failed, President Kennedy wrote a memorandum in which he explained, "I expect the Joint Chiefs of Staff to present the military viewpoint in governmental councils in such a way as to assure that the military factors are clearly understood before decisions are reached."[33]

The Joint Chiefs' assessment of the Bay of Pigs operation is a vivid example of how foreign policy analysts can become targets of criticism as a result of leaving their assessments of uncertainty vague. As we saw in the book's introduction, the Joint Chiefs summed up their views of the invasion plan by writing that it had a "fair chance of ultimate success."[34] We have already seen how the author of this report and Secretary McNamara both claimed that the "fair chance" phrase was supposed to be a warning, yet several members of the Kennedy administration (including the president himself) interpreted the "fair chance" language as a statement of support. But this semantic confusion was only one aspect of the report failed to offer a clear assessment of uncertainty. Upon close inspection of the relevant documents, it turns out that a "fair chance of ultimate success" did not actually refer to the chances that the Bay of Pigs invasion would ultimately succeed.

[32] For similar discussions of this point, see Michael Morell, *The Great War of Our Time: the CIA's Fight against Terrorism from Al Qa'ida to ISIS* (New York: Twelve, 2014), pp. 102–103. Betts, *Enemies of Intelligence*, p. 116; Jervis, *Why Intelligence Fails*, p. 44.

[33] National Security Action Memorandum 55, "Relations of the Joint Chiefs of Staff to the President in Cold War Operations," 28 June 1961.

[34] "Memorandum from the Joint Chiefs of Staff to Secretary McNamara," *Foreign Relations of the United States [FRUS] 1961–1963*, Vol. X, Doc 35 (3 February 1961).

The Joint Chiefs' report began by explaining that its goal was to evaluate the plan "to effect the overthrow of the Castro regime." But in the last paragraph of the document's second appendix, the Joint Chiefs explained that their definition of "ultimate success" only referred to the "objective stated in paragraph 2b." Understanding this cryptic statement requires consulting another section of the report, in which the Joint Chiefs defined that specific objective as "hold[ing] a beachhead long enough to establish a provisional government, act[ing] as a rallying point for volunteers and a catalyst for uprisings throughout Cuba."[35] This outcome was substantially more limited than toppling Fidel Castro, let alone doing so in a manner that concealed U.S. involvement.[36]

Moreover, the Joint Chiefs' assessment only applied to the original concept for the invasion, known as the Trinidad Plan. The concept that the United States actually implemented, known as the Zapata Plan, involved a different order of battle, a new landing site, and substantially less U.S. air support. Neither the Joint Chiefs nor any of President Kennedy's other advisers prepared a formal assessment of the plan that was actually set in motion.[37]

The documents used to justify the Bay of Pigs invasion thus came nowhere near providing a clear assessment of the chances that the invasion would work. Some participants claim that these documents were actually intended to warn the president about the invasion's risks; the assessments applied to tactical outcomes rather than strategic objectives; and these assessments referred to a plan that was substantially different from the one that President Kennedy implemented. According to this conventional wisdom about the politics of uncertainty and blame, these are exactly the kinds of vague, indirect assessment of

[35] *FRUS 1961–1963*, Vol. X, Doc 35 (3 February 1961).

[36] This nuance was clearly lost on some CIA planners. A CIA briefing paper thus states: "The Joint Chiefs of Staff have evaluated the military aspects of the plan . . . . They have concluded that 'this plan has a fair chance of ultimate success' (that is of detonating a major and ultimately successful revolt against Castro)." Although that is the most intuitive way of interpreting the Chiefs' stated views, it is not what their report actually said. "Paper Prepared in the Central Intelligence Agency," *FRUS 1961–1963*, Vol. X, Doc 46 (17 February 1961).

[37] President Kennedy and Secretary McNamara understood that the Joint Chiefs would object to the withholding of air support, in particular, but they did not know how strong this objection would be. Secretary McNamara acknowledged in a post-mortem discussion that "the Chiefs never knew about" the decision to cancel air strikes and that this was an issue about which "they all felt strongly." "Memorandum for the Record," *FRUS 1961–1963*, Vol. X, Doc 199 (3 May 1961). Yet, even after the fact, it is hard to determine what the Joint Chiefs might have said about the last-minute change. Thus, when Joint Chiefs Chairman Lyman Lemnitzer was asked to explain how his assessment of the Zapata Plan might have deviated from the original "fair chance" estimate, he replied: "I could put words together and say that we said that Trinidad had a fair chance and that Zapata had less than a fair chance, but actually we felt that Zapata had a fair chance but of a lower grade than Trinidad." "Memorandum for the Record," *FRUS 1961–1963*, Vol. X, Doc 221 (18 May 1961).

uncertainty that should shield foreign policy analysts from criticism. As historian James Rasenberger puts it, the documentary record in this case reflects "a triumph of bureaucratic equivocation over clarity."[38]

Yet President Kennedy did not grant his advisers any benefit of the doubt when it came to assigning accountability for the invasion's failure. Instead, President Kennedy emerged from this crisis with the view that he could not trust the Joint Chiefs to provide sound advice. "Those sons of bitches," he remarked to an aide, had "just sat there nodding, saying it would work."[39] This was not a stray remark: several historians have argued that this episode created a rift between the president and his uniformed military leadership that continued to grow throughout the early stages of the Vietnam War.[40] Thus, whatever the Joint Chiefs intended to achieve by offering vague and indirect assessments of the Bay of Pigs invasion, their equivocation ultimately backfired, enabling a major foreign policy blunder while eroding credibility with the White House.

The Cuban Missile Crisis

The onset of the Cuban Missile Crisis is often labeled an intelligence failure because the Intelligence Community did not identify the presence of nuclear weapons on the island until five months after their emplacement had begun. Yet the Intelligence Community had frequently addressed the possibility that the Soviets would put missiles in Cuba. A January 1962 Special National Intelligence Estimate argued that such a development was "unlikely" and that, to the Soviets, the value of placing nuclear missiles in Cuba "would probably not be great enough to override the risks involved."[41] A March 1962 NIE similarly stated, "We believe it unlikely that the [Soviet] Bloc will provide Cuba with strategic weapons systems."[42] An August NIE noted Cuba's military buildup but argued it was "unlikely" that the Soviets would provide Cuba "with the capability to undertake major independent military operations" or that "the Bloc will station in Cuba Bloc combat units of any description" within the next year.[43]

Throughout the summer of 1962, the Intelligence Community continued to report on the Soviets' growing military buildup in Cuba, but never changed its

---

[38] James Rasenberger, *The Brilliant Disaster: JFK, Castro, and America's Doomed Invasion of the Bay of Pigs* (New York: Scribner, 2011), p. 119.

[39] Richard Reeves, *President Kennedy: Profile of Power* (New York: Simon and Schuster, 1993), p. 103.

[40] See, for example, H. R. McMaster, *Dereliction of Duty: Lyndon Johnson, Robert McNamara, the Joint Chiefs of Staff, and the Lies That Led to Vietnam* (New York: HarperCollins, 1997), ch. 1.

[41] SNIE 80-62, *The Threat to U.S. Security Interests in the Caribbean Area* (January 17, 1962).

[42] NIE 85-62, *The Situation and Prospects in Cuba* (March 21, 1962).

[43] NIE 85-2-62, *The Situation and Prospects in Cuba* (August 1, 1962).

baseline assessment regarding the prospect of Moscow bringing nuclear weapons to Cuba. In September, the Kennedy administration restricted U-2 overflights of Cuba, fearing that additional surveillance would not be valuable enough to justify the political risk of the U-2s being detected. Director of Central Intelligence John McCone protested this restriction, and when U-2 flights resumed in October, they spotted the Soviet missiles.[44]

The problem with the intelligence assessments was not that they were overconfident or overprecise. Saying that missile emplacement was "unlikely" or that the Soviets "probably" would not think this was worth the risk hardly ruled out the prospect. Yet the analysts' vague language enabled readers, both before and after the fact, to believe that the risk of the Soviets sending nuclear weapons in Cuba was not worth worrying about. Even if intelligence analysts had estimated that there was just a ten percent chance of nuclear missile installation in Cuba, it would have been difficult for decision makers to pass off the blame for failing to study the subject further. Intelligence analysts might still have received criticism for not offering a stronger warning, but they could not have been accused of glossing over major risks.

The October War

Egypt and Syria invaded Israel in October 1973. Although U.S. analysts had tracked the mobilization of Arab armies throughout the year, most national security officials believed that Egypt's President Anwar Sadat was simply orchestrating those moves to create leverage for ongoing political negotiations.

Even if U.S. analysts did not believe that war was likely, they frequently acknowledged that this outcome was possible. For example, a May 1973 NIE titled "Possible Egyptian-Israeli Hostilities" explained that Egypt's military movements "are consistent with both preparations to fight Israel and with political/psychological efforts to stimulate diplomatic activity leading to a settlement." The NIE stated that "substantial Egyptian-Israeli hostilities appear unlikely in the next few weeks"; it warned that "the danger will probably rise if [negotiations] pass without any results" but cautioned that "this does not mean that hostilities will then become inevitable or even probable."[45] All of these statements proved to be true. And while the last phrase implied that conventional war would remain

<hr/>

[44] On the U-2 overflight controversy, see Max Holland, "The 'Photo Gap' That Delayed Discovery of Missiles," *Studies in Intelligence*, Vol. 49, No. 4 (2005), pp. 15–30. On intelligence estimates regarding missiles in Cuba and decision makers' engagement with that information, see Jonathan Renshon, "Mirroring Risk: The Cuban Missile Estimation," *Intelligence and National Security*, Vol. 24, No. 3 (2009), pp. 315–338.

[45] NIE 30-73, *Possible Egyptian-Israeli Hostilities: Determinants and Implications* (May 17, 1973).

unlikely moving forward, it only said that war was not *necessarily* more likely than not. Almost any probability of war in the medium- to long-run would have been consistent with the language of this NIE.

Intelligence reports continued to offer vague and cautious predictions leading up to the war's onset on October 6. A U.S. Intelligence Board estimate from October 4 stated, "We continue to believe that an outbreak of major Arab-Israeli hostilities remains unlikely for the immediate future, although the risk of localized fighting has increased slightly." An October 5 CIA Bulletin described the Egyptian military buildup but argued that it "do[es] not appear to be preparing for a military offensive against Israel." An October 6 Bulletin stated: "For Egypt a military initiative makes little sense at this critical juncture."[46]

Each of these statements indicated that intelligence analysts did not see the outbreak of war as being more likely than not. But none of these statements provided a clear or confident prediction that war would *not* in fact take place. Once again, vague descriptions of uncertainty allowed decision makers to draw the conclusion that the risk was too small to worry about, even though that is not what intelligence analysts had actually said. This is, in fact, one lesson that the CIA itself took away from the crisis: the agency's official post-mortem on its own performance during the October War argued that analysts had offered "rather timid cautionary advice" and that it would have been better to have explicitly assessed the risk of war.[47]

The Iranian Revolution

The Iranian Revolution is often described as an intelligence failure because U.S. analysts failed to understand that opposition forces would topple the Shah until it was too late to intervene. Protests against the Shah began in October 1977, intensified throughout 1978, and then the opposition sacked the government in January 1979. Throughout this period, U.S. analysts had generally assumed that the Shah would crack down on any protests that seriously threatened his rule. The analysts thus interpreted the government's lack of

---

[46] Combined Watch Report of the U.S. Intelligence Board, No. 1206 (October 4, 1973); CIA Bulletin (October 5, 1973); CIA Bulletin (October 6, 1973). For commentary on these and other relevant documents, see Director of Central Intelligence, *The Performance of the Intelligence Community before the Arab-Israeli War of October 1973* (December 20, 1973); and Matthew T. Penney, "Intelligence and the 1973 Arab-Israeli War," in *President Nixon and the Role of Intelligence in the 1973 Arab-Israeli War* (Washington, D.C.: Center for the Study of Intelligence, 2013), pp. 6–13.

[47] The CIA post-mortem is reprinted in Director of Central Intelligence, *Performance of the Intelligence Community before the Arab-Israeli War.*

firmness in handling the situation as evidence that there was no major crisis. As the U.S. Embassy in Tehran explained in August 1978, "At some point, the Shah may be forced to repress an outbreak with the iron fist and not the velvet glove if Iran is to retain any order at all. We have no doubt that he will do so if that becomes essential."[48]

Intelligence reporting throughout this period suggests that analysts took this logic for granted, seemingly dismissing out of hand the prospect of governmental collapse. The National Foreign Assessment Center (NFAC) reported in April 1978 that "the riots, demonstrations, and sabotage in many cities in towns in recent weeks are no threat to government stability." An August 1978 NFAC assessment argued that "Iran is not in a revolutionary or even a 'prerevolutionary' situation . . . this does not at present threaten the government." Reflecting the prevailing view that state repression was the Shah's trump card in reserve, a September 1978 assessment stated that Iranian security forces possessed "a monopoly of coercive force in the country" and thus they retained "the ultimate say about whether the Shah stays in power."[49]

Judged with the benefit of hindsight, these statements demonstrate clear overconfidence. Yet these statements did not really assess uncertainty at all, apparently taking the shah's stability for granted. In his analysis of the episode, Robert Jervis explains that a systematic problem during this period was that intelligence products largely stuck to reporting on current events instead of developing deeper analyses of long-term prospects that might have revealed weak points in the conventional wisdom.[50] Jervis therefore concludes that "the case of Iran reveals a need for analysts to make sharp and explicit predictions."[51] Even if

[48] For post-mortems on intelligence about the Iranian Revolution, see Robert Jervis, *Why Intelligence Fails: Lessons from the Iranian Revolution and the Iraq War* (Ithaca, N.Y.: Cornell University Press, 2010), ch. 2; and William J. Daugherty, "Behind the Intelligence Failure in Iran," *International Journal of Intelligence and CounterIntelligence*, Vol. 14, No. 4 (2001), pp. 449–484. The quote in this paragraph is from Jervis, *Why Intelligence Fails*, p. 70.

[49] These and other relevant assessments are quoted in Jervis, *Why Intelligence Fails*, ch. 2.

[50] For example, the U.S. Intelligence Community did not produce a NIE analyzing the Shah's prospects. Intelligence officials began drafting an NIE during the summer of 1978, but shelved the effort well before potential publication.

[51] Jervis, *Why Intelligence Fails*, p. 46. Jervis (p. 49) furthermore explains how vague estimates not only prevented analysts from conveying uncertainties to decision makers, but that this practice may have also hindered analysts from adapting to new information. Part of the difficulty of analyzing the Iranian protests was that there was no single moment that made clear that faith in the Shah was misplaced. Instead, Jervis writes, discrepant information "arrived bit by bit over an extended period of time." Because analysts never explicitly assessed the probability of regime change, they had no way to keep track of these minor adjustments as they built up over time. This is another reason why Jervis concludes that "explicit predictions would have been especially helpful," allowing analysts to make and account for incremental revisions to the status quo.

analysts had assessed the chances of regime change to be small, they could not have been accused of false certainty or of dismissing the protests' viability out of hand.

Summary

This section has examined the empirical record of perceived U.S. intelligence failures since World War II. Only the 1949 Soviet nuclear test supports the notion that analysts expose themselves to preventable criticism by making clear and honest assessments of uncertainty. In nine other cases, by contrast—the eight absences of warning described in Figure 5.1 and the Iranian Revolution— intelligence analysts received criticism because they did not appear to assess key elements of uncertainty at all. After the Bay of Pigs invasion and the assessments of Iraq's WMD programs, vague assessments of uncertainty backfired by allowing critics to make analysts' judgments seem more mistaken than they really were. And in the cases of the Cuban Missile Crisis and the October War, vague assessments of uncertainty appeared to create the impression that analysts did not believe that high-stakes risks were worth worrying about.[52]

Altogether, this experience suggests that the conventional wisdom about the politics of uncertainty and blame may have it exactly backward: rather than shielding intelligence analysts from preventable attacks, vague probability assessments have generally allowed critics to claim that the Intelligence Community had neglected potential surprises, presented conclusions with false confidence, or downplayed important risks. And despite the inherent limitations of drawing these kinds of inferences directly from the historical record, the next section will replicate these findings in an experimental context where it is possible to draw sharper causal inferences about why critics judge some assessments of uncertainty more harshly than others.

---

[52] The other five cases provide less insight into the politics of uncertainty in blame, but they are generally consistent with the notion that decision makers interpret vague assessments of low probabilities as an indication that a risk is not worth worrying about. In some cases, as with the Soviet invasion of Czechoslovakia or Saddam Hussein's invasion of Kuwait, intelligence analysts *did* provide decision makers with relatively clear advance warnings, supporting the argument that the politics of uncertainty and blame have less to do with analysts' actual assessments than with policy outcomes that are outside their control. See Jeffrey A. Friedman, "Probability Assessment and National Security Decision Making: The Politics of Uncertainty and Blame," paper presented to the 2016 annual meeting of the American Political Science Association (Philadelphia, Penn.).

Experimental Evidence

In order to gain a clearer picture of the causal dynamics behind the politics of uncertainty and blame, I designed a survey experiment for a nationally representative sample of 3,000 respondents.[53] I chose to focus this experiment on the general public because, out of all of the potential sources of criticism that foreign policy analysts face, I expect the general public to evaluate assessments of uncertainty in a manner that is the least sophisticated and thereby the most problematic. Thus, as with the experiments discussed in chapter 4, I deliberately designed this research in a manner that should be most likely to support pessimistic views about the constraints on assessing uncertainty in international politics.[54]

As explained in chapter 4, survey experiments can never replicate the complexity and intensity of real foreign policy debates. Yet by isolating specific variables within an experimental framework, it is possible to generate rigorous insights about how respondents intuitively evaluate assessments of uncertainty. This method makes it possible to observe how critics naturally calibrate their levels of criticism depending on subtle changes in probability estimates; to compare how much these judgments are shaped by judgmental accuracy as opposed to factors such as policy outcomes; and to examine whether critics intuitively criticize explicit probability estimates more harshly than equivalent qualitative expressions.[55] The results from this experiment reinforce the historical patterns described in the previous section. The data show that vague assessments of

[53] I administered this survey through Survey Sampling International on April 22–23, 2016. Fifty-four percent of respondents were female; 11 percent were black or African American; and 14 percent were Hispanic. Respondents' average age was 44. All results presented in this section are robust to employing survey weights. Unless otherwise noted, the results presented below only include data for the respondents who passed the survey's recall questions. Appendix section 3b demonstrates that all results are robust to including respondents at any level of minimum performance on the recall questions.

[54] Of course, even if we can expect the public to be the least sophisticated critics of national security analysis, their criticism might also be less political than the kinds of adversarial arguments made by elected officials and pundits. As explained in this chapter's first section, however, adversarialism should actually *reduce* incentives to leave foreign policy analysis vague, on the grounds that adversarial critics should be more likely to exploit elastic redefinition to make analysts' judgments seem worse than they really were.

[55] In this respect, the survey experiment presented in this section resembles the manner in which other international relations scholars have examined the determinants of public attitudes toward foreign policy decision making. The literature on "audience costs" in international relations is particularly germane, as the main thrust of this literature is to explore the conditions under which leaders suffer public criticism, and the use of survey experiments to study these dynamics is well-established. See, for example, Michael R. Tomz and Jessica L. P. Weeks, "Public Opinion and the Democratic Peace," *American Political Science Review*, Vol. 107, No. 4 (2013), pp. 849–865; and Joshua D. Kertzer and Ryan Brutger, "Decomposing Audience Costs," *American Journal of Political Science*, Vol. 60, No. 1 (2016), pp. 234–249.

Scenario	Source of uncertainty	Potential error of commission	Potential error of omission
A hostage rescue mission to rescue U.S. captives held by a rebel group	The probability that the hostages are in a suspected location	Placing soldiers at risk if the hostages are not in fact present	Missing an opportunity to rescue the hostages, who could be moved to another location
Restricting commercial air travel in response to a rumored terrorist plot	The probability that the plot is real as opposed to a hoax	Restricting air travel in response to a false alarm would cause unnecessary panic and economic distress	Missing an opportunity to stop a terrorist plot
A proposed arrest of a foreign official suspected of embezzling U.S. development aid	The probability that the suspect is guilty	Arresting an innocent official would cause diplomatic controversy	Missing an opportunity to apprehend a corrupt official
A drone strike targeting a suspected high-ranking terrorist	The probability that the target is an innocent civilian	The drone strike could kill an innocent civilian	Missing an opportunity to kill a high-ranking terrorist

Figure 5.2 Description of scenarios.

uncertainty tend to leave foreign policy analysts worse-off, and that the prospect of criticism does not necessarily distort their incentives in the manner the conventional wisdom suggests.

Experimental Design

The experiment involved four decision scenarios: a proposed hostage-rescue mission, a decision about whether to restrict commercial air travel in light of a rumored terrorist threat, the prospect of arresting a foreign official accused of embezzling U.S. development aid, and a drone strike against a person suspected of being a high-ranking terrorist. Figure 5.2 summarizes key elements of these scenarios, and the appendix provides their full texts.[56]

---

[56] See appendix section 3a.

Each vignette began with a paragraph describing the basic decision problem. For example, here is the first paragraph of the vignette involving a rumored terrorist plot:

> U.S. intelligence analysts receive information about a potential terrorist attack on passenger airliners. Informants warn that terrorists may be preparing use a new form of explosive against several flights departing from California. If this is true, then it poses an immediate threat to passenger safety. However, there are reasons to doubt that the plot is real. In particular, terrorists may be planting false information to trick the U.S. government into restricting air travel, which would cause panic and economic damage.

The next paragraph of each vignette contained four experimental manipulations. First, I randomized whether or not respondents saw probability estimates expressed using numeric percentages or words of estimative probability. This provides direct evidence about how critics respond to elastic redefinition. Next, I randomized what analysts' assessments of uncertainty in these scenarios entailed.[57] This makes it possible to examine the extent to which larger judgmental errors drew greater levels of criticism. I also randomized whether or not decision makers chose to act on the information that analysts provided and whether or not that decision proved to be justified. This makes it possible to determine the extent to which respondents criticized analysts on the basis of policy outcomes, as opposed to the accuracy of the judgments that analysts actually provided.

Here are three different versions of the second paragraph of the terrorism scenario, which provide examples of how these randomized pieces of information would have appeared to survey respondents:

- Analysts conclude that there is a 40 percent chance that this plot is real. Decision makers review the information and decide to halt all flights leaving California for one week. This move costs the airline industry more than $1 billion and creates national alarm. The threat is later revealed to have been a hoax, and stopping air travel appears to have saved no lives.

---

[57] Within each of these conditions, respondents saw a range of possible probability assessments, varying from zero to one hundred percent (and their verbal equivalents). See appendix section 3a for details.

- Analysts conclude that it is unlikely that this plot is real. Decision makers review the information and decide to allow air travel to continue. The threat is later revealed to have been a hoax.
- Analysts conclude that there is a 10 percent chance that this plot is real. Decision makers review the information and decide to allow air travel to continue. Days later, four airliners leaving California are destroyed in explosions, killing several hundred passengers.

After each scenario, the survey asked respondents to say how much criticism analysts deserved for the way they had assessed uncertainty. The survey elicited these responses on scales from zero to one hundred.[58] The mean for this variable was 36, with a standard deviation of 34.[59]

The Downside of Elastic Redefinition

Earlier in the chapter, I explained how the conventional wisdom about the politics of uncertainty and blame posits that foreign policy analysts should receive more criticism for making explicit probability assessments than for offering equivalent, qualitative judgments. I explained how the logic behind this argument is dubious, as it requires supposedly adversarial critics to offer analysts the benefit of the doubt. Then I showed how that claim is inconsistent with the historical record of modern U.S. intelligence failures, in which critics have tended to make vague judgments seem worse than they really were. The experimental data that I collected reinforce the argument that vague probability assessments expose foreign policy analysts to more criticism than they prevent. I found that respondents assigned *less* criticism, on average, to explicit probability assessments. Though this difference was not substantively

[58] Eliciting numeric assessments, rather than using a coarser rating scale, is important for examining potentially nonlinear effects. It is not possible to conduct a direct experimental test of whether public opinion resembles a strictly proper scoring rule without eliciting granular responses.

[59] I chose to ask respondents to provide levels of criticism—as opposed to using a response scale that would have allowed respondents to express both positive and negative impressions—because scholars of blame avoidance in public policy generally assume that pressures to reduce criticism outweigh incentives to claim credit. Scholars also generally believe that this so-called negativity bias is especially strong in national security, where secrecy ensures that analysts' failures are typically more public than their successes. Actions that raise average scores on a feeling thermometer could run contrary to public officials' interests if they intensify negative opinions. Directly eliciting negative opinions is thus the most appropriate way to evaluate the key drivers of the politics of uncertainty and blame. On negativity bias in public policy analysis, see Hood, *Blame Game*, pp. 9–14; and Weaver, "Politics of Blame Avoidance."

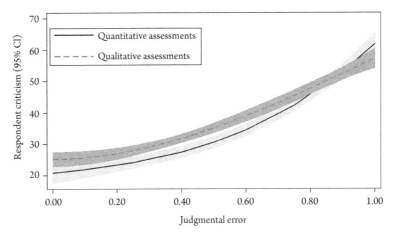

Figure 5.3 Criticism versus judgmental error.

large—roughly three points, on average—it was statistically significant at the $p < 0.01$ level.[60]

Figure 5.3 presents a more granular depiction of how respondents evaluated assessments of uncertainty. The horizontal axis represents judgmental error, and the vertical axis represents the average level of criticism that analysts received.[61] Survey respondents almost always assigned higher levels of criticism to analysts who left their probability assessments vague. The only exception to this pattern came when analysts made mistaken judgments with probabilities of either one hundred percent or zero percent (such that their judgmental error reached the maximum of 1.0). Of course, these judgments all expressed *certainty*, not uncertainty. These data thus provide no indication that critics consistently offer foreign policy analysts the benefit of the doubt when assessing vague probability assessments. If anything—and consistent with the historical evidence presented in the previous section—it appears as though the conventional wisdom on this subject has it exactly backward.

[60] These results reflect a two-way, paired sample t-test. I also asked respondents to say how much criticism they believed the *decision makers* deserved in each scenario. Clearer assessments of uncertainty led to small reductions of blame assigned to decision makers, too, an effect that was also statistically significant at the $p < 0.01$ level.

[61] To capture the judgmental error associated with qualitative probability assessments, I randomly assigned each judgment a numeric value inside the range by which the National Intelligence Council defines that term. See chapter 1 on how the National Intelligence Council defines words of estimative probability according to seven equally-spaced segments of the number line. All results presented below hold if I instead defined words of estimative probability using the Director of National Intelligence's guidelines, or interpret verbal terms using the number at the midpoint of each term's respective range.

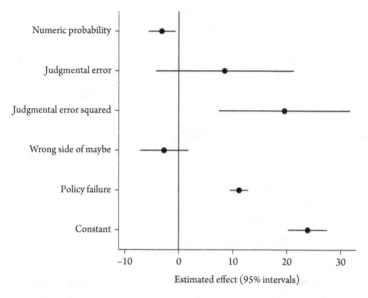

Figure 5.4 Why respondents criticize some assessments of uncertainty more harshly than others. The figure shows the impact each randomized variable exerted on the amount of criticism respondents assigned to foreign policy analysts. Ordinary least squares regression with robust standard errors and respondent fixed effects (N = 5,151).

Multivariate Analysis

To build a more complete picture of the factors that shape the politics of uncertainty and blame, I conducted a multivariate analysis that took the following randomized factors into account: (i) whether analysts expressed their judgments using numbers versus words; (ii) the judgmental error associated with each probability assessment; (iii) the square of judgmental error, which is the key parameter underpinning the Brier score; (iv) an indicator capturing whether or not a probability assessment fell on the "wrong side of maybe," such that its judgmental error exceeded fifty percent; and (v) whether or not decision makers ended up making the right choice on the basis of analysts' assessments.[62]

Figure 5.4 summarizes the results from this analysis.[63] The first row of the figure shows, once again, that respondents assigned less criticism, on average, to numeric probability assessments.[64] The next three lines of Figure 5.4 show that

[62] That is, whether decision makers made one of the errors of omission or commission described in Figure 5.2. If we instead measure the treatment effects associated with errors of omission and commission separately, those effects prove to be nearly identical. In Figure 5.3, those respective coefficients (standard errors) would be 11.51 (1.08) and 10.85 (1.10).

[63] The model is ordinary least squares regression, with robust standard errors and respondent fixed effects.

[64] This finding is statistically significant at the $p = 0.01$ level.

respondents' judgments were not systematically influenced by the crude heuristic of whether or not analysts' judgments fell on the "wrong side of maybe."[65] Instead, we see that criticism increased with the square of judgmental error. Recall that this is how the Brier score operates, too—proper evaluations of probabilistic judgments *should* increase with the square of judgmental error, and we will return to this issue later in the section.

The second-to-last row of Figure 5.4 shows that respondents evaluated foreign policy analysts in a manner that was heavily conditioned by policy outcomes. The coefficient on the "policy failure" variable is very large: it is roughly equivalent to shifting a probability estimate from thirty-three percent to sixty-seven percent (and vice versa), or changing a correct prediction made with certainty to a fifty-fifty judgment.[66] These results thus show how the way respondents evaluated foreign policy analysts was far more sensitive to the outcomes of the decision makers' choices than to the content of the judgments that the analysts actually made. This fact may be unfair to analysts. But, as we saw earlier in the chapter, it contradicts the idea that analysts possess strong incentives to distort the content of their judgments.[67]

To my knowledge, the data shown in Figure 5.4 provide the first systematic picture of the public's intuitive "penalty function" for evaluating assessments of uncertainty. Figure 5.5 then compares this function to a strictly proper scoring rule based on the Brier score.[68] I divided these data into different plots depending on how respondents performed on four recall questions posed at the end of the survey. These questions asked respondents to reproduce specific information about each scenario they had previously seen.[69] We can treat the number of recall questions each respondent answered correctly as an indication of how closely that respondent engaged with the survey. This makes it possible to examine not just how respondents evaluated probability assessments on the

[65] This finding ($p = 0.24$) falls well short of the standard threshold for statistical significance.

[66] Since respondent criticism increased with the square of judgmental error, it is not possible to equate this "outcome failure" penalty to any specific amount of judgmental error. Thus, the penalty associated with an extra ten percentage points' worth of judgmental error would be different depending on the original amount of judgmental error entailed.

[67] Again, see Gurdal, Miller, and Rustichini, "Why Blame?," on this point.

[68] Any multiple of the Brier score is also a strictly proper scoring rule. The right-hand panel of Figure 5.4 thus multiplies the Brier score by a coefficient that minimizes the difference between respondents' data and a strictly proper scoring rule.

[69] These questions were substantially more challenging than simple "attention checks," in which respondents are asked to give a particular answer in order to ensure that they are reading instructions at all. For example, I asked whether survey-takers could recall the specific probability estimate which analysts gave in each case.

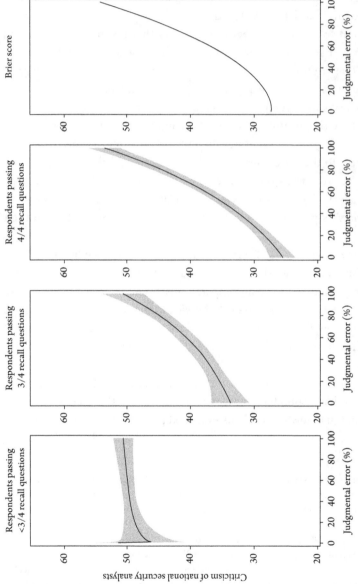

Figure 5.5 Respondents' intuitive scoring rule. The figure plots the relationship between judgmental error and the criticism respondents assigned to those judgments, or what I have called the respondents' "intuitive scoring rule." The first three plots indicate that as respondents pay more attention to the scenarios (as measured by the number of recall questions they passed), their scoring rule becomes steeper and more convex. The fourth panel compares their performance to a strictly proper scoring rule based on a transformation of the Brier score.

whole, but how their evaluations changed as a result of closer engagement with substantive material.

Figure 5.5 shows that the more closely respondents engaged with the details of the survey, the more their responses approximated the Brier score.[70] On the far-left panel of Figure 5.5, plotting data for respondents who answered fewer than three of four recall questions correctly (32 percent of respondents overall), we see that judgmental error only weakly predicts variations in respondent criticism, and that this relationship is essentially linear. In the second panel of the survey, plotting data for respondents who answered three of four recall questions correctly (26 percent of respondents), the relationship between judgmental accuracy and respondent criticism becomes steeper and it accelerates more quickly. In the third panel of the survey, capturing responses from the 42 percent of participants who answered all four recall questions correctly, the empirical relationship between judgmental accuracy and respondent criticism is almost identical to the Brier score.

Conclusion

These patterns refute the common notion that ordinary people lack the capacity to evaluate assessments of uncertainty in reasonable ways. Without any training or special instructions on how to approach this challenge, a nationally representative sample of respondents calibrated their reactions to judgmental error about as well one could possibly hope for. On the whole, these data do not reflect knee-jerk, over-the-top reactions. Instead respondents' views were sensitive to nuance and they rewarded analysts for making judgments that were clearer and more accurate.

Although this is still a far cry from claiming that people are fully rational when it comes to evaluating the quality of foreign policy analysis, these findings contradict a range of prominent concerns about how the prospect of criticism distorts incentives for assessing uncertainty in international politics. If anything, the qualitative and quantitative evidence presented in this chapter suggests that vague probability assessments expose foreign policy analysts to more criticism than they prevent. More generally, the chapter explained that just because foreign policy analysts receive unfair criticism, this does not necessarily distort analysts' incentives to assess uncertainty in clear and structured ways. Perceptions to the contrary appear to reflect another area in which the conventional wisdom exaggerates the obstacles to assessing uncertainty in foreign policy discourse.

---

[70] I plotted these relationships using fractional polynomials, which is a flexible method for defining curves that best fit empirical data.

6

Analysis and Decision

The book's previous chapters have examined the logic, psychology, and politics of assessing uncertainty in international affairs. Those chapters explained how foreign policy analysts can assess subjective probabilities in clear and structured ways that add meaningful information to high-stakes policy debates. This chapter now takes a closer look at how decision makers can use probability assessments to evaluate high-stakes foreign policy choices.

The chapter begins by showing how probabilistic reasoning can inform foreign policy choices through a logic called "break-even analysis." Then the chapter presents a longer and more nuanced argument that explains how subjective probabilities are especially important when it comes to evaluating foreign policy decisions that play out over extended periods of time. In some cases, it can actually be impossible to make rigorous judgments about the extent to which policies are making acceptable progress without assessing subjective probabilities in detail. This argument is significant because it departs from a large body of existing scholarship on learning in international politics which assumes that leaders can use a straightforward logic of trial and error to determine to update their beliefs about policy effectiveness. In this way, the chapter explains that even rationalist scholars of international politics underestimate the importance of transparent probabilistic reasoning in foreign policy analysis.

Probability Assessment and Break-Even Analysis

The central challenge of decision making under uncertainty is to determine whether or not an action's expected benefits exceed its expected costs.[1] If we

---

[1] Another key element of decision making under uncertainty, which the chapter does not discuss, involves determining whether it is better to decide on a course of action immediately as opposed to delaying that choice in order to gather additional information. To simplify this discussion, the chapter treats the opportunity costs of forgoing additional information as only one component of a decision's

use the letter C to represent an action's expected costs, the letter B to represent the benefits a decision maker expects to receive if the action is successful, and the letter p to represent the probability that the action will in fact succeed, then the decision is worthwhile so long as $pB > C$.[2] We can rewrite this expression to say that a decision is worthwhile as long as its probability of success is greater than the ratio of costs to benefits ($p > C/B$).

In an ideal world, decision makers would estimate each of these factors precisely.[3] But that is not actually necessary in order to make sound choices, so long as decision makers can make informed judgments regarding which side of this inequality is greater than the other. The more precisely decision makers estimate *either* their probability of success *or* the ratio of costs and benefits, the more ambiguity they can accept when dealing with the other.

This logic is called *break-even analysis*. The game of poker provides a classic example of how break-even analysis can simplify decision making under uncertainty.[4] The central challenge in poker is determining the chances that your cards are good enough to win the hand. But poker players do not need to determine these chances precisely to make sound bets. Poker players always know how much money they need to bet to stay in the game (C), and they always know how much money they will win if the bet pays off (B). The ratio of these costs and benefits (C/B) is known in poker as "pot odds." As long as players believe that their chances of winning the hand are larger than the hand's pot odds, then it is in their interest to make a bet.

For instance, if there is $100 in the pot and it takes $10 to call, then the benefits of winning the hand will be ten times greater than the costs of attempting to do so. With a cost-benefit ratio of $10/100$ (or 0.10), a player would need to believe that she has more than a ten percent chance of success to make the gamble

---

overall expected costs. For more complete normative foundations of decision making under uncertainty, readers should consult John W. Pratt, Howard Raiffa, and Robert Schlaifer, *Introduction to Statistical Decision Theory* (Cambridge, Mass.: MIT Press, 1995); and Robert L. Winkler, *Introduction to Bayesian Inference and Decision*, 2nd ed. (Sugar Land, Tex.: Probabilistic Publishing, 2003), among others.

[2] A more generalizable version of this logic would be to start by identifying all outcomes a decision might entail, and to estimate the costs and benefits associated with realizing each of those possibilities. This makes the analysis more demanding in a technical sense, but it does not change the basic theoretical logic of break-even analysis.

[3] On the normative foundations for estimating each of these parameters, see Pratt, Raiffa, and Schlaifer, *Introduction to Statistical Decision Theory*.

[4] On the theory of break-even analysis, see Winkler, *Introduction to Bayesian Inference and Decision*, ch. 6. For a rigorous application of this idea in a national security context, see John Mueller and Mark G. Stewart, *Terror, Security, and Money: Balancing the Risks, Benefits, and Costs of Homeland Security* (New York: Oxford University Press, 2011). See also Richard Posner, *Catastrophe: Risk and Response* (New York: Oxford University Press, 2004).

worthwhile.[5] It does not matter whether the player is uncertain about whether her chances of success lie somewhere between twenty percent and forty percent, since every possibility within this range is high enough to clear the break-even point. If, instead, there is $40 in the pot and it takes $20 to call, then a player will need at least a fifty percent chance of success to justify trying to win the hand. Once again, it would not matter if the player is uncertain about whether her chances of success are between twenty and forty percent. All possibilities within this range would now lie *below* the break-even point, and it would be in the player's interest to fold.

Of course, the logic of break-even analysis is harder to apply in areas of decision making, like international politics, where costs and benefits are tough to measure. The national interest is notoriously difficult to define.[6] When President Obama and his advisers met to consider striking Osama bin Laden's compound in Abbottabad, for instance, they would have had to consider the strategic value of damaging al Qaeda, the political value of capturing or killing bin Laden himself, the risk that soldiers and civilians would be harmed in the operation, and the damage that the operation would do to U.S.-Pakistani relations. There is no objective way to measure any of these factors, let alone to combine them into a single index.[7] Thus, while poker players can quickly calculate their "pot odds" for winning any hand, foreign policy decision makers almost always face substantial ambiguity in determining what their chances of success would have to be to make a risky action worthwhile.

In these cases, it can be more useful to conduct break-even analysis from the opposite direction: instead of using the ratio of costs and benefits to determine what the probability of success would need to be to make the choice worthwhile, decision makers can begin by estimating their probability of success, and they can use that judgment to ask what the ratio of costs and benefits would have to look like to justify a risky choice. This approach is attractive because, unlike trying to estimate every factor that plays into the national interest, a decision's probability of success represents a single parameter. As we saw in chapter 2, decision makers can always estimate this parameter precisely if they are willing to approach the challenge in clear and structured ways.

---

[5] I have simplified this discussion by omitting risk preferences. Formally, the costs and benefits in this case are determined by the *utility* that poker players attach to different monetary outcomes, and not the monetary outcomes themselves.

[6] On the "conceptual chaos" of valuing outcomes in international relations, see David A. Baldwin, "Success and Failure in Foreign Policy," *Annual Reviews of Political Science*, Vol. 3 (2000), pp. 167–182.

[7] It is always possible to reduce multi-attribute utility functions to numeric indices, but this is an inherently subjective task. See Ralph L. Keeney and Howard Raiffa, *Decisions with Multiple Objectives: Preferences and Value Tradeoffs* (New York: Wiley, 1976).

We have already seen that President Obama said he thought the odds that bin Laden was living at Abbottabad were similar to a coin flip. This would represent a probability estimate of fifty percent, or 0.50. If a decision is worthwhile when its probability of success is greater than its cost-benefit ratio ($p > C/B$), then as soon as President Obama determined that there was a fifty percent chance that bin Laden was at Abbottabad, he should have also believed that a raid on the compound was justified as long as he thought that the decision's ratio of costs to benefits was less than one-half.[8] This makes it possible to hone President Obama's decision problem to the question of whether or not the prospective benefits of killing or capturing bin Laden were at least twice as large as the prospective costs of sending U.S. forces to Abbottabad.

Making this determination may be inherently subjective, but that is a far cry from saying that the problem is intractable. Indeed, I find it difficult to believe that any senior foreign policy official, if presented with this question directly, would have argued that the benefits of killing or capturing bin Laden were not twice as large as the raid's expected costs. We have also seen how President Obama's assessment of the chances that bin Laden was living at Abbottabad was deliberately cautious. Chapter 2 explained how a simple average of estimates expressed at this meeting would have produced a probability estimate that was closer to two in three. In that case, the raid would have been justified if the benefits of killing or capturing bin Laden were only one-and-a-half times as great as the raid's expected costs.

Of course, the challenges of grappling with the uncertainty surrounding the bin Laden raid did not prevent President Obama from achieving one of his signature national security accomplishments. The episode nevertheless demonstrates how senior leaders struggled with a conceptual challenge that was, in fact, relatively straightforward to resolve. There might have been no "right answer" when it came to estimating the chances that Osama bin Laden was living in Abbottabad (at least, not on the basis of the information available to U.S. leaders at the time). But as long as decision makers are willing to address such ambiguity in a principled manner, they can always use that information to evaluate difficult trade-offs. And there are many other cases in which the struggles that foreign

---

[8] In making this calculation, I have assumed that a Special Forces raid on the Abbottabad compound would certainly kill or capture bin Laden if he were present. As then Secretary of Defense Robert Gates wrote in his memoir, "I had total confidence in the ability of the SEAL team to carry out the mission. My reservations lay elsewhere." Robert Gates, *Duty: Memoirs of a Secretary at War* (New York: Alfred A. Knopf, 2014), p. 540. However, adding uncertainty about the chances of the raid's success would not make the decision problem much more difficult. We could thus reframe the critical probability estimate as being the chances that a Special Forces raid on the compound would kill or capture bin Laden, as opposed to the chances that bin Laden was present.

policy officials encounter in managing similar challenges can meaningfully impact decision outcomes.

For instance, in spring 2014, U.S. intelligence officials learned that Islamic State militants might be holding American citizens hostage in a compound near Raqqa, Syria. Like the intelligence on Abbottabad, the information on the Raqqa compound was suggestive but incomplete, and decision makers reportedly struggled to determine whether the information they had was sound enough to justify taking action. President Obama eventually ordered a Special Forces team to raid the compound in July, but by that point the hostages were gone. U.S. officials concluded that Islamic State militants had moved the hostages less than seventy-two hours before U.S. forces arrived. The Islamic State later broadcast the execution of two of those hostages, James Foley and Steven Sotloff, to a global audience. Public outrage over these executions played a significant role in driving the Obama administration to escalate its military involvement in Iraq and Syria.[9]

Compared to the Abbottabad raid, there is much less publicly available information about the Obama administration's attempt to rescue the hostages in Raqqa. There were also some plausible justifications for delaying the Raqqa mission until early July. For example, some officials later explained that the mission was timed to coincide with a new moon, when darkness would make it easier for U.S. forces to approach the Islamic State compound undetected. Narrowly missing the hostages may have thus had more to do with minimizing the risks to U.S. forces than with the difficulty of determining whether the available intelligence was strong enough to warrant an attempt a rescue mission.

The Raqqa mission nevertheless serves as a cautionary example of how foreign policy officials must make high-stakes decisions under real time pressure. In the Abbottabad case, the Obama administration achieved a major policy success despite months of deliberation. In the Raqqa case, when decision makers confronted similar conceptual challenges in determining whether their assessments of uncertainty justified authorizing a Special Forces mission, saving as little as seventy-two hours might have averted a major foreign policy crisis. These experiences highlight the importance of cultivating efficient methods of making decisions under uncertainty, and the need to avoid unnecessary confusion wherever possible. If decision makers are willing to assess the uncertainty surrounding their choices in clear and structured ways, then there is no reason why these problems should seem intractable.

---

[9] On the details of this hostage-rescue attempt, see Adam Entous, Julian E. Barnes, and Siobhan Gorman, "Intelligence Gaps Crippled Mission in Syria to Rescue Hostages James Foley, Steven Sotloff," *Wall Street Journal*, September 5, 2014; Karen DeYoung, "The Anatomy of a Failed Hostage Rescue Deep in Islamic State Territory," *Washington Post*, February 14, 2015.

Subjective Probability and Strategic Assessment, I

The previous section showed that transparent probabilistic reasoning can provide helpful leverage for evaluating foreign policy decisions. The remainder of the chapter explains that there are some situations in which this kind of reasoning is also logically necessary to make sound choices. The core of this argument is that many foreign policies involve cumulative dynamics that impede forming intuitive judgments about strategic progress. The following sections explain that it can be difficult to draw even rudimentary inferences about this matter without assessing subjective probabilities in detail. Especially since this claim departs from the conventional wisdom among international relations scholars, I develop the theoretical argument over the course of two sections. I then illustrate this argument with examples drawn from the U.S. occupation of Iraq.

Throughout this discussion, I use the term *strategic assessment* as shorthand to describe the challenge that foreign policy decision makers face in judging how long it might take or how much it might cost to achieve their desired goals.[10] A large body of international relations scholarship explores this issue.[11] Much of this literature focuses on rational actors forming and revising beliefs about the viability of military strategies, but similar conceptual challenges surround the application of economic sanctions, democracy promotion, or any other foreign policy that builds toward a strategic objective over time. The central challenge in this field is that, even when foreign policy analysts can directly observe tactical outcomes (such as winning battles in a war), it generally remains unclear how those outcomes relate to a policy's strategic objectives (such as wearing down an opponent's resolve). This is what creates uncertainty about how long it might take or how much it might cost for a foreign policy to succeed.

The most common way that international relations scholars study this issue is to disaggregate armed conflict into "rounds of fighting." (Again, we can apply analogous logic to any other major foreign policy. For instance, the application

---

[10] Two important studies describing the challenges of strategic assessment are Scott Sigmund Gartner, *Strategic Assessment in War* (New Haven, Conn.: Yale University Press, 1997); and Ben Connable, *Embracing the Fog of War* (Santa Monica, Calif.: Rand, 2012).

[11] Prominent examples of the modeling frameworks that I describe in this section include R. Harrison Wagner, "Bargaining and War," *American Journal of Political Science*, Vol. 44, No. 3 (2000), pp. 469–484; Darren Filson and Suzanne Werner, "A Bargaining Model of War and Peace," *American Journal of Political Science*, Vol. 46, No. 4 (2002), pp. 819–838; Branislav Slantchev, "The Principle of Convergence in Wartime Negotiations," *American Political Science Review*, Vol. 97, No. 4 (2003), pp. 621–632; Robert D. Powell, "Bargaining and Learning While Fighting," *American Journal of Political Science*, Vol. 42, No. 2 (2004), pp. 344–361; and Alastair Smith and Allan C. Stam, "Bargaining and the Nature of War," *Journal of Conflict Resolution*, Vol. 48, No. 6 (2004), pp. 783–813.

of economic sanctions could be divided into periods of time, and progress in democracy promotion could be measured over the course of election cycles.) In some models, rounds of fighting reflect individual battles fought to control a particular location or resource, under the assumption that a combatant must surrender once it loses all of the resources in its possession. In other models, a "round of fighting" is more abstract, the basic idea being that every time combatants engage each other in a bout of armed conflict, this induces some chance that either side will collapse. Either way, combatants enter conflict with uncertainty about the chances that they can defeat their opponents in any given round of fighting. Rational decision makers then update their perceptions based on the information they observe as an armed conflict unfolds.

To render this framework tractable, most scholars make a crucial simplifying assumption. This assumption is that, even if combatants are initially uncertain about their chances of defeating an opponent in any given round of fighting, they can at least assume that this probability remains fixed and repeated from one round of fighting to the next.[12] This premise radically simplifies the challenge of strategic assessment, for two reasons. First, every round of fighting in these models provides meaningful information that helps decision makers to form more accurate assessments of their overall strategic prospects.[13] Second, these models allow decision makers to learn and adapt in an intuitive manner, becoming more optimistic about their strategic prospects every time they win a round of fighting and becoming more pessimistic about their strategic prospects every time they conclude a round of fighting without achieving their objectives.[14]

[12] In some models, those probabilities are allowed to change in a manner that is common knowledge. But this is effectively the same as arguing that the probability of success in each round of fighting is a known function of a common parameter, which itself does not change from one round of fighting to the next.

[13] Thus, Smith and Stam, "Bargaining and the Nature of War," p. 627, write: "The act of waging war reveals information about the relative strength of each side." Filson and Werner, "Bargaining Model of War and Peace," p. 820, explain that "war itself provides the information necessary for disputants to reach a settlement to end the war." This notion that war automatically provides credible information is accepted by a broad range of international relations scholars. For example, H. E. Goemans explains that "war makes agreement possible because war provides information . . . . As the war progresses, at least one side must learn that its estimate [of the balance of power] was wrong." H. E. Goemans, *War and Punishment* (Princeton, N.J.: Princeton University Press, 2000), pp. 27–28. Or Dan Reiter, "Exploring the Bargaining Model of War," *Perspectives on Politics*, Vol. 1, No. 1 (2003), p 31, writes: "Combat can reduce uncertainty by providing combatants with information about the actual balance of power."

[14] Slantchev, "Principle of Convergence," p. 627, thus argues that "it is impossible for the uninformed player to become optimistic with time" as combat unfolds. Similarly, Powell, "Bargaining and Learning," p. 349, writes that each time a round of fighting passes without causing an opponent to collapse, a rational decision maker "becomes more confident that it is facing the more powerful type [of opponent] . . . . Indeed, the odds of facing [the more powerful opponent] increase with each round

This approach to modeling strategic assessment reflects the standard logic of what decision theorists call *Bayesian updating*. The logic of Bayesian updating can be described using the following thought experiment. Imagine an urn that contains one hundred marbles. Some of those marbles are blue and the rest are red. Your goal is to guess these marbles' proportion as accurately as possible, but you are not allowed to inspect the urn's contents for yourself. Instead, you will watch as an experimenter reaches into the urn, removes one marble at random, and shows you that marble before returning it to the urn.

Every marble that the experimenter draws in this experiment provides information about the urn's overall mix of colors. For example, imagine that you begin the experiment believing that the urn contains twenty-five red marbles. Yet as the experimenter draws marbles at random from the urn, you note that every marble she produces is blue. The first few times this happens, it may not influence your overall expectations a great deal. Over time, however, the more blue marbles the experimenter draws from the urn, the harder it becomes to believe that one-quarter of the urn's contents are actually red. As the experiment proceeds, you will thus gradually lower your estimate of how many red marbles the urn contains. While the mathematics of Bayesian updating can tell you exactly how much you should adjust your judgment as the experiment proceeds, the basic intuition behind this process is simple. Every time you see a blue marble, it should raise your estimate of the number of blue marbles in the urn; and every time you see a red marble, it should lower your estimate of the number of blue marbles in the urn.

This is basically how international relations scholars model the challenge of strategic assessment. The manner in which these scholars assume that each round of fighting induces the same probability of defeating an opponent is conceptually equivalent to assuming that each draw from the urn produces the same probability of drawing a red marble. When combatants go a round of fighting without defeating their opponents, that is conceptually equivalent to having the experimenter pull a blue marble from the urn. Following the standard logic of Bayesian updating, we can thus infer that every time combatants go a round of fighting without defeating their opponents (or, every time a policy fails to achieve its intended objectives), they should become more pessimistic about their chances of achieving positive outcomes in the future. By contrast, every time a combatant

---

of fighting . . . . This is the sense in which fighting conveys information." Again, it is straightforward to adapt this logic to other policy areas. For example, we could argue that every time an opponent resists the pressure of economic sanctions for a year, it should reduce decision makers' estimates of the chances that the opponent will concede moving forward. Or, we could argue that every time a country holds a corrupt election, this should reduce the perceived chances that this country will conduct a fair contest in the future.

wins a battle (or every time a policy produces some tactical success), that should make her more optimistic about her broader strategic prospects. Mathematical logic can formalize how much decision makers should update these beliefs, but the direction of that updating is straightforward and intuitive.

These assumptions are extremely useful for building game-theoretic models. Yet it is clearly implausible to argue that a military strategy's chances of succeeding remain fixed and repeated over time. For that matter, it is hard to conceive of *any* major foreign policy for which that assumption actually holds, and I am unaware of any scholar who has ever attempted to substantiate such a claim. When leaders design military strategies, apply economic sanctions, pursue democracy promotion, or implement many other major foreign policies, they usually understand that those policies have virtually no chance of succeeding in the short run. Instead, the assumption is that, over time, these policies will make gradual progress toward a desired goal.

For example, when the Johnson administration debated committing U.S. combat forces to Vietnam in 1965 (see chapter 1), few senior officials believed that the Communists would surrender right away. Secretary of Defense Robert McNamara captured the views of U.S. military leaders in writing that "none of them expects the [Viet Cong] to capitulate or to come to a position acceptable to us, in less than six months."[15] Assistant Secretary of State William Bundy similarly argued that "we may have to hang on quite a long time before we can hope to see an improving situation in South Viet-Nam," let alone before the South Vietnamese regime would be able to stand on its own.[16] When intelligence estimates predicted the impact of ground-force commitments, they typically stated that the escalations would not cause the Communists to buckle immediately. "The real test," according to one report, "would be that of combat," and it was only if "the tide of battle runs against the Viet Cong for a substantial period" that the Communists might possibly resort to negotiations.[17]

These statements express a logic that is very different from the standard assumptions international relations scholars use to model strategic assessment, which hold that every round of fighting provides meaningful information that helps decision makers to resolve uncertainty. If McNamara, Bundy, and other senior officials truly believed there was no chance that the Vietnamese Communists would concede in the short run, then the fact that the Communists

---

[15] Robert McNamara to President Johnson, April 21, 1965, *Foreign Relations of the United States, 1964–1968*, Vol. II, Doc 265.

[16] William P. Bundy, "Where Are We Heading?" *Pentagon Papers* (Gravel edition), February 18, 1965, Vol. III, Doc 252.

[17] Directorate of Intelligence, "Memorandum: Reactions to a Further US Buildup in South Vietnam," 10 June 1965: *Estimative Products on Vietnam*, pp. 255–260.

continued to fight throughout this period would not have provided any new information about their capabilities and resolve. Of course, this does not preclude saying that decision makers could have drawn on other kinds of information to revise their beliefs about the chances that their strategy would succeed. The point is instead that the mere act of continued fighting would not have helped the Johnson administration to update its strategic assessments in the straightforward manner scholars have traditionally assumed. This is a clear sense in which the cumulative dynamics of armed conflict depart from conventional wisdom on learning in international politics.

Yet the place where the cumulative dynamics of international politics diverge most sharply from the standard logic of strategic assessment is in how they allow actors to update their beliefs in different directions, even as they observe identical experiences. The next section will describe the theoretical foundations of this claim in more detail. But to build basic intuitions on this subject, consider Napoleon's invasion of Russia in 1812. The French Army won the opening battles in this war. The conventional wisdom on learning in international politics would thus say that Napoleon should have become progressively more optimistic about his chances of continuing to defeat his opponents in future battles, and that Russia should have become progressively more pessimistic about its own strategic prospects. Yet Russia's leaders knew that Napoleon's chances of success would not remain fixed and repeated from one battle to the next. As Napoleon's invasion dragged on, his army lost manpower, supplies, and morale. Indeed, Russia's defensive strategy depended on the notion that these cumulative losses would drain momentum from Napoleon's invasion. In this sense, it was entirely plausible—and, indeed, accurate—for Russian leaders to believe that their strategy was working at a strategic level, even as the Russian Army lost one battle after another.

In principle, scholars could amend standard models of strategic assessment to anticipate this dynamic: for example, by drawing assumptions about how France's probability of winning battles could decline by a particular amount from one round of fighting to the next. In practice, however, there are an infinite number of ways in which one could capture these potential trends, and there is no reason why French and Russian leaders should have held similar perceptions of what those trends entailed.[18] Indeed, the fact that the French and Russian leaders could have held different assumptions about this issue implies that both

---

[18] On the ambiguity surrounding perceptions of relative power, see Jonathan Kirshner, "Rationalist Explanations for War?" *Security Studies*, Vol. 10, No. 1 (2000), pp. 143–150. Slantchev, "Principle of Convergence," p. 623n6, acknowledges that relative power might change from one round of fighting to the next, but states that "it is not clear *a priori*" how this would happen, and so he brackets the issue. Note that the indeterminacy of these relative power shifts is exactly

sides could have simultaneously believed that their strategies were working. If the French leaders believed that their probability of success remained relatively constant from one battle to the next, then they would have seen their early performance as an optimistic indication of eventual strategic victory. Meanwhile, if Russian leaders believed that their probability of success would rise over time, then they might have seen the outcome of these early battles as being largely irrelevant to the war's ultimate outcome. The next section delves further into this argument, showing how these kinds of probability assessments can lead rational decision makers to draw starkly different lessons from observing the same experience.

Subjective Probability and Strategic Assessment, II

Consider a second thought experiment that involves drawing marbles from an urn. There are two differences between this thought experiment and the one presented in the last section. First, your goal in this experiment is not to assess the urn's overall mix of colors, but rather to estimate how many marbles the urn contains. Second, once the experimenter has withdrawn a marble from the urn, she will not put it back. As the experiment proceeds, you will be asked to update your beliefs about how many marbles remain in the urn. The experiment will continue until the urn's contents are exhausted.

To connect this experiment with the theoretical logic of strategic assessment, we can say that the number of marbles in the urn represents the "rounds of fighting" a combatant can sustain before being forced to surrender. The fact that you are uncertain about the number of marbles in the urn represents the difficulty of knowing how long it might take or how much it might cost for a military strategy (or any other major foreign policy) to succeed.[19] The way in which you are asked to revise these perceptions over time thus reflects a different way of framing the challenge leaders face in updating their beliefs about strategic prospects over time.

To ground this logic with a straightforward example, consider that you begin the experiment believing that the urn contains anywhere from ten to one hundred marbles. Figure 6.1 shows how you should update your beliefs as the experiment proceeds. The solid line in Figure 6.1 represents your estimate of the total

what leads the analysis presented in this chapter to depart from conventional models of strategic assessment.

[19] Thus, we could represent this logic in terms of the number of years it might take for economic sanctions to coerce opponents into making a concession, or the number of electoral cycles it might take before a regime is willing to conduct a fair contest.

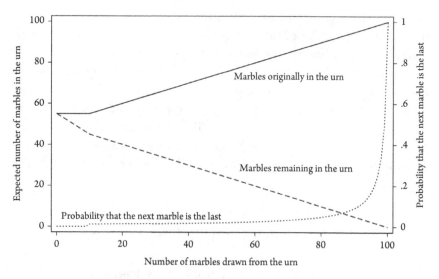

Figure 6.1 Rational updating under cumulative dynamics.

number of marbles that were originally in the urn. For the first ten draws, you should have no reason to update this judgment, because you did not believe that the urn could contain fewer than ten marbles. This is similar to the notion that U.S. officials had no reason to update their beliefs about the breaking point of the Vietnamese Communists as a result of the fighting that immediately followed their decision to escalate the war. We have already seen how this contrasts with conventional notion that every round of fighting should provide rational decision makers with an opportunity to revise their initial assessments of uncertainty.

The dashed line in Figure 6.1 represents your estimate of the number of marbles remaining in the urn. This is equivalent to asking how much longer it will take or how much more it will cost to achieve your intended objectives. Note how the dashed line shows that your estimate of this quantity will continually *decline* as the experiment continues. The intuition behind this pattern is that, even if you initially underestimated the number of marbles remaining in the urn, every draw brings you one step closer to the point where the urn's contents are exhausted. The dotted line in Figure 6.1 represents the probability that the next marble drawn from the urn will prove to be the last. Note that this probability continually *increases* as the experiment continues. Every time the experimenter pulls a marble from the urn, it progressively depletes the urn's remaining contents, just as military officials might assume that every round of fighting degrades an opponent's remaining capabilities and resolve.

The purpose of this thought experiment is not to say that foreign policy decision makers should myopically become more optimistic as they implement their policies. Indeed, one of the central ways in which this theoretical logic departs from the conventional wisdom on strategic assessment is that once we relax the assumption that a policy's chances of success remain fixed and repeated over time, then tactical experience no longer provides unambiguous lessons for evaluating strategic prospects.

To see why this is the case, compare how two different individuals would approach our thought experiment given different sets of prior beliefs. Analyst A has the same initial assumptions represented in Figure 6.1: at the start of the experiment, she believes that the urn contains anywhere from ten to one hundred marbles. By contrast, Analyst B believes that the urn contains *either* ten marbles *or* one hundred marbles. She believes that each possibility is equally likely, but they are the only two outcomes she finds to be credible.

Note that there is a sense in which both analysts start the experiment with similar expectations. Both would begin the experiment by saying that the urn contains fifty-five marbles, on average. But as the experiment proceeds, these analysts will update their beliefs in very different ways. In particular, consider what happens after the experimenter pulls the eleventh marble from the urn. We saw earlier how Analyst A should become slightly more optimistic that the next marble will be the last. But Analyst B would draw a fundamentally different lesson from learning that the urn contains more than ten marbles. Specifically, Analyst B now concludes that the urn originally contained one hundred marbles. Analyst B's estimate of the number of marbles remaining in the urn will thus sharply increase.

Such diverging expectations should be impossible according to the standard logic international relations scholars use to model rational learning. According to this conventional wisdom, two analysts observing the same experience should always agree about how to interpret that information, and thus their overall conclusions should strictly converge over time. But as we have seen, that conclusion depends on the premise that leaders are observing a process in which the probability of realizing some outcome remains fixed and repeated. Once we relax that constraint, we see how rational actors can draw different lessons from observing identical experience.

Figure 6.2 shows that these diverging perceptions can, in fact, emerge as a result of subtle differences in probability estimates. Figure 6.2 demonstrates this point using four graphs.[20] The horizontal axis in each graph indicates different levels of cost that decision makers might have to pay to achieve some strategic objective. We can express this cost using any units we like, such as money, casualties, time, or abstract "rounds of fighting." The shaded regions in

---

[20] For an extended and more formal discussion of these arguments, see Jeffrey A. Friedman, *Cumulative Dynamics and Strategic Assessment*, Ph.D. diss. (Cambridge, Mass.: Harvard University, 2013).

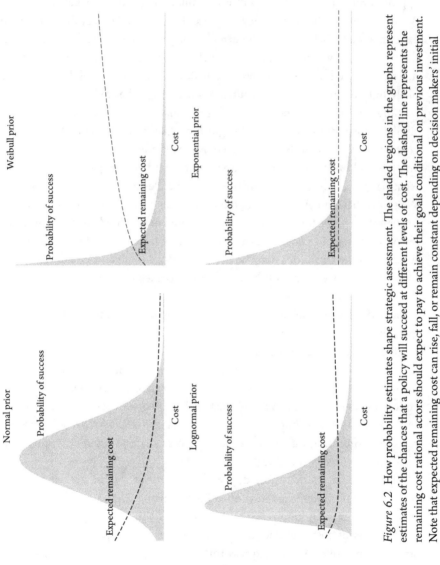

Figure 6.2 How probability estimates shape strategic assessment. The shaded regions in the graphs represent estimates of the chances that a policy will succeed at different levels of cost. The dashed line represents the remaining cost rational actors should expect to pay to achieve their goals conditional on previous investment. Note that expected remaining cost can rise, fall, or remain constant depending on decision makers' initial assumptions.

each graph represent a decision maker's initial perceptions of the chances that a policy will succeed at each potential level of investment. The dashed line in each graph represents a parameter that we can call *expected remaining cost*. This is the amount of further investment rational decision makers would expect to pay before achieving their strategic objectives, conditional on already committing a certain level of resources toward that goal.

The upper-left panel of Figure 6.2 shows how a decision maker should adapt her expectations over time if her initial beliefs about the cost that might be required to achieve her objectives follow a normal distribution: the bell-shaped curve that social scientists often use to model uncertainty.[21] This graph shows how estimates of expected remaining cost will continually decrease for a decision maker whose prior beliefs correspond to the normal distribution. By contrast, the upper-right panel of Figure 6.2 shows how decision makers should adjust their perceptions of uncertainty based on prior beliefs that correspond to the heavy Weibull distribution. A decision maker who holds these initial beliefs about the way her chances of success will rise and fall over time should continually become more pessimistic about expected remaining cost. The bottom-right panel in Figure 6.2 shows how perceptions of expected remaining cost will hold constant over time if a decision makers' prior assumptions follow the exponential distribution.[22] And the bottom-left panel in Figure 6.2 shows how expected remaining cost can fluctuate based on a prior assumption that follows the lognormal distribution. Here, we see that expected remaining cost initially falls, but subsequently begins to rise.

I chose to present the four probability distributions in Figure 6.2 not because I think that they necessarily reflect common assumptions about the uncertainty that surrounds foreign policy decision making, but because these distributions are so similar. The normal and lognormal distributions on the left side of Figure 6.2 are closely related to each other, as are the exponential and Weibull distributions on the right side of Figure 6.2. These graphs thus indicate how subtle differences in probability assessments carry diverging implications for rational learning in international politics.[23]

---

[21] Unlike the assumptions presented in the stylized thought experiments, the normal distribution is unbounded, such that it assigns some probability to every possible value of a given variable (in this case, the cost that leaders might have to pay to achieve their strategic goals).

[22] This provides a more general result, which is that expected remaining cost should only rise when a decision maker's initial assumptions have a heavier tail than the exponential distribution.

[23] There is an extensive debate among international relations theorists over whether rational actors can enter war (or any other form of coercive bargaining) without holding "common priors" about the uncertainty surrounding the resolution of disputes. This debate lies outside the scope of the chapter's analysis. The logic presented here is premised instead on the descriptive observation that combatants often *do* enter armed conflict and other coercive bargaining situations with different expectations about their strategic prospects. For more on the common priors debate in international

Conceptual Summary

This section has examined the logic of strategic assessment in international politics. The discussion focused, in particular, on how tactical outcomes shape perceptions of strategic progress. Of course, this is only one source of information that leaders can use to update their beliefs about the viability of military strategies or other foreign policies. Nevertheless, the relationship between tactical experience and strategic expectations looms large over the theory and practice of international politics. We saw in chapter 1 that the Kennedy and Johnson administrations devoted enormous effort to surveying tactical outcomes in Vietnam, in the hopes that this information would help to optimize U.S. military strategy.[24] And this chapter has described how contemporary scholarship on strategic assessment, in large part, revolves around the question of how leaders can use tactical successes and failures to improve their estimates of how much longer it might take or how much more it might cost to achieve their strategic goals.

This scholarship underestimates the analytic challenges of strategic assessment. The standard approach to this topic assumes that tactical outcomes provide unambiguous signals that naturally eliminate uncertainty about a policy's strategic prospects. Yet this logic relies on the implausible assumption that a policy's chances of success remain fixed and repeated. By relaxing that assumption, this section explained how the strategic lessons that rational actors should draw from tactical outcomes are conditional on their beliefs about how a policy's chances of success might change over time. If leaders do not agree on what those probability estimates entail, then there is no reason to expect their expectations to converge. The chapter's final section illustrates this problem with examples drawn from the U.S. occupation of Iraq.

politics, see Mark Fey and Kristopher Ramsay, "Mutual Optimism and War," *American Journal of Political Science*, Vol. 51, No. 4 (2007), pp. 738–754; Branislav Slantchev and Ahmer Tarar, "Mutual Optimism as a Rationalist Explanation for War," *American Journal of Political Science*, Vol. 55, No. 1 (2011), pp. 135–148; Kirshner, "Rationalist Explanations for War?"; Mark Fey and Kristopher Ramsay, "The Common Priors Assumption," *Journal of Conflict Resolution*, Vol. 50, No. 4 (2006), pp. 607–613, draw a similar distinction between the descriptive fact that combatants often enter disputes without possessing common priors and the normative question of whether or not noncommon priors can be rational.

[24] The recent wars in Iraq and Afghanistan have generated renewed interest in the question of what leaders can (and cannot) learn from collecting these kinds of data. Jim Baker, "Systems Thinking and Counterinsurgencies," *Parameters*, Vol. 26, No. 4 (2006/07), pp. 26–43; Jonathan Schroden, "Measures for Security in a Counterinsurgency," *Journal of Strategic Studies*, Vol. 32, No. 5 (2009), pp. 715–744; Connable, *Embracing the Fog of War.*

Cumulative Dynamics and Strategic Assessment in Iraq, 2003–2011

According to the U.S. Army's official history of the occupation of Iraq, "conditions in Iraq proved to be wildly out of synch with prewar assumptions."[25] Despite the U.S. government's initially optimistic pronouncements that the war would be relatively quick and cheap, the occupation lasted more than eight years. During this time, Iraq experienced one of the longest and deadliest civil wars in modern history. With the return of large-scale violence following U.S. withdrawal, Iraq remains one of the most dangerous countries in the world. In many ways, the history of debates about U.S. strategy in Iraq is a story of how decision makers and their critics struggled to develop a common understanding of these strategic problems.

This section divides debates about U.S. strategy in Iraq into three phases. The first phase took place between the end of conventional operations in April 2003 and the summer of 2006. During this period, critics of the war effort argued that Iraq was becoming a quagmire, while proponents of U.S. strategy believed that they were on track to reversing the trends of rising violence. By the end of 2006, the Bush administration had accepted that its original approach was not viable, and it turned to a new strategy known as the "Surge." This precipitated a second phase of debate, in which the key question was whether or not the Surge could return violence to manageable levels within a feasible time frame. By the end of 2008, with violence in Iraq having fallen to its lowest point since before the invasion, a third phase of debate asked whether Iraq could now sustain its relative stability without direct support from the U.S. military. Figure 6.3 describes how violence trends evolved in Iraq throughout these periods, measured in terms of fatalities sustained both by Coalition Forces and by Iraqi civilians.[26]

In each of these three phases of debate, opponents of the U.S. occupation argued that previous violence trends predicted future events. Thus, when violence in Iraq was high from 2003–2007, critics inferred that U.S. strategy was failing, and when violence settled at lower levels from 2008–2011, they inferred that Iraq was ready to stand on its own. By contrast, proponents of maintaining a robust U.S. presence in Iraq generally based their arguments on the expectation that violence trends were subject to change. When violence was high, they argued that U.S. efforts could precipitate some kind of tipping point that would

[25] Donald P. Wright and Timothy R. Reese, *On Point II: Transition to the New Campaign* (Ft. Leavenworth, Kans.: Combat Studies Institute, 2008), p. 153.

[26] Coalition casualty data are from the website iCasualties.org, Iraq Coalition Casualties Count, http://www.icasualties.org. Iraqi civilian casualties data are from the website Iraq Body Count, http://www.iraqbodycount.org. I downloaded both data sets on October 20, 2016.

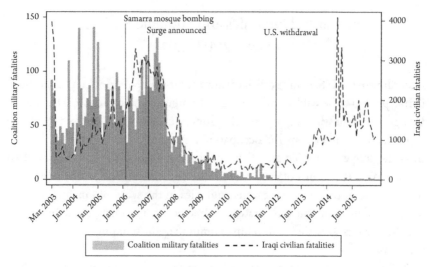

Figure 6.3 Violence trends in Iraq, 2003–2015.

reverse unfavorable trends, and when violence declined, they argued that Iraq's relative stability remained too fragile to last without external support.

My purpose in describing these debates is not to stake claims about which side was correct in evaluating any specific period of the war. The purpose of this section is instead to show how proponents and critics of U.S. strategy each presented internally coherent logics based on diverging beliefs about how long it might take or how much it might cost to create a stable Iraq. These contrasting assessments of uncertainty allowed observers to draw fundamentally different lessons from observing the same experience. Those assumptions were always subjective and open to dispute. But without resolving those disputes, decision makers and their critics could not agree about whether or not U.S. strategy was making progress, let alone whether that progress was sufficient to stabilize Iraq at acceptable cost. This is the sense in which probabilistic reasoning lies at the heart of strategic assessment, and how disputes about this reasoning can prevent drawing even rudimentary judgments about the extent to which foreign policies are worthwhile.

Debating U.S. Strategy in Iraq, 2003–2006

U.S. officials devoted relatively little effort to planning postinvasion operations in Iraq.[27] This was partly because most senior leaders expected that post-invasion

---

[27] On this point, see Aaron Rapport, *Waging War, Planning Peace: U.S. Noncombat Operations and Major Wars* (Ithaca, N.Y.: Cornell University Press, 2015), ch. 3. Other secondary sources that shaped my discussion of this debate include Gordon Rudd, *Reconstructing Iraq: Regime Change, Jay*

operations would be brief and painless. President George W. Bush, Secretary of Defense Donald Rumsfeld, and Director of Central Intelligence George Tenet each acknowledged in their memoirs that they were surprised to see organized violence emerge after U.S. forces ousted Saddam Hussein's regime.[28] Their surprise was widely shared throughout the government. As the U.S. Army's official history of the Iraq War explains, "None of the organizations involved in [the planning] effort came to the conclusion that a serious insurgent resistance would emerge after a successful Coalition campaign against the Baathist regime."[29] Nevertheless, violence in Iraq continually rose throughout the four years following the invasion.

Critics of the war effort saw this trend as indicating that the United States was headed into a quagmire in Iraq. From the beginning of the war, these critics had worried that deposing Saddam Hussein could set off a chain reaction of instability, particularly by unleashing long-standing animosity between the country's Sunni and Shiite populations. Seen from this perspective, the worse Iraq's violence grew, the harder it would be to restrain the vicious cycle of intercommunal fear and reprisal.[30]

Proponents of U.S. strategy in Iraq saw matters differently. To them, the violence in Iraq was a symptom of the country's political problems, especially the lack of a legitimate government and the nationalist resistance to the U.S. military presence. U.S. strategy sought to mitigate these problems by progressively improving Iraq's political and military capabilities, allowing the United States to reduce the size of its "footprint" wherever possible. The expectation was that as the United States transferred responsibility to the Iraqi government, and as the Iraqi government gradually proved its legitimacy, this process would eliminate the grievances that were driving the insurgent violence.[31]

Garner, and the ORHA Story (Lawrence, Kans.: University Press of Kansas, 2011); Michael Gordon and Bernard E. Trainor, *Endgame: The Inside Story of the Struggle for Iraq, from George W. Bush to Barack Obama* (New York: Pantheon, 2012); and Wright and Reese, *On Point II*.

[28] See George W. Bush, *Decision Points* (New York: Broadway, 2010), p. 258; Donald Rumsfeld, *Known and Unknown: A Memoir* (New York: Sentinel, 2011) pp. 520, 664; George Tenet, *At the Center of the Storm: My Years at the CIA* (New York: HarperCollins, 2007), p. 318.

[29] Wright and Reese, *On Point II*, pp. 88–89.

[30] Conceptually, this idea reflected a bimodal conception of uncertainty surrounding strategic prospects in Iraq: if the United States were unable to contain violence at the early stages of the occupation, then the chances of stabilizing the situation would rapidly deteriorate. Thus, the longer that the war dragged on, and the higher that violence climbed, the greater were the chances that the United States was headed into a quagmire.

[31] Gordon and Trainor, *Endgame*, p. 56, thus explain: "At the White House, the hope was that the push toward sovereignty would soothe the Iraqis' grievances over the occupation and take the steam out of the insurgency. Politics, in effect, was to enable the military strategy."

U.S. strategy in Iraq was thereby premised on the notion that current trends did *not* reliably predict future prospects. As Secretary Rumsfeld wrote in a 2005 memorandum to President Bush, the "key question" surrounding the war effort was "when there will be a clearly discernible 'tipping point.' Eventually, more and more Iraqi people will decide that they will no longer side with the enemies of the legitimate Iraqi government and move to the middle. And the people in the middle, at some point, will decide that there is going to be a legitimate, free Iraqi government."[32]

Thus, even as the Bush administration acknowledged that the postinvasion violence had been far more extensive than anticipated, senior officials did not see these trends as reflecting basic flaws in their overall strategy. President Bush wrote in his memoirs that while "the chaos and violence we witnessed were alarming . . . I refused to give up on our plan before it had a chance to work."[33] Meanwhile, the administration pointed to several indicators of Iraq's political progress. Iraqi leaders approved an interim constitution in March 2004. Three months later, Iraq formally regained its legal sovereignty. In January 2005, the country held its first democratic elections. In October 2005, Iraq adopted a new democratic constitution via national referendum.

Of course, none of these events proved to be the turning points for which the Bush administration had hoped. In hindsight, it was clearly wrong to believe that security conditions in Iraq were closely coupled to political benchmarks. But the flaw in this reasoning had little to do with drawing inferences from the violence trends themselves. Rather, the basic question driving debates about U.S. strategy in Iraq was estimating the probability that U.S. and Iraqi efforts could reverse those trends. Critics and proponents of U.S. strategy held different assumptions about whether those chances were growing larger or smaller over time. These assumptions, in turn, led foreign policy analysts to draw different conclusions about the viability of U.S. strategy even though they were observing the same experience. Without resolving the controversy surrounding these assumptions, the Bush administration had no reason to abandon its belief that U.S. strategy was making progress in Iraq. After all, there is nothing inherently implausible about arguing that political and military efforts can help to reverse problematic trends—indeed, that is exactly what happened during the next phase of the conflict.

[32] Donald Rumsfeld, "Progress in Iraq," memorandum to President Bush, 29 November 2005.
[33] Bush, *Decision Points*, p. 259.

Debating the Surge, 2006–2007

The Bush administration began to make fundamental changes to its Iraq policy starting in the fall of 2006. Although it is commonly argued that violence skyrocketed in Iraq during this period, that is not entirely right. As shown in Figure 6.3, trends in both Coalition and civilian casualties throughout 2006 were essentially a continuation of the steady, upward climb that had characterized prior years. What was different about Iraq's violence in 2006 was not so much its trajectory as its character. In particular, it became increasingly difficult to ignore that this violence was rooted in sectarian fear, not just political grievance.

The key event in sparking this change occurred when Al Qaeda in Iraq (AQI) bombed the Al-Askari Mosque in Samarra, one of the country's holiest Shiite sites. AQI conducted this bombing to exacerbate Iraq's sectarian conflict. This gambit achieved its intended outcome. Following the Samarra mosque attack, Shiite militias launched aggressive campaigns to eject Sunnis from Baghdad, while the Iraqi government's predominantly Shiite security forces were frequently caught conducting extrajudicial abuses against Sunni civilians.

In this context, it was no longer debatable whether or not Iraq was embroiled in a sectarian civil war. It thus became untenable to argue that U.S. strategy would succeed by transitioning authority to the Iraqi government, which was widely seen as privileging Shiite interests. In his memoirs, President Bush explains how his thinking shifted during the summer of 2006. "In the months after the Samarra bombing," he writes, "I had started to question whether our approach matched the reality on the ground. The sectarian violence had not erupted because our footprint was too big. . . . And with the Iraqis struggling to stand up, it didn't seem possible for us to stand down."[34]

By the end of 2006, the Bush administration had altered its strategy on several important dimensions.[35] U.S. forces assumed direct responsibility for protecting Iraqi civilians through the use of large-scale, manpower-intensive patrols. The White House began to place more coercive pressure on the Iraqi government,

[34] Bush, *Decision Points*, pp. 363, 393. Secretary Rumsfeld recalled the situation in a similar way. "Looking back," he wrote, "it is now clear that the effect of the [Samarra] bombing proved a game changer in Iraq." Rumsfeld, *Known and Unknown*, p. 660.

[35] A large number of excellent sources describe both the internal and public debates about the Surge. The following sources were especially helpful in grounding my discussion: Bob Woodward, *The War Within* (New York: Simon and Schuster, 2008); David Ucko, *The New Counterinsurgency Era* (Washington, D.C.: Georgetown University Press, 2009); Thomas Ricks, *The Gamble* (New York: Penguin, 2009); Peter D. Feaver, "The Right to Be Right: Civil-Military Relations and the Iraq Surge," *International Security*, Vol. 35, No. 4 (Spring 2011), pp. 87–125; Peter Mansoor, *Surge* (New Haven, Conn.: Yale, 2013); and Gordon and Trainor, *Endgame*.

led by Prime Minister Nouri al-Maliki, in an effort to restrain that government's sectarian tendencies. And, in January 2007, the Bush administration announced a temporary "surge" of thirty thousand soldiers to Iraq, who would provide a year and a half of additional manpower to combat violence in Iraq's most dangerous areas.

At this point, debates about U.S. policy in Iraq shifted into a second phase, which largely revolved around uncertainty over whether or not the new strategy could return the violence in Iraq to manageable levels before the Surge's time limit had expired. Critics of the Surge argued that this goal was infeasible, and they once again saw short-term violence trends as supporting their perspective. As shown in Figure 6.3, civilian casualties in Iraq continued to rise during the first six months of the Surge. And though Coalition casualties began to fall around the time the Surge was announced, the initial trajectory of this decline was much too slow to return to pre-2006 levels by the time the Surge forces would have to come home. Critics used these trends to support their argument that the Surge was failing and that seeing the strategy through to its completion would be a needless waste of resources.

Proponents of the Surge, by contrast, argued that the strategy simply needed more time to achieve its intended goals. In this view, U.S. soldiers had to build credibility with Iraqi civilians before those civilians would support this new phase of the war effort. Surge advocates also argued that one of the main reasons why Coalition casualties remained high was because those forces were now fighting much more aggressively. In this view, the initial costs of the Surge reflected an up-front investment designed to improve the probability of shifting the war's strategic dynamics. Figure 6.3 shows that this is indeed what happened—Iraq's violence fell by a factor of ten over the following year. By 2009, both Coalition and civilian casualties were lower than at any point since the invasion.

There is still substantial uncertainty about why violence declined in Iraq during this period and, in particular, whether the U.S. troop surge was necessary for precipitating this outcome.[36] Later in this section, we will see that there are also reasons to doubt whether it was ever possible to sustain this relative stability in the long run. In this sense, the reduction in violence in Iraq in 2007–2008 was, at best, an operational success and not a strategic victory.

Nevertheless, the decline in violence during the Surge provides another example of how it can be misleading to assume that tactical outcomes provide a

---

[36] Elsewhere, I have argued that the Surge strategy was a necessary but insufficient component for reducing Iraq's violence, though it remains unclear whether additional forces were necessary for this strategy to take effect. See Stephen Biddle, Jeffrey A. Friedman, and Jacob N. Shapiro, "Testing the Surge: Why Did Violence Decline in Iraq in 2007?" *International Security*, Vol. 37, No. 1 (2012), pp. 7–40.

reliable indicator of strategic prospects. Once again, the trend lines in violence offered little direct support to either the critics or the proponents of the Surge. The central challenge in evaluating this strategy was estimating the probability that these trends would shift within a relevant time frame, and there was no logical reason to assume that those chances had to remain fixed and repeated over time. Thus, while the conventional wisdom among international relations scholars holds that tactical outcomes provide unambiguous signals that resolve uncertainty about a policy's strategic prospects, debates about the Iraq Surge show that this causal relationship can work in the exact opposite direction: because proponents and critics of the Surge held very different perceptions of this strategy's overall prospects, they drew fundamentally different lessons from observing the same tactical experience.

Debating Withdrawal, 2009–2011

After violence settled at relatively low levels following the Surge, debates over U.S. strategy entered a third phase, in which the key question was the extent to which Iraq could now stand on its own without a major foreign military presence.[37] This debate became increasingly urgent over time, given that the Status of Forces Agreement (SOFA), which granted the United States a legal basis to station military forces in Iraq, was set to expire at the end of 2011. President Obama and Prime Minister Maliki could not come to terms in negotiating a new SOFA, and in December 2011, the United States formally withdrew its military presence from Iraq.

As SOFA negotiations collapsed, proponents and critics of continuing the U.S. military presence in Iraq engaged in yet another debate about the extent to which existing violence trends predicted strategic prospects. Advocates of withdrawal pointed out that Iraq had, by the end of 2011, experienced four years of relative stability. By this point, the U.S. presence in Iraq was down to forty thousand troops (less than a quarter of the 2007 deployment), and those force levels would surely have continued to decline under a new SOFA. Meanwhile, since the United States had formally ended combat operations in Iraq in 2010, its forces were already stationed outside the country's major population centers, and their role was mostly limited to training, equipping, and advising the Iraqi security forces. Advocates of withdrawal thus believed that the United States was no longer in a position to provide Iraq with critical support, and that it was safe to

[37] Again, many excellent sources describe the debates about U.S. politics during this period along with the breakdown of the SOFA negotiations specifically. Particularly useful for information my discussion here are Emma Sky, *The Unraveling* (New York: PublicAffairs, 2015); David Kilcullen, *Blood Year* (New York: Oxford University Press, 2016); and articles by Stephen Biddle and Ali Khedery.

withdraw from a country that had not seen large-scale violence in several years. Extrapolating from this past experience, withdrawal advocates assumed that the probability of renewed violence in Iraq would remain low into the future.

Proponents of maintaining a U.S. military presence in Iraq were unconvinced that Iraq's relative stability would continue. In their view, even a limited number of U.S. forces played an important role in bolstering Iraq's military and police, and in restraining Prime Minister Maliki's sectarian tendencies. By removing this support, they argued, U.S. withdrawal could raise the probability that Iraq's Sunnis and Shiites would return to the cycle of conflict that drove large-scale violence during the occupation's earlier years. In that sense, proponents of maintaining a U.S. presence in Iraq argued that recent violence trends were misleading, and that the country still required substantial assistance in order to continue consolidating its progress in politics and security.

It remains difficult to judge which of these predictions proved to be more accurate. After another year of relative stability following U.S. withdrawal, sectarian violence rose in 2013, and then reached unprecedented levels as Islamic State militants seized several of the country's Sunni population centers in 2014. Proponents of withdrawing U.S. forces from Iraq were clearly mistaken in believing that Iraq was in a position to consolidate progress on its own. Yet it is also hard to predict the extent to which a limited number of U.S. forces in a noncombat role could have prevented the Islamic State's rise. A foreign military presence during this period might even have proved to be counterproductive if it exacerbated resentment or encouraged Iraqi leaders to shirk their responsibility for managing domestic problems.

It thus remains an open question how much longer it would have taken or how much it would have cost the United States to have left Iraq on a sustainable footing or whether this goal was ever feasible at all. Once again, resolving this uncertainty had little to do with extrapolating trends in tactical outcomes. Instead, the key issue shaping strategic decisions lay with estimating the probability that U.S. forces could help Iraq reach a point where it could stand on its own within a feasible time frame. Though any attempt to estimate those chances would have been inherently subjective, it is impossible to evaluate the wisdom of withdrawing from Iraq without tackling that issue.

Conclusion

This chapter has shown that assessments of subjective probability provide crucial foundations for learning and adaptation in international politics. Although international relations scholars believe that leaders' perceptions should naturally converge as they observe foreign policies in action, we have seen that this argument relies on the premise that a policy's chances of success remain fixed and repeated over time.[38] I explained why that assumption is implausible, and how it leads scholars to underestimate the genuine analytic challenge of strategic assessment. Tactical results in armed conflict or other areas of international politics do not provide unambiguous signals about a policy's future outcomes. Instead, the chapter showed that the lessons leaders draw from observing tactical successes and failures are conditioned by the way that those leaders assess their strategic prospects. Without reaching consensus about what this uncertainty entails, we cannot expect foreign policy analysts and decision makers to agree on even rudimentary issues like whether or not a military strategy is making acceptable progress.

The problem, of course, is that assessments of strategic prospects are inherently subjective. There is almost never an obvious "right way" to estimate how a foreign policy's chances of success will rise and fall over time. Yet to say that these beliefs are subjective is different from saying they are meaningless. We have seen throughout the book that foreign policy analysts always possess a theoretically coherent and empirically justifiable basis for assessing subjective probabilities. This chapter showed that those judgments can provide useful— indeed, sometimes crucial—foundations for structuring hard choices. The next chapter concludes by drawing additional practical implications from the book's analysis and by describing directions for future research.

---

[38] Or that these probabilities change in predictable ways that are known to decision makers in advance.

7

Placing Probability Front and Center in Foreign Policy Discourse

After the terrorist attacks on September 11, 2001, many national security officials worried that the next strike could be far worse. The nightmare scenario involved a nuclear weapon being detonated on U.S. soil. After a receiving a briefing about al Qaeda's attempts to acquire a nuclear device from Pakistan, Vice President Richard Cheney concluded: "If there's a one percent chance that Pakistani scientists are helping al Qaeda build or develop a nuclear weapon, we have to treat it as a certainty in terms of our response." The journalist Ron Suskind famously labeled Cheney's statement the "One Percent Doctrine." In a best-selling book by that name, Suskind argued that the One Percent Doctrine characterized the heightened priority that U.S. foreign policy officials have assigned to managing low-probability, high-consequence risks in an age of global terrorism.[1]

On its face, the logic of the One Percent Doctrine seems absurd. If the damage that a risk could cause is sufficiently high, and if policymakers have feasible options for reducing that danger, then a one percent chance of catastrophe could easily be large enough to justify a major response. From this perspective, treating a one percent chance as a certainty is not careful thinking: it just inflates the risk by two orders of magnitude.[2] Foreign policy decisions are hard enough without deliberately distorting assumptions. How could anyone justify debating high-stakes choices in this manner?

There are at least two ways to answer that question. The first is that public officials did not believe that they could justify their preferred policies based on merit alone. In this view, consciously inflating low-probability threats could have been a rhetorical strategy for overriding reasonable opposition, in much the same way that Harry Truman's secretary of state, Dean Acheson, famously

---

[1] Ron Suskind, *The One Percent Doctrine* (New York: Simon and Schuster, 2006).

[2] For a broader, related criticism of public discourse on the risk of terrorism, see John Mueller and Mark Stewart, *Chasing Ghosts: The Policing of Terrorism* (New York: Oxford University Press, 2016).

argued that leaders sometimes need to present hard choices to the public in a manner that is "clearer than truth."[3] Treating a one percent chance as a certainty could thus be a tactic for avoiding open and honest discourse, impairing other people's abilities to make sound decisions.[4]

Yet one can also interpret the One Percent Doctrine as a tactic for *improving* other people's abilities to make sound decisions, and I suspect that is closer to what the doctrine's proponents had in mind. The premise behind this view is that most people struggle to assess and interpret subjective probabilities. Thus, even if a one percent chance of catastrophe deserved a major policy response, it might be difficult for leaders and voters to prioritize combating threats that seem so unlikely.[5] Treating a one percent chance as a certainty could be a patronizing but productive way to navigate difficult conceptual terrain.

In this respect, the One Percent Doctrine reflects an extreme example of the aversion to probabilistic reasoning described throughout this book. The book has explained that many scholars and practitioners believe there is no coherent way to assess uncertainty in international politics, that making these assessments provides no meaningful information, that transparent probabilistic reasoning biases analysts or decision makers, that it exposes public officials to excessive criticism, and that subjective probabilities are simply irrelevant to structuring hard choices. We have also seen that these arguments do not withstand scrutiny. Even though the most important assessments of uncertainty in international politics are inherently subjective, the book has shown that it is always possible to deal with this challenge in clear and structured ways, and that foreign policy analysts and decision makers handle this challenge best when they confront it head-on.

In some cases, placing greater emphasis on assessing uncertainty can directly influence major foreign policy decisions. When the Joint Chiefs of Staff argued that the Bay of Pigs invasion had "a fair chance of ultimate success," they enabled one of the worst U.S. foreign policy blunders of the Cold War. The Pentagon sent hundreds of thousands of soldiers to Vietnam without carefully analyzing the risks of doing so. And even though intelligence analysts technically acknowledged

---

[3] Dean Acheson, *Present at the Creation: My Years at the State Department* (New York: Norton, 1969), p. 375.

[4] Joshua Rovner, *Fixing the Facts: National Security and the Politics of Intelligence* (Ithaca, N.Y.: Cornell University Press, 2011); Chaim Kaufmann, "Threat Inflation and the Failure of the Marketplace of Ideas," *International Security*, Vol. 29, No. 1 (2004), pp. 5–48; John Mueller, *Overblown* (New York: Free Press, 2006).

[5] On the challenges that policymakers and the general public face in dealing with low-probability, high-consequence threats, see Richard Posner, *Catastrophe: Risk and Response* (New York: Oxford University Press, 2004); Cass R. Sunstein, *Worst-case Scenarios* (Cambridge, Mass.: Harvard University Press, 2007); and Robert Meyer and Howard Kunreuther, *The Ostrich Paradox: Why We Underprepare for Disasters* (Philadelphia, Penn.: University of Pennsylvania Press, 2017).

the presence of uncertainty regarding the status of Saddam Hussein's weapons of mass destruction programs, they framed their judgments in a manner that short-circuited debates about what their doubts entailed and whether the invasion of Iraq was justified in light of them.

Beyond these specific examples, the book has argued that aversion to probabilistic reasoning exacts a consistent toll across a broad range of foreign policy analysis and decision making. These costs may not be readily apparent when examining any individual intelligence report, military plan, op-ed, or policy debate. Nevertheless, the book has shown that conventional approaches to assessing uncertainty in international politics sacrifice meaningful information, withhold details that shape decision makers' evaluation of risky choices, and expose foreign policy analysts to unnecessary blame.

These are all serious problems. Yet each of the book's chapters conveys a positive message, too. By reconsidering the logic, psychology, and politics of assessing uncertainty in international affairs, the book has shown how it is possible to *add* meaningful information to foreign policy debates, to provide details that *help* decision makers to evaluate risky choices, and to *limit* critics' ability to make controversial judgments seem more mistaken than they really are. While no one should believe that assessing uncertainty in international politics is easy or uncontroversial, the book has shown that it is possible to improve these judgments in nearly any area of foreign policy discourse. The book now concludes by describing some of the practical implications of its findings and by suggesting priorities for further research.

Developing Basic Standards for Assessing Uncertainty in International Politics

The best way to improve probabilistic reasoning in international politics is to establish strong norms that favor placing assessments of uncertainty front and center in high-stakes policy debates. These norms should have at least four components. Together, these components comprise what I will call the *basic standard* for assessing uncertainty.

The first element of the basic standard is that foreign policy analysts should describe the uncertainty surrounding any prediction or policy recommendation that they make. It is especially important to describe the chances that policy recommendations will achieve their intended objectives.[6] These judgments should not be viewed as caveats or add-ons, but rather as a fundamental

---

[6] An added benefit to this component of the basic standard is that it would require policy advocates to be clear about what their objectives entail.

requirement of rigorous foreign policy analysis. Just as it would be unacceptable to support a policy without having a clear idea of its objectives or its potential costs, any proposal that does not assess the chances that high-stakes decisions will succeed should be viewed as incomplete and unsound.

The second component of the basic standard is that scholars, practitioners, and pundits should never justify predictions or policy recommendations using the practices that chapter 1 called "relative probability" and "conditioning." At best, these judgments are uninformative; at worst, they can bias high-stakes decisions. Costly actions cannot be justified simply because they seem necessary, or because they would improve effectiveness, or because they present the best prospects for achieving important goals. Instead, the book has argued that it is always crucial to explain *how much* risky choices would improve effectiveness and to estimate what their prospects for success actually are.

The third component of the basic standard is that assessments of uncertainty should be clear enough for readers to reliably understand what they mean. By far the easiest way to accomplish this goal is for foreign policy analysts to supplement key judgments with numeric percentages. This would not require changing any language in existing analyses, only providing additional clauses, parentheticals, or footnotes to clarify what assessments of uncertainty mean.[7] This would eliminate prospects for miscommunication, prevent foreign policy analysts from sacrificing relevant insight, stop critics from characterizing analysts' language unfairly, and foreclose opportunities to advance vague judgments that sound more meaningful than they really are.

If foreign policy analysts prefer to assess uncertainty using purely qualitative language, then it is important to ensure that these analysts employ a common lexicon. This lexicon should discriminate among at least 10 levels of probability. Decision makers should be given systematic instruction in interpreting what these terms mean, and foreign policy organizations should ensure that analysts use these terms in ways that match their intended definitions. These are all nontrivial challenges that the U.S. government has been unable to solve. In light of this experience—and given the book's findings—foreign policy organizations might be better served by asking analysts to supplement their judgments with explicit assessments of uncertainty.

The fourth and final element of the basic standard is that foreign policy analysts should consistently distinguish between assessments of probability and confidence. Chapter 2 explained that probability and confidence are distinct concepts with independent implications for high-stakes decision making.

---

[7] Expressing numeric percentages in intervals of 5 percentage points might be a decent rule of thumb for all but the most extreme judgments. The data in chapter 3 suggest that anything less than this level of precision would systematically sacrifice meaningful information.

We have nevertheless seen several examples of how foreign policy analysts often conflate probability and confidence, and how they rarely assess these concepts simultaneously. The most straightforward way to solve this problem is for foreign policy analysts to provide a clear statement of the chances that a judgment is true, accompanied by a brief description of how the analysts arrived at that conclusion.[8] The difficulty of distinguishing between assessments of probability and confidence provides another reason to favor making those judgments as explicit as possible.

None of the recommendations described here is particularly complicated. The basic standard is essentially a matter of being transparent about the uncertainty that lies behind predictions and policy recommendations. Implementing the basic standard would nevertheless represent a fundamental shift in the character of foreign policy discourse, both in and out of government. Chapter 1 showed that even analytically inclined policymakers like the Whiz Kids fail to meet the basic standard in the vast majority of their policy analyses. Similarly, when one scans policy recommendations presented in newspaper op-eds or on the pages of major policy journals, it is rare to see scholars, practitioners, and pundits place assessments of uncertainty front and center in their analysis.

Government agencies possess the most obvious opportunities to establish these norms. Chapter 1 explained how virtually all intelligence and military organizations develop official guidelines for assessing uncertainty. Those guidelines could be changed at any time to incorporate the basic standard. Media outlets possess similar opportunities to set rules of the road for policy debates. Just as it is reasonable to expect that military planners should carefully assess the chances that any dangerous operation will succeed, it is worth asking scholars, practitioners, and pundits to thoughtfully describe the uncertainty that surrounds any policy recommendation they offer in public forums. Editorial boards can develop and enforce publishing guidelines that prevent making hard choices seem clearer than truth. Journalists who cover foreign policy debates can press policy advocates to describe the uncertainty their recommendations entail.

Decision makers can take steps to implement the basic standard by directing their staffs to incorporate clear assessments of uncertainty into policy analyses. The book has described several cases in which decision makers learned this

---

[8] Chapter 2 explained that rigorous discussions of analytic confidence should include at least three components: the reliability of the available evidence supporting a judgment, the range of reasonable opinion surrounding that judgment, and the degree to which that judgment might change in response to new information. While it may be infeasible to require that foreign policy analysts assess these elements of uncertainty for every judgment they make, this standard of rigor is appropriate for particularly high-stakes judgments, such as estimating the chances that Osama bin Laden was living in Abbottabad, or estimating the chances that Saddam Hussein was pursuing nuclear weapons.

lesson the hard way. Thus, after the Bay of Pigs invasion collapsed, President Kennedy wrote a National Security Action Memorandum that required the Joint Chiefs of Staff "to present the military viewpoint in governmental councils in such a way as to assure that the military factors are clearly understood before decisions are reached."[9] Of course, decision makers would ideally implement these lessons *before* major crises occur. Adopting the basic standard is one way to do that.

What about cases in which neither analysts nor decision makers are naturally inclined to provide transparent assessments of uncertainty? In this context, multiple advocacy can help to foster rigorous policy debates.[10] Any time one side of a policy debate seeks to make matters clearer than truth, their opponents should have incentives to bring relevant doubts into better focus.

This kind of multiple advocacy can play out in a wide range of forums, including Congressional testimony, television commentary, and debates in the White House Situation Room. Critics who oppose a policy can always press their rivals to assess the chances that this policy will succeed and to defend that judgment against scrutiny. If policy analysts are unable or unwilling to do this, then critics can point out that they do not possess a valid basis for recommending that decision makers place lives and resources at risk.[11] The fact that policy analysts do not systematically press each other to justify their arguments in this fashion helps to emphasize that the goal of improving foreign policy analysis is not just a matter of setting better standards for intelligence analysts and military planners. Scholars, journalists, and pundits can also play an important role in helping to place assessments of uncertainty at the center of foreign policy discourse.

Directions for Further Research

This book has examined the logic, psychology, and politics of assessing uncertainty in international affairs. But a truly comprehensive study of

---

[9] National Security Action Memorandum 55, "Relations of the Joint Chiefs of Staff to the President in Cold War Operations," 28 June 1961.

[10] Alexander L. George and Eric K. Stern, "Harnessing Conflict in Foreign Policy Making: From Devil's to Multiple Advocacy," *Presidential Studies Quarterly*, Vol. 32, No. 3 (2002), pp. 484–508.

[11] Indeed, the fact that scholars, practitioners, and pundits do not pursue this kind of multiple advocacy more often provides one of the strongest indications of how aversion to probabilistic reasoning in foreign policy discourse does not simply reflect cynical avoidance of controversial issues. To the extent that a policy's critics do not make more effort to probe the uncertainty surrounding high-stakes choices, it can only be because critics do not naturally consider this line of questioning, or because they do not think that line of questioning will be productive.

this topic would engage many questions that the book did not address. In closing, I will highlight four such issues: organizational culture, effort, emotion, and values.

Chapter 2 argued that rigorously assessing uncertainty in international politics conflicts with the traditional emphasis that foreign policy analysts place on objectivity. Indeed, chapter 2 explained why rigor and objectivity are all but impossible to achieve simultaneously when debating foreign policy decisions, given that foreign policy decisions almost always depend on subjective probabilities. Of course, saying that assessments of uncertainty are subjective does not imply that they are meaningless. It is nevertheless important to acknowledge that placing these judgments front and center in foreign policy discourse would clash with many analysts' and decision makers' natural impulse to value objectivity. Further research on organizational culture could provide valuable insights about how to manage this tension.[12]

Another limitation of the book's analysis is that it relied on experiments that captured respondents' intuitive responses to foreign policy issues. All things being equal, this is a strength of the book's research design: responses provided on the basis of limited effort should generally underestimate the value of careful probabilistic reasoning. Yet this also means that the book does not describe the true frontiers of human capabilities in this area. Accomplishing that goal requires merging the methodological tools described in the book with actual analytic efforts conducted by foreign policy professionals.[13]

A third way to expand the book's research program would draw upon insights from the study of values and emotions in international politics. Some observers might see the book's focus on subjective probability as representing an overly narrow focus on the rationalist elements of foreign policy analysis. There is indeed a great deal of evidence that emotion and rationality are complements, not

[12] Relevant studies in this area include Rob Johnston, *Analytic Culture in the U.S. Intelligence Community* (Washington, D.C.: Center for the Study of Intelligence, 2005); James Marchio, "The Intelligence Community's Struggle to Express Analytic Certainty in the 1970s," *Studies in Intelligence*, Vol. 58, No. 4 (2015), pp. 31–42; and Alan Barnes, "Making Intelligence Analysis More Intelligent," *Intelligence and National Security*, Vol. 31, No. 1 (2016), pp. 327–344.

[13] For examples of important work already being conducted in this area, see David R. Mandel and Alan Barnes, "Accuracy of Forecasts in Strategic Intelligence," *Proceedings of the National Academy of Sciences*, Vol. 111, No. 30 (2014), pp. 10984–10989, who analyze experimental work conducted by Canada's Intelligence Assessment Secretariat; and Bradley J. Stasny and Paul E. Lehner, "Comparative Evaluation of the Forecast Accuracy of Analysis Reports and a Prediction Market," *Judgment and Decision Making*, Vol. 13, No. 2 (2018), pp. 202–211, who analyze experimental work conducted by the U.S. Intelligence Advanced Research Projects Agency (IARPA). On IARPA's broader efforts to improve assessments of uncertainty in intelligence analysis, see Philip E. Tetlock and Daniel Gardner, *Superforecasting: The Art and Science of Prediction* (New York: Crown, 2015).

substitutes, when it comes to making sound decisions.[14] Improving the rigor of probabilistic reasoning would not be desirable if this crowded out other, less-quantifiable elements of good judgment.[15]

This is a valid concern which is also consistent with the book's central message. Privileging rationalist rigor in foreign policy analysis would surely be counterproductive if it creates illusions of certainty or objectivity.[16] And that mindset is exactly what this book seeks to counteract. The main purpose of placing probabilities front and center in foreign policy discourse is to emphasize the *lack* of certainty that surrounds high-stakes choices, and to highlight the inherently subjective nature of major foreign policy decisions.

Moreover, the book has shown how aversion to probabilistic reasoning allows foreign policy analysts and decision makers to avoid engaging some of the most morally charged elements of international politics. U.S. officials did not refrain from describing the chances of failure in Vietnam because they disapproved of cost-benefit analysis. They were, after all, the Whiz Kids—some of the most methodologically zealous individuals who have ever guided U.S. foreign policy. Instead, chapter 1 argued that senior leaders avoided assessing their strategic prospects in Vietnam because that would have conflicted with their desire to make foreign policy decisions in a scientific manner. The Whiz Kids' main weakness was not that they were too rigorous, but that they privileged seemingly-objective analyses over the kinds of subjective judgments that were far more important for evaluating U.S. strategy.

Similarly, it is hard to believe that proponents of the Iraq War avoided providing clearer assessments of uncertainty surrounding Saddam Hussein's WMD programs because they worried that this would overshadow important value judgments. Quite the opposite, I argued that more transparent probabilistic reasoning in this case would have triggered deep questions about what level of certainty should be required to justify preventive war, and what the

---

[14] See, for example, James Druckmann and Rose McDermott, "Emotion and the Framing of Risky Choice," *Political Behavior*, Vol. 30, No. 3 (2008), pp. 297–321; and Jennifer Lerner et al., "Emotion and Decision Making," *Annual Review of Psychology*, Vol. 66 (2015), pp. 799–823. On the argument that emotion and rationality are complements, not substitutes, see Antonio Damasio, *Descartes' Error: Emotion, Reason, and the Human Brain* (New York: Putnam, 1994).

[15] For an important collection of essays on the extent to which rational conceptions of "good judgment" apply to foreign policy decision making, see Stanley A. Renshon and Deborah Welch Larson, eds., *Good Judgment in Foreign Policy* (Lanham, Md.: Rowman and Littlefield, 2003).

[16] Prominent articulations of this concern include Stanley Hoffmann, *Gulliver's Troubles: Or, the Setting of American Foreign Policy* (New York: McGraw Hill, 1968), pp. 87–175; Alexander Wendt, "Driving with the Rearview Mirror: On the Rational Science of Institutional Design," *International Organization*, Vol. 55, No. 4 (2001), pp. 1019–1049; Peter Katzenstein and Lucia Seybert, "Protean Power and Uncertainty: Exploring the Unexpected in World Politics," *International Studies Quarterly*, Vol. 62, No. 1 (2018), pp. 80–93.

remaining doubts about Iraq's WMD programs entailed. In this sense, placing assessments of uncertainty front and center in debates about the Iraq War would have provoked contentious value judgments rather than pushing those issues aside. Identifying the best ways to grapple with these judgments is another area in which further research can provide substantial insights for shaping foreign policy discourse.[17]

There are thus many potential avenues for expanding the book's analysis. Each of these issues also highlights how debates about assessing uncertainty in international politics are only partly a matter of developing pragmatic standards for communicating key judgments. These controversies ultimately revolve around theoretical and empirical questions about what assessments of uncertainty mean and how they can be useful.

By helping to answer some of these questions, I hope that *War and Chance* leaves readers with an optimistic outlook. Skeptical views of probabilistic reasoning are understandable, but they are also overblown, and they do not preclude making meaningful judgments about major foreign policy issues. The main reason to be concerned with existing approaches to assessing uncertainty in international politics is not just because the current state of affairs is surrounded by vagueness and confusion, but because it is genuinely possible to do better.

---

[17] On the relationship between assessments of probabilities and values in high-stakes decision making, see Robyn M. Dawes, *Rational Choice in an Uncertain World* (San Diego, Calif.: Harcourt Brace Javonovich, 1988).

Appendix

SUPPORTING INFORMATION
FOR CHAPTERS 3–5

Contents

1. Supplementary Materials for Chapter 3

1a. Methodology for Estimating Returns to Precision in Probability Assessment

The methodology for estimating returns to precision described in chapter 3 involves evaluating the accuracy of probability assessments using the Brier score.

The Brier score for a given forecasting problem, X, is given by the formula $Brier(X) = \sum_x (\theta_x - p_x)^2 / N$. In this formula, x denotes the outcomes foreign policy analysts are predicting; θ_x takes a value of 1 if outcome x occurs and a value of 0 if outcome x does not occur; p_x is the probability that the analyst assigned to outcome x; and N is the number of outcomes that the analyst is considering as part of the forecasting problem.[1]

My colleagues and I adopted a deliberately conservative approach to statistical analysis by calculating an *aggregate Brier score* (A) for each forecasting problem in our data set. We calculated this score using the formula $A_{\gamma j} = mean_{i \in \gamma}[mean_{k \in K_{ij}}(Brier_{ijk})]$, where i is an individual forecaster; γ is a broader group of forecasters to which this individual belongs (e.g., superforecasters, trained groups, all forecasters); j is a forecasting question; k is a day in the forecasting tournament; $mean(\cdot)$ is the mean of a vector; K_{ij} is the set of all forecasts made by forecaster i on question j while the question remained open;[2] and $Brier_{ijk}$ is the Brier score for an estimate made by a given forecaster on a given question on a given day. Thus, $A_{\gamma j}$ provides an aggregated estimate of forecast accuracy among all forecasters belonging to group γ with respect to question j.

We calculated *rounding errors* for each forecasting question by measuring the proportional changes in Brier scores when we rounded individual forecasts into bins of different widths. Thus, we defined $\tilde{A}_{\gamma j B}$ as the aggregate forecasting accuracy for group γ on question j, having rounded respondents' forecasts to the midpoints of B bins. For example, we estimated the rounding error associated with transforming probabilities into three-stepconfidence levels as $\left(\tilde{A}_{\gamma j B=3} - A_{\gamma j}\right) / A_{\gamma j}$.

---

[1] All of the forecasting problems analyzed in chapter 3 have binary outcomes. The Brier score for these forecasting problems is thus equivalent to $(1 - p_1)^2$, where p_1 is the probability the analyst assigned to the observed outcome.

[2] With a maximum of one forecast per day, recorded as a forecaster's most recent estimate prior to midnight, U.S. Eastern Time.

1b. Logarithmic Scoring and Replication of Results

The logarithmic scoring rule represents an alternative method for evaluating the accuracy of probability assessments. Denote p_1 as the probability that the analyst assigned to the outcome that eventually occurred. The logarithmic scoring rule assigns a score of $\ln(p_1)$ for each forecasting problem.[3]

The logarithmic scoring rule is much more sensitive than the Brier score to fine-grained distinctions at the extreme edges of the probability spectrum (e.g., 0.01 versus 0.001 or 0.99 versus 0.999). The Brier score, by contrast, is more sensitive to variations in the middle of the probability spectrum (e.g., between 0.30 and 0.70) One drawback to logarithmic scoring is that it assigns infinite penalties to probability estimates that respondents offer with false certainty. Thus, if an analyst assigns a zero percent probability to a statement that proves to be true, then her logarithmic score for this estimate would be $\ln(0) = -\infty$.

Since this would render many probability estimates unusable, and since most probability estimates analyzed in the book's empirical chapters fall into the middle of the probability spectrum,[4] I use the Brier score as the main measure for evaluating the accuracy of probability assessments throughout chapters 3 and 4. However, all the results presented in the book are also robust to employing the logarithmic scoring rule, provided that estimates of 0.0 or 1.0 are either removed from the data set or shifted to nearby values like 0.01 and 0.99.

For instance, Table A.1 compares aggregate rounding errors estimating using the Brier score versus the logarithmic scoring rule. In both cases, we see that superforecasters lose predictive accuracy when we round their judgments into any word of estimative probability and that non-superforecasters demonstrate returns to precision on all estimates that do not fall into the extreme segments of the number line. This is the same finding that was reported in Table 3.2.

1c. Robustness of Empirical Results across Time Horizons

Chapter 3 described how returns to precision are robust across the following four categories of forecasts: (a) *Lay-Ups*, forecasts made within two weeks of a

---

[3] Unlike the Brier score, higher values are better when applying the logarithmic scoring rule.

[4] The questions used in the GJP were deliberately selected to produce estimates that fell in this range. If the actual rate of occurrence for the outcomes that these forecasters predicted was too extreme (i.e., too high or too low) then much larger volumes of data would have been required to estimate forecasting accuracy.

Table A.1. **Comparison of Aggregate Rounding Errors, Brier versus Logarithmic Scoring**

Group		Remote (.00–.14)	Very unlikely (.15–.28)	Unlikely (.29–.42)	Even chance (.43–.56)	Likely (.57–.71)	Very likely (.72–.85)	Almost certain (.86–1.0)
Rounding Errors via Brier Scoring								
All forecasters	Mean:	3.4%	4.3%	2.3%	1.3%	2.3%	4.3%	3.4%
	Median	-0.5%	3.7%	2.2%	1.1%	2.2%	3.7%	-0.5%
Superforecasters	Mean:	85.8%	16.2%	7.0%	1.8%	7.0%	16.2%	85.8%
	Median	32.2%	12.1%	4.1%	1.0%	4.1%	12.1%	32.2%
Rounding Errors via Logarithmic Scoring								
All forecasters	Mean:	-1.1%	3.5%	1.6%	0.9%	1.6%	3.5%	-1.1%
	Median	-7.5%	3.7%	1.7%	0.8%	1.7%	3.7%	-7.5%
Superforecasters	Mean:	70.4%^	9.9%	4.4%	1.2%	4.4%	9.9%	70.4%^
	Median	55.0%	9.4%	3.1%	0.7%	3.1%	9.4%	55.0%

Note: The table examines how rounding probability estimates into seven equal bins influences predictive accuracy for forecasts within different segments of the number line. Unless otherwise indicated, all findings in this table are statistically distinct from zero at the $p < 0.001$ level.

^This statistic is not statistically significant at the $p < 0.05$ level.

question's closing date and with no more than five percent probability or no less than ninety-five percent probability; (b) *Period I* forecasts, made up to 36 days prior to a question's closing date, but excluding Lay-Ups; (c) *Period II* forecasts, made anywhere from 37 to 96 days prior to a question's closing date; and (d) *Period III* forecasts made more than 96 days prior to a question's closing date. There were 109,240 Lay-Ups in the data set, and 259,696 forecasts in the other three categories, respectively. Table A.2 analyzes returns to precision within each category.[5]

1d. Attributes Used to Examine Variation in Returns to Precision across Individuals

Chapter 3's analysis of returns to precision across individuals involved measuring the following attributes:

- *Brier score*: Each respondent's median Brier score.
- *Number of Questions*: The number of distinct forecasting problems a respondent completed.
- *Average Revisions per Question*: The average number of times a respondent updated his or her predictions for each forecasting problem.
- *Granularity*: The proportion each respondent's forecasts that were not multiples of ten percentages points.
- *Probabilistic Training*: An indicator that takes a value of 1 if a respondent was (randomly) assigned to receive training in probabilistic reasoning as part of his or her participation in the Good Judgment Project (GJP).
- *Group Collaboration*: An indicator that takes a value of 1 if a respondent was (randomly) assigned to collaborate with other forecasters as part of his or her participation in the GJP.
- *Education Level*: A four-category variable capturing a respondent's highest academic degree (no bachelor's degree, bachelor's degree, master's degree, doctorate). If a respondent participated in multiple years of the forecasting competition, we averaged Education values across years.
- *Numeracy*: Each respondent's score on a series of word problems designed to capture mathematical fluency.[6]

---

[5] Note that forecasters receive larger rounding penalties for Period II forecasts than for Period I forecasts: this is because we removed Lay-Ups from the Period I forecasts, whereas the Period II forecasts retain substantial numbers of small-probability estimates.

[6] See Ellen Peters et al. "Numeracy and Decision Making," *Psychological Science*, Vol. 17, No. 5 (2006), pp. 407–413. The GJP changed numeracy tests between years 2 and 3 of the competition.

Table A.2. **Returns to Precision across Time Horizons**

Reference class		Brier score across all numerical forecasts	Rounding Errors 7 WEPs, 2015 version	7 WEPs, evenly spaced	Confidence levels (3 bins)	Estimative verbs (2 bins)
Lay-Ups						
All forecasters	Mean:	0.065	42.4%***	436.4%*	2578.1%**	5865.1%***
	Median:	0.009	2.3%***	40.4%***	267.9%***	628.3%***
Superforecasters	Mean:	0.046†	869.4%	5334.5%	2.9e4%***	$6.6\mathrm{e}^{-4}$%***
	Median:	$2.4\mathrm{e}^{-4}$	278.9%***	2047.9%***	1.2e4%***	$2.6\mathrm{e}^{-4}$%***
Period I forecasts: Forecasts registered up to 36 days prior to question closing						
All forecasters	Mean:	0.114	1.6%***	8.1%***	45.7%***	118.0%***
	Median:	0.064	1.2%***	4.3%*	15.8%***	46.9%***
Superforecasters	Mean:	0.073†	4.41%***	29.1%***	174.0%***	422.7%***
	Median:	0.006	6.9%**	68.5%***	432.2%***	1032.5%***
Period II forecasts: Forecasts registered between 37 and 96 days prior to question closing						
All forecasters	Mean:	0.148	1.0%***	3.8%	21.0%***	55.6%***
	Median:	0.104	1.0%***	1.9%*	8.5%***	22.0%***
Superforecasters	Mean:	0.119	32.0%***	215.2%*	1251.6%***	2869.9%***
	Median:	0.047	2.5%**	14.5%***	97.3%***	255.1%***
Period III forecasts: Forecasts registered at least 97 days prior to question closing						
All forecasters	Mean:	0.187	0.7%***	1.2%	6.6%**	18.3%***
	Median:	0.155	0.9%***	0.8%*	3.7%***	11.8%***
Superforecasters	Mean:	0.119	0.9%***	13.5%**	78.2%***	204.4%***
	Median:	0.047	0.7%**	6.3%***	22.6%***	72.9%***

Note: $p < 0.05$, ** $p < 0.01$, *** $p < 0.001$. † On some questions, superforecasters' average prediction was zero, creating a negatively infinite rounding penalty. We dropped those observations in order to create the estimates shown here. WEPs = words of estimative probability.

- *Raven's Progressive Matrices*: An index in which higher scores indicate better reasoning ability.[7]
- The *Expanded Cognitive Reflection Test (CRT)*: An index on which higher scores indicate an increased propensity to suppress misleading intuitive reactions in favor of more accurate, deliberative answers.[8]
- *Fox-Hedgehog*: An index capturing respondents' self-assessed tendency to rely on ad hoc reasoning versus simplifying frameworks.[9]
- *Need for Cognition*: An index of respondents' self-assessed preference for addressing complex problems.[10]

We also included control variables for *Age*, an indicator capturing whether or not a respondent was *Female*, and an indicator capturing whether or not a respondent was designated as a *Superforecaster* in any tournament year.

1e. Full Analysis of Variation in Returns to Precision across Individuals

Table A.3 presents ordinary least squares regressions predicting individual thresholds of estimative precision using different combinations of variables. All non-binary independent variables in this table are standardized. Each coefficient in Table A.3 thus reflects the extent to which we would expect a respondent's threshold of estimative precision to change when we increase each predictor by one standard deviation, or if we change a binary variable from 0 to 1.

For example, Model 1 shows that if a respondent's Brier score improves by one standard deviation, then we would expect that respondent to be able to

We standardized numeracy test results so that they represent comparable indices. If a respondent participated in multiple years of the forecasting competition, we averaged Numeracy values across years.

[7] See W. Arthur Jr. et al., "College-Sample Psychometric and Normative Data on a Short Form of the Raven Advanced Progressive Matrices Test," *Journal of Psychoeducational Assessment*, Vol. 17, No. 4 (1999), pp. 354–361.

[8] Jonathan Baron et al., "Why Does the Cognitive Reflection Test (Sometimes) Predict Utilitarian Moral Judgment (and Other Things)?" *Journal of Applied Research in Memory and Cognition*, Vol. 4, No. 3 (2015), pp. 265–284.

[9] Mellers et al., "Psychological Strategies for Winning a Geopolitical Forecasting Tournament."

[10] J. T. Cacioppo and R. E. Petty, "The Need for Cognition," *Journal of Personality and Social Psychology*, Vol. 42, No. 1 (1982), pp. 116–131. If a respondent participated in multiple competition

Table A.3. **Predicting Individual-Level Returns to Precision**

	Model 1	Model 2	Model 3	Model 4	Model 5[†]
Targets for Cultivation					
Brier score	−1.62 (.15)***	−1.57 (.16)***	−1.80 (.24)***	−1.74 (.26)***	−1.77 (.26)***
Number of Questions		1.15 (.09)***		1.09 (.10)***	1.09 (.10)***
Average Revisions per Question		0.34 (.17)*		0.41 (.26)	0.41 (.26)
Granularity		−0.19 (.10)		−0.06 (.14)	−0.05 (.14)
Probabilistic Training (dummy)		0.66 (.15)***		0.65 (.19)***	0.63 (.19)***
Group Collaboration (dummy)		0.38 (.16)*		0.52 (.20)*	0.50 (.20)*
Targets for Selection					
Numeracy			−0.00 (.10)	−0.04 (.09)	
Education Level			0.05 (.10)	−0.02 (.10)	
Raven's Progressive Matrices			0.12 (.11)	0.04 (.11)	
Cognitive Reflection Test			0.04 (.11)	0.04 (.11)	
Fox-Hedgehog			0.06 (.09)	0.02 (.09)	
Need for Cognition			0.12 (.10)	0.15 (.09)	
Additional controls					
Age	0.17 (.07)	−0.01 (.07)	0.43 (.10)***	0.16 (.10)	0.01 (.01)
Female (dummy)	−0.23 (.19)	0.01 (.18)	−0.21 (.24)	0.13 (.23)	0.12 (.23)
Superforecaster (dummy)	7.05 (.64)***	5.56 (.59)***	7.71 (.72)***	6.01 (.71)	6.11 (.71)***
Constant	3.64 (.09)***	3.04 (.14)***	3.85 (.11)***	2.94 (.18)***	2.57 (.31)***
N	1,821	1,821	1,307	1,307	1,307
R^2	0.32	0.41	0.37	0.45	0.45
AIC	9,547	9,299	6,905	6,733	6,725

Note: Ordinary least squares regression predicting thresholds of estimative precision across respondents. Non-binary independent variables standardized. Robust standard errors. $p < 0.05$, $p < 0.01$, $p < 0.001$.

[†]Model 5 only retains observations available in Models 3–4.

parse her probability assessments into somewhere between 1 and 2 additional bins. Model 1 also demonstrates that a simple model featuring forecasting skill and our three controls predicted substantial variation in individual-level returns to precision ($R^2 = 0.32$).

Model 2 shows how adding the other Targets for Cultivation variables substantially improved model fit ($R^2 = 0.41$).[11] By contrast, Model 3 shows that the Targets for Selection variables predicted little individual-level variation in returns to precision when controlling for respondents' Brier scores.

Model 4 combines all predictors into a single regression. Here, we see that all of the Targets for Selection variables remain statistically insignificant. The Average Revisions per Question ($p = 0.12$) variable lost statistical significance as well, but skill, experience, training, and collaboration all remained consistent predictors of respondents' returns to precision.

Model 5 then replicates the analysis of the Targets for Cultivation using only observations for which we have data on all variables. Model 5 returned an R^2 value just 0.002 below that of Model 4, thereby showing just how little predictive power the Targets for Selection adds to understanding individual-level returns to precision.[12]

2. Supplementary Materials for Chapter 4

2a. Respondent Demographics (Experiments 1–4)

Table A.4 describes respondent demographics for each of the six groups that participated in the survey experiments described in chapter 4.[13]

---

years, we averaged values across years. The GJP changed CRT tests after year 2 of the competition, so we standardized each test's results in order to provide comparable measures.

[11] Adding a squared term for Number of Questions is statistically significant ($p < 0.01$), but improves R^2 by less than 0.01. A model containing all targets for cultivation less the Brier score has a model fit of $R^2 = 0.17$ for the full sample and for the 1,307 observations for which we have full data.

[12] Estimating Model 1 in a sample with those same 1,307 observations only returns R^2 and AIC scores of 0.37 and 6,898, respectively.

[13] Because of concerns about protecting respondent anonymity among military officers, we were able to ask fewer demographic questions of the elite sample respondents, and the questions we were allowed to ask those respondents varied by cohort.

Table A.4. **Respondent Demographics across Survey Experiments Presented in Chapter 4**

Sample	1	2	3	4	5	6
	Elite (NWC)	Non-elite (AMT)	Elite (NWC)	Non-elite (AMT)	Elite (NWC)	Non-elite (AMT)
N	208	1,458	199	1,561	183	1,208
Experiment(s)	1, 2, 3	1, 2	2	3	4	4
Date	Aug. 2015	Aug. 2015	May 2015	Aug. 2015	Aug. 2016	Aug. 2016
% Female	15%	52%	-	52%	12%	48%
% White	82%	80%	-	81%		82%
% College degree	100%	61%	100%	61%	100%	60%
% U.S. citizen	87%	99%	86%	99%	89%	99%
% Current military service	75%	0.8%	78%	0.4%	71%	0.6%
% Current or former military service	84%	6%	-	5%	11%	5%
Age (average)	-	35	-	35	-	35
Age (standard deviation)		11		11		11

Note: The *Experiments* row reflects the experiments in which each sample participated. NWC = National War College; AMT = Amazon Mechanical Turk; N = "Number of respondents."

2b.　Text of Drone and Security Force Scenarios (Experiments 1–2)

Chapter 4 presented the full text of the hostage-rescue scenario that was presented to respondents in Experiments 1 and 2. Figures A.1a and A.1b present the full text for the other two vignettes involved in these experiments, involving a drone strike and a decision to aid local security forces in counterinsurgency, respectively.

The Central Intelligence Agency uses drones to monitor houses in Yemen believed to be used by AI Qaeda in the Arabian Peninsula (AQAP). CIA analysts report that an unusual number of people have recently been gathering at one of these houses. At any given time, there are at least 8–12 individuals inside the house. All of these individuals appear to be male, but it is impossible to confirm their identities. Recent intercepted communications have indicated that AQAP's senior leadership was planning to convene in this area.

Intelligence analysts stress that their judgments are subjective and that they are based on incomplete information. However, based on all available intelligence, analysts assess that it is likely that the house contains members of AQAP's senior leadership. Drone operators are standing by to attack the house. They believe it is very likely that a drone strike on the house would kill everyone inside.

Analysts warn that it is possible, though unlikely, that the house contains women and children. If U.S. forces strike this target, then it is almost certain that AQAP would not meet again anywhere in this region. This would compromise ongoing surveillance efforts in the area. It is not clear when U.S. intelligence will have another lead like this one.

Summary of estimated chances:

- The house contains member of AI Qaeda's senior leadership: *Likely*
- A drone strike on the house would kill everyone inside: *Very likely*
- The house contains women and children: *Unlikely*
- The drone strike will compromise ongoing surveillance efforts in the area: *Almost certainly*

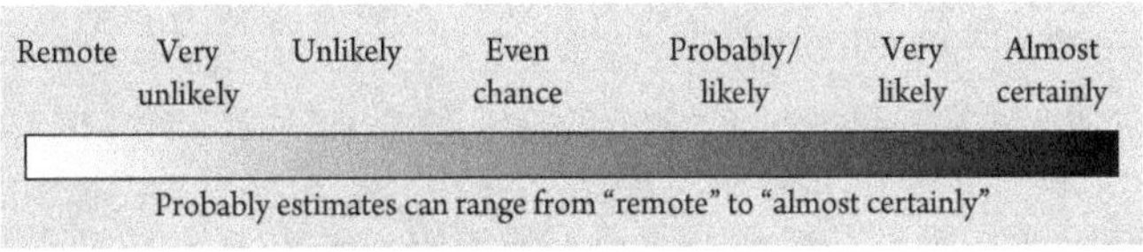

Remote	Very unlikely	Unlikely	Even chance	Probably/ likely	Very likely	Almost certainly

Probably estimates can range from "remote" to "almost certainly"

Figure A.1a Drone-strike scenario (neutral version, qualitative assessment condition).

An Afghan leader named Ghamay Jan recently approached U.S. officials. Jan offered to mobilize 500 followers to combat the Taliban along a dangerous stretch of the border with Pakistan located in Khost Province. Jan requests that the United States provide him funding, equipment, and permission to use Force against the Taliban.

Intelligence analysts stress that their judgments are subjective and that they are based on incomplete information. Nevertheless, they believe it is likely that Jan can mobilize the forces he has promised. Moreover, Jan's followers have substantial military experience and extensive family ties in Khost Province. If they cooperate with the United States, analysts believe it is likely that they would prevent the Taliban from crossing the nearby border.

Yet Ghamay Jan is a controversial figure. Intelligence analysts believe there is an even chance that he previously assisted the Taliban to establish a presence in this part of Khost Province. They also say it is very likely that Jan would use the authority he requests to facilitate illegal smuggling. If the United States supports Ghamay Jan, analysts say it is unlikely that they can retain the backing of other local leaders in Khost Province. Yet those leaders have been unable to secure their border with Pakistan in the past.

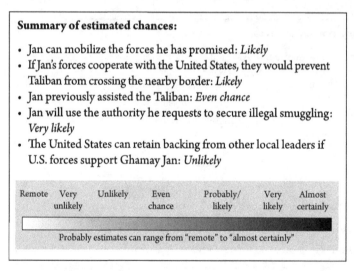

Summary of estimated chances:

- Jan can mobilize the forces he has promised: *Likely*
- If Jan's forces cooperate with the United States, they would prevent Taliban from crossing the nearby border: *Likely*
- Jan previously assisted the Taliban: *Even chance*
- Jan will use the authority he requests to secure illegal smuggling: *Very likely*
- The United States can retain backing from other local leaders if U.S. forces support Ghamay Jan: *Unlikely*

Remote	Very unlikely	Unlikely	Even chance	Probably/ likely	Very likely	Almost certainly

Probably estimates can range from "remote" to "almost certainly"

Figure A.1b Security forces scenario (neutral version, qualitative assessment condition).

2c. Randomization of Probability Assessments (Experiments 1–2)

Participants in Experiment 1 saw one of three versions of each scenario. Each scenario version involved a different set of probability assessments. Table A.5 describes the assessments that appeared in the "pessimistic," "neutral," and "optimistic" versions of each scenario.

Table A.5. **Variations in Probability Assessments across Scenario Versions**

Assessment	Probability Assessments across Scenario Versions		
	Pessimistic	Neutral	Optimistic
Hostage-Rescue Scenario			
Hostages at compound	Even chance (50%)	Likely (65%)	Very likely (80%)
Special forces can retrieve hostages	Likely (65%)	Very likely (80%)	Almost certain (95%)
Soldiers wounded on mission	Likely (65%)	Even chance (50%)	Unlikely (35%)
Collateral damage	Even chance (50%)	Unlikely (35%)	Very unlikely (20%)
Hostages killed if mission fails	Almost certain (95%)	Almost certain (95%)	Almost certain (95%)
Drone Strike Scenario			
House contains Qaeda leaders	Even chance (50%)	Likely (65%)	Very likely (80%)
Drone strike kills occupants	Very likely (80%)	Very likely (80%)	Very likely (80%)
House contains women/ children	Likely (65%)	Unlikely (35%)	Remote chance (5%)
Strike compromises surveillance	Almost certain (95%)	Almost certain (95%)	Almost certain (95%)
Local Security Forces Scenario			
Jan can mobilize forces	Even chance (50%)	Likely (65%)	Very likely (80%)
Jan's forces can secure border	Unlikely (35%)	Likely (65%)	Almost certain (95%)
Jan previously assisted Taliban	Very likely (80%)	Even chance (50%)	Very unlikely (20%)
Jan will secure illegal smuggling	Almost certain (95%)	Very likely (80%)	Likely (65%)
U.S. can retain local leaders' support	Very unlikely (20%)	Unlikely (35%)	Even chance (50%)

Table A.6. **Survey Results from Elite Sample B**

	Support for hostage rescue (1–7 scale)	Support for delaying decision (1–7 scale)	Confidence in assessment (1–7 scale)
Qualitative assessments	5.33 (1.56)	3.14 (1.97)	5.18 (1.19)
Quantitative assessments	4.53 (1.86)	4.11 (2.07)	5.13 (1.26)
	p = 0.001	p = 0.001	p = 0.793

Note: The p-values in this table reflect two-way t-tests comparing differences in means.

2d. Full Results for Supplementary Elite Sample (Experiment 2)

Table A.6 presents two-way t-tests analyzing responses to a neutral hostage scenario by respondents in the second elite sample described in Experiment 2 (Elite Sample B). These results show that quantifying probability assessments reduced support for risky action, increased support for gathering additional information, and had no significant impact on respondents' confidence levels. These results are identical to those of the larger experimental study presented in chapter 4.

2e. Question Lists (Experiments 3–4)

Experiment 3 presented respondents with 35 randomly ordered questions:

- In your opinion, what are the chances that Afghanistan's literacy rate is currently above 50 percent?
- In your opinion, what are the chances that Saudi Arabia currently exports more oil than all other countries in the world combined?
- In your opinion, what are the chances that the United States currently has a longer life expectancy than Jamaica?
- In your opinion, what are the chances that the United States currently operates a military base in Ethiopia?
- In your opinion, what are the chances that the United States has an active territorial claim in Antarctica?
- In your opinion, what are the chances that France currently has more soldiers stationed in Afghanistan than any NATO member besides the United States?

- In your opinion, what are the chances that more than 20 countries currently operate nuclear power plants?
- In your opinion, what are the chances that Japan is currently a member of the International Whaling Commission?
- In your opinion, what are the chances that Russia is a member of the Nuclear Nonproliferation Treaty?
- In your opinion, what are the chances that the United States currently has free trade agreements in place with fewer than 30 countries?
- In your opinion, what are the chances that fewer than 80 countries currently recognize Taiwan's independence from China?
- In your opinion, what are the chances that ISIS draws more foreign fighters from Egypt than from any other country outside of Iraq and Syria?
- In your opinion, what are the chances that Russia's economy grew in 2014?
- In your opinion, what are the chances that Haiti has the lowest per capita income of any Latin American country?
- In your opinion, what are the chances that there are currently more Muslims in the world than there are Roman Catholics?
- In your opinion, what are the chances that Sweden is a member of NATO?
- In your opinion, what are the chances that Tokyo's stock exchange is the second largest stock exchange in the world?
- In your opinion, what are the chances that the U.S. State Department currently lists Iran as a state sponsor of terrorism?
- In your opinion, what are the chances that the Arabic media organization al-Jazeera currently operates bureaus in more countries than does CNN?
- In your opinion, what are the chances that the United States currently possesses more than 2,000 nuclear warheads?
- In your opinion, what are the chances that the economy of North Korea is larger than the economy of New Hampshire?
- In your opinion, what are the chances that German President Angela Merkel is currently the longest-serving head of government in Western Europe?
- In your opinion, what are the chances that there are currently more refugees living in Lebanon than in any other country in the world?
- In your opinion, what are the chances that the United States currently conducts more trade with Mexico than with the European Union?
- In your opinion, what are the chances that the largest U.S. Embassy is currently located in Beijing?
- In your opinion, what are the chances that the U.S. defense budget is more than five times as large as China's defense budget?
- In your opinion, what are the chances that the United States currently operates more aircraft carriers than all other countries in the world combined?

- In your opinion, what are the chances that Israel receives more foreign aid than any other country in the world?
- In your opinion, what are the chances that more than 3 million people live within the borders of the Palestinian territories of the West Bank and Gaza?
- In your opinion, what are the chances that more than 5,000 people died as a result of the Ebola outbreak in West Africa in 2014?
- In your opinion, what are the chances that within the next six months, Syrian President Bashar al-Assad will be killed or no longer living in Syria?
- In your opinion, what are the chances that within the next six months, the Iraqi Security Forces will reclaim control of either Ramadi or Mosul (or both) from ISIS?
- In your opinion, what are the chances that there will be a new Pope within the next six months?
- In your opinion, what are the chances that more than 50,000 U.S. citizens will travel to Cuba within the next six months?
- In your opinion, what are the chances that more than 10 U.S. soldiers will be killed fighting ISIS within the next six months?

Experiment 4 presented respondents with 30 randomly-ordered questions:

- In your opinion, what are the chances that Nigeria has the largest population of any African country?
- In your opinion, what are the chances that Turkey currently provides more United Nations peacekeeping troops than any other country?
- In your opinion, what are the chances that Afghanistan currently produces more than half of the world's opium?
- In your opinion, what are the chances that the International Committee of the Red Cross has more full-time staff members than the U.S. Department of State?
- In your opinion, what are the chances that more than one-third of the world's population is currently under the age of 15?
- In your opinion, what are the chances that India tested its first nuclear weapon in 1998?
- In your opinion, what are the chances that Norway has a larger economy than New Jersey?
- In your opinion, what are the chances that Iraq's President is required by law to be Kurdish?
- In your opinion, what are the chances that Morocco is a member of the African Union?
- In your opinion, what are the chances that the United States has provided more official development assistance than any other country since 2010?

- In your opinion, what are the chances that Pope Francis is currently over the age of 75?
- In your opinion, what are the chances that the United States currently spends more money on national defense than on Social Security?
- In your opinion, what are the chances that Pakistan has a larger active-duty military than Iran?
- In your opinion, what are the chances that the United States currently has a lower unemployment rate than Vietnam?
- In your opinion, what are the chances that Transparency International currently ranks the United States as being more corrupt than the average country?
- In your opinion, what are the chances that the U.S. Department of Homeland Security's annual budget is less than $100 billion?
- In your opinion, what are the chances that the United States is currently holding fewer than 100 detainees in the Guantanamo Bay prison camp?
- In your opinion, what are the chances that North Korea's Kim Jong Un is currently the world's youngest head of government?
- In your opinion, what are the chances that the 2015 Paris Climate Agreement requires all signing countries to cut carbon emissions by at least 2 percent?
- In your opinion, what are the chances that Russia withdrew its support for the International Space Station in 2014?
- In your opinion, what are the chances that Saudi Arabia currently produces more oil than any other country?
- In your opinion, what are the chances that jihadi terrorists have killed more people in France than in the United States over the last decade?
- In your opinion, what are the chances that the International Criminal Court has never issued a conviction?
- In your opinion, what are the chances that the United States is the only country whose military possesses stealth aircraft?
- In your opinion, what are the chances that more than 50,000 Americans traveled to Cuba over the past year?
- In your opinion, what are the chances that there are currently more than 3 million registered refugees from the Syrian Civil War?
- In your opinion, what are the chances that the global number of people living on less than $2 per day has declined over the past twenty years?
- In your opinion, what are the chances that the United States currently maintains economic sanctions on more than 50 countries?
- In your opinion, what are the chances that Brazil's President, Dilma Rousseff, currently faces criminal charges as part of her impeachment proceedings?

- In your opinion, what are the chances that the United States currently conducts more trade with Canada than with Mexico?

2f. Method for Comparing the Accuracy of Qualitative and Quantitative Probability Assessments (Experiments 3–4)

To compare the accuracy of verbal and numeric probability assessments, it is necessary to score those assessments in equivalent terms. Our method for addressing this challenge involved four steps.

Step 1: Select a particular word of estimative probability (WEP). As described in chapter 4, Experiments 3–4 asked respondents to use a WEP spectrum that divides the number line into seven equal segments.

Step 2: For each question posed to respondents in a given survey, calculate the mean of all numeric assessments that correspond to each WEP.

For example, the WEP "remote chance" covers the first 1/7 of the probability spectrum (i.e., probabilities from zero to fourteen percent). For each question in the data set, we would thus calculate the mean of all probability estimates that fell between 0.00 and 0.14. We can generalize this approach using the formula $\mu_{q,w} = \sum_{w_{low}}^{w_{high}} p / N$, where $\mu_{q,wep}$ is the mean value for all numeric estimates corresponding to WEP w on question q, w_{low} and w_{high} represent the lowest and highest possible percentages correspondent to WEP w; p is a probability assessment; and N is the quantity of numeric probabilities respondents provided that fell between w_{low} and w_{high} on question q.

We chose to estimate these empirical means—instead of pegging the value of each WEP to a fixed point—so that the inferred meaning of each WEP could vary by context. For instance, the WEP "remote chance" spans probabilities ranging from zero to fourteen percent. The midpoint of this range is 0.07. But if we asked a question on which most respondents in the numeric assessment condition gave extremely small probability estimates (e.g., between 0.00 and 0.02), then we would expect that most qualitative assessors (and most consumers of this analysis) might also be inclined to interpret a "remote chance" as reflecting a value toward the bottom of the acceptable range.[14]

---

[14] On how interpretations of verbal probabilities can vary by context, see Ruth Beyth-Merom, "How Probable Is Probable? A Numerical Translation of Verbal Probability Expressions," *Journal of Forecasting*, Vol. 1, No. 3 (1982), pp. 257–269.

However, this particular aspect of the scoring method is not crucial to the results presented in chapter 4. All findings reported in chapter 4 are robust to translating WEPs into the midpoints of each bin; to defining WEPs based on survey research that indicates how respondents typically interpret what those terms are supposed to mean;[15] and to defining WEPs based on the midpoints of definitions recommended by the U.S. Director of National Intelligence.[16]

Step 3: The previous step in the analysis assigned a single numeric value to each WEP in the data set. Because there is no such constraint on the values that numeric percentages can take in the quantitative assessment condition of this experiment, the latter set of responses involve greater variance. It is necessary to eliminate that extra variance in order to score qualitative and quantitative judgments on a level playing field. We thus round all numeric probability estimates that correspond to a particular WEP to the same $\mu_{q,wep}$ values estimated above.

Step 4: We have now transformed the data so that we can compare the accuracy of verbal and numeric probability estimates on equivalent grounds. The results presented in chapter 4 evaluate these judgments using the Brier scores. These findings are also robust to evaluating the accuracy of probability estimates using the logarithmic scoring rule.

2g. Relationship between Certitude and Judgmental Accuracy (Experiment 3)

The results of Experiment 3 showed that foreign policy analysts who assessed subjective probabilities using numbers instead of words tended to provide answers that were more extreme and less accurate. Figure A.2 demonstrates how these attributes related to one another.[17]

---

[15] We based these definitions on "inferred probabilities" collected by Frederick Mosteller and Cleo Youtz, "Quantifying Probabilistic Expressions," *Statistical Science*, Vol. 5, No. 1 (1990), pp. 2–12. For a similar method applied in more recent work, see David R. Mandel, "Accuracy of Intelligence Forecasts from the Intelligence Consumer's Perspective," *Policy Insights from the Behavioral and Brain Sciences*, Vol. 2, No. 1 (2015), pp. 111–120.

[16] The Director of National Intelligence's alternative WEP spectrum is described in chapter 1, Figure 1.2. For more detail on these robustness checks, see Jeffrey A. Friedman, Jennifer S. Lerner, and Richard Zeckhauser, "Behavioral Consequences of Probabilistic Precision: Experimental Evidence from National Security Professionals," *International Organization*, Vol. 71, No. 4 (2017), pp. 803–826.

[17] Indeed, in a statistical sense, the tendency for numeric assessors to make more extreme judgments *entirely* explains the gap in performance between groups.: See Friedman, Lerner, and Zeckhauser, "Behavioral Consequences of Probabilistic Precision."

National security officials

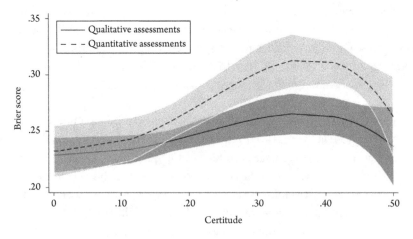

Amazon Mechanical Turk respondents

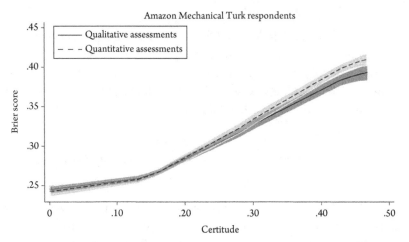

Figure A.2 Accuracy, certitude, and analytic precision. The graphs display the relationship between the certitude respondents attached to their probability assessments and the accuracy of those assessments (as measured by Brier scores, with 95 percent intervals). The performance gap between qualitative and quantitative assessors grows as respondents became more certain in their judgments.

The horizontal axes in Figure A.2 reflect the *certitude* that respondents attached to their probability estimates, defined as the absolute difference between each probability estimate and fifty percent (such that estimates of ten percent and ninety percent reflect the same levels of certitude).[18] The vertical axes in

---

[18] The data in these graphs do not extend all the way to 100 percent given the scoring method described in the previous section, which rounds each probability estimate in the data set to the nearest $\mu_{q,w}$ benchmark.

Figure A.2 represent the average Brier scores associated with probability estimates at each level of certitude. Note that the gap between Brier scores steadily grows as probability estimates become more extreme.[19]

2h. Informational Treatment and Placebo (Experiment 4)

Figures A.3a and A.3b present the training materials and placebo information provided to respondents in Experiment 4. These materials each appeared on three separate pages of the online survey.

All of the information provided in these training materials is accurate based on information collected from Experiment 3. Respondents in the qualitative assessment condition received similar feedback (though the results described calibration statistics based on verbal terms such as "remote chance" and "almost certainly").

2i. Full Analysis of Experiment 4

Table A.7 describes the results of Experiment 4. The accuracy of respondents' probability assessments is measured through average Brier scores. Table A.7 shows how these Brier scores correlated with (a) assessment of qualitative versus quantitative probabilities and (b) assignment to the training condition versus the placebo condition. These treatments were randomized independently.

3. Supplementary Materials for Chapter 5
3a. Text of Experimental Vignettes

The survey experiment presented in chapter 5 contained four vignettes, each of which involved experimental manipulations regarding: (a) whether probability assessments were expressed using numbers versus words; (b) the magnitude of each probability assessment; (c) whether or not decision makers chose to take action; and (d) the true outcome of the parameter about which analyst were uncertain. Here is the full text of each scenario, with the experimental manipulations in brackets:

---

[19] Figure A.2 plots these relationships using fractional polynomials with 95 percent confidence intervals.

Instructions (1 of 3)

The goal of this portion of the survey is to understand how respondents assess uncertainty. We will ask you to assess the chances that 30 statements are true. For example, we might ask you "what are the chances that the population of Russia is greater than 100 million people?"

We ask you to provide your answers using numeric percentages. If you are almost certain that this statement is true, then you would give an answer close to 100%, if you think there is only a remote chance that a statement is true then you would give an answer close to 0%, and if you have no idea either way then you would give an answer close to 50%.

Instructions (2 of 3)

In previous experiments, we have found that most people are substantially overconfident when they provide these answers. For example, when respondents said that they thought a statement was 90% likely to be true, we found that those statements were actually true about 65% of the time. When respondents said that they thought a statement had a 0% chance of being true, we found that those statements were actually true about 25% of the time.

Overall, we found that <u>99 out of every 100 respondents would have given more accurate judgments by making those judgments more cautious</u> (that is, by making their estimates closer to 50%). We will present the results from the present survey in lecture on August 19.

Instructions (3 of 3)

In the graph below, we show data evaluating respondents' judgments from prior surveys. If respondents were conveying their judgments effectively, then the data would form a diagonal line. Here you will see that respondents' judgments would have been substantially more informative if they were more cautious about assigning extreme estimates.

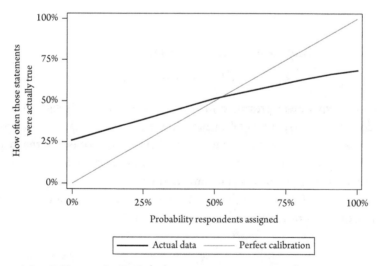

Figure A.3a Calibration feedback (numeric assessment condition).

Instructions (1 of 3)

The goal of this portion of the survey is to understand how respondents assess uncertainty. We will ask you to assess the chances that 30 statements are true. For example, we might ask you "what are the chances that the population of Russia is greater than 100 million people?"

We will ask about a range of issues relating to foreign policy, economics, and national security. We hope that you find these questions to be interesting.

Instructions (2 of 3)

We ask you to provide your answers using numeric percentages. If you are almost certain that this statement is true, then you would give an answer close to 100%, if you think there is only a remote chance that a statement is true then you would give an answer close to 0%, and if you have no idea either way then you would give an answer close to 50%.

Instructions (3 of 3)

We will use the results of this experiment to understand how well individuals "calibrate" their probability assessments. For example, when respondents say that they think a statement is 90% likely to be true, we can examine whether these statements are actually true about 90% of the time. Or when respondents say that they think a statement is 25% likely to be true, we can examine whether those statements are true roughly 25% of the time. We will present the results from this survey in lecture on August 19.

Figure A.3b Placebo information (numeric assessment condition).

Hostage-Rescue Vignette

The U.S. military is searching for five American citizens held hostage by a rebel group overseas. They receive information suggesting that the hostages are being held in a rural compound. Analysts can tell that the compound is being used by the rebel group, but they have difficulty confirming that the hostages are present. There is pressure to act quickly and little opportunity to gain additional information. Special Forces expect that a raid on the compound will meet armed resistance.

After careful deliberation, analysts report that [probability manipulation] that the hostages are being held in the compound. Decision makers review the available information and [decision manipulation].

Probability manipulations: There is a 40 percent chance; there is a 50 percent chance; there is a 60 percent chance; there is a 75 percent chance; there is a 90 percent chance; there is a 100 percent chance; it is possible but unlikely; there is an even chance; it is likely; it is very likely; they are almost certain; they are certain.

Decision manipulations: (i) choose to raid the compound. When special forces enter the compound, they find that the hostages were not in fact present, and two soldiers are killed in the resulting firefight; (ii) choose to raid the compound. When Special Forces enter the compound, they locate and retrieve the hostages, though two soldiers are killed in the resulting firefight; (iii) decline to raid the compound. It is later determined that the hostages were not in fact

Table A.7. **Impact of Training on Judgmental Accuracy**

	No Feedback	With Feedback	Difference
Qualitative assessors	0.257 (.05) N = 46	0.246 (.03) N = 47	4.3% better with feedback (p = 0.21)
Quantitative assessors	0.283 (.05) N = 44	0.265 (.05) N = 45	6.4% better with feedback (p = 0.13)
Difference	10.2% better using words (p = 0.03)	7.8% better using words (p = 0.03)	

Brier Scores for Amazon Mechanical Turk Respondents
Brier Scores for National Security Officials

	No Feedback	With Feedback	Difference
Qualitative Assessors	0.291 (.05) N = 312	0.281 (.04) N = 289	3.5% better with feedback (p = 0.005)
Quantitative Assessors	0.303 (.05) N = 283	0.282 (.05) N = 324	7.0% better with feedback (p < 0.001)
Difference	4.4% better using words (p = 0.002)	0.6% better using words (p = 0.63)	

The p-values in this table reflect two-way t-tests comparing differences in means.

present. Their location remains unknown; (iv) decline to raid the compound. It is later determined that the hostages were in fact present. They have since been moved to another unknown location.

Terrorism Vignette

U.S. intelligence analysts receive information about a potential terrorist attack on passenger airliners. Informants warn that terrorists may be preparing use a new form of explosive against several flights departing from California. If this is true, then it poses an immediate threat to passenger safety. However, there are reasons to doubt that the plot is real. In particular, terrorists may be planting false information to trick the U.S. government into restricting air travel, which would cause panic and economic damage.

Analysts conclude that [probability manipulation] that this plot is real. Decision makers review the information and decide [decision manipulation].

Probability manipulations: there is a 0 percent chance; there is a 10 percent chance; there is a 25 percent chance; there is a 40 percent chance; there is a 50 percent chance; there is a 60 percent chance; it is impossible; there is a remote chance; it is possible but very unlikely; it is possible but unlikely; there is an even chance; it is likely.

Decision manipulations: (i) to halt all flights leaving California for one week. This move costs the airline industry more than $1 billion and creates national alarm. The threat is later revealed to have been a hoax, and stopping air travel appears to have saved no lives; (ii) to halt all flights leaving California for one week. This move costs the airline industry more than $1 billion and creates national alarm. However, the threat is confirmed to be real, law enforcement agents disrupt it, and this saves several hundred lives; (iii) to allow air travel to continue. The threat is later revealed to have been a hoax; (iv) to allow air travel to continue. Days later, four airliners leaving California are destroyed in explosions, killing several hundred passengers.

Corruption Vignette

U.S. intelligence analysts are tracking Afghan government officials suspected of embezzling more than $100 million in U.S. development aid. One suspect, Babrak Ghafar, is currently visiting the United States. U.S. officials could apprehend Ghafar before he leaves. But arresting a prominent Afghan government official would cause major political controversy if Ghafar turns out to be innocent.

After careful deliberation, intelligence analysts report that [probability manipulation] that Ghafar is embezzling funds. Decision makers review the available information and [decision manipulation].

Probability manipulations: There is a 40 percent chance; there is a 50 percent chance; there is a 75 percent chance; there is a 90 percent chance; there is a 100 percent chance; it is possible but unlikely; there is an even chance; it is likely; it is very likely; they are almost certain; they are certain.

Decision manipulations: (i) choose to arrest Ghafar. It is later determined that Ghafar was in fact part of the corruption ring; (ii) choose to arrest Ghafar. It is later determined that Ghafar was not part of the corruption ring. The incident draws substantial international criticism of U.S. intervention in Afghan politics; (iii) decline to arrest Ghafar. It is later determined that Ghafar was not part of the corruption ring; (iv) decline to arrest Ghafar. It is later determined that Ghafar was in fact part of the corruption ring. His current whereabouts are unknown.

Drone-Strike Vignette

U.S. intelligence officials are attempting to locate a high-ranking terrorist. Drone operators say that they have found a man who meets their target's description. He is driving alone, in a deserted area. Drone operators may not get another shot as clean as this one. But it is always difficult to confirm a target's identity using remote surveillance. U.S. officials worry that the man could be an innocent civilian.

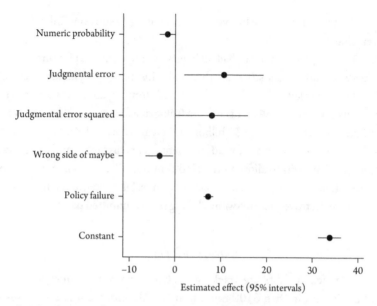

Figure A.4 Replication of Figure 5.4, with no excluded responses. The figure shows the impact each randomized variable exerted on the amount of criticism the respondents assigned to foreign policy analysts. These data do not exclude any respondents who failed attention checks. Ordinary least squares regression with robust standard errors and respondent fixed effects (N = 11,793).

After careful deliberation, intelligence officials assess that[probability manipulation] that this man is an innocent civilian. Decision makers review the available information and [decision manipulation].

Probability manipulations: there is a zero percent chance; there is a 10 percent chance; there is a 25 percent chance; there is a 40 percent chance; there is a 50 percent chance; there is a 60 percent chance; it is impossible; there is a remote chance; it is possible but very unlikely; it is possible but unlikely; there is an even chance; it is likely.

Decision manipulations: (i) choose to authorize a drone strike. It is later determined that the man was, in fact, an innocent civilian; (ii) choose to authorize a drone strike. It is later determined that the man was, in fact, a high-ranking terrorist; (iii) decline to authorize a drone strike. It is later determined that the man was, in fact, an innocent civilian; (iv) decline to authorize a drone strike. It is later determined that the man was, in fact, a high-ranking terrorist.

3b. Robustness of Empirical Results to Attention Check Completion

Figure A.4 replicates the findings presented Table 5.4, using all respondents in the data set—that is, without dropping respondents who did not pass all four attention checks.

INDEX